# COUNSELING THE ABLE DISABLED

## Rehabilitation Consulting In Disability Compensation Systems

Lawrence J. Deneen, Ph.D.
San Francisco/Oakland, California

Thorvald A. Hessellund, Ed.D.
San Leandro, California

First Edition

REHAB PUBLICATIONS, San Francisco, California

**COUNSELING THE ABLE DISABLED**

**Rehabilitation Consulting In Disability Compensation Systems**

By Lawrence J. Deneen and Thorvald A. Hessellund

Published by:

Rehab Publications
P.O. Box 22606
San Francisco, California 94122


First Printing 1986, Second Printing 1989, Third Printing 1992
Printed in the United States of America

Library of Congress Catalog Card Number: 86-61254

ISBN 0-9614877-1-2

## ABOUT THE AUTHORS

**Lawrence J. Deneen, Ph.D.,** Member, Board of Rehabilitation Certification, Commissioner on Insurance Rehabilitation Specialist Certification, Former Chairman of Ethics and Appeals Committee, President of Martin-Deneen Associates, Inc. a prominent private consulting firm. He actively counsels with disabled workers. He is the author of many publications in the field and is a well known vocational expert. Dr. Deneen has lectured at seminars for claims persons, nurses, counselors, and attorneys, in California, Arizona, Illinois, Georgia, and Florida. He has taught many consultants how to be more successful and effective as professionals in business.

**Thorv A. Hessellund, Ed.D.,** Founder and President of Rehabilitation Associates, Inc., prominent private consulting firm established in 1975. He served as President of the California Association of Rehabilitation Professionals, 1977. As Director of Education for Insurance Technology Company, Dr. Hessellund implemented training programs for claims divisions and insurance carriers. A consultant to private industry for many years, he is known nationally as an authority in all aspects of the rehabilitation process. He has lectured at seminars in California, Arizona, and New York.

Dr. Deneen and Dr. Hessellund were prompted to write this book because of their success and the success of their clients. Many of their friends, noting their success, approached them for their formula. Now they are revealing to you the inside story on rehabilitation cousulting ... the source of new beginnings for the able disabled.

## WARNING -- DISCLAIMER

This book is designed to provide information in regard to the subject matter covered. It is sold with the understanding that the publisher and authors are not engaged in rendering legal, accounting, or other professional services. If legal or other expert assistance is required, the services of a competent professional should be sought. The authors are certified vocational rehabilitation counselors. They qualify as experts in the field of vocational rehabilitation and their consultant services are available on a fee basis.

It is not the purpose of this text to reprint all the information that is otherwise available to the authors and/or publisher but to compliment, amplify and supplement other texts. For more information, see the many references in the Appendix.

Every effort has been made to make this text as complete and as accurate as possible. However, there **may be mistakes** both typographical and in content. Therefore, this text should be used only as a general guide and not as the ultimate source of rehabilitation consulting information. Furthermore, this text contains information on rehabilitation consulting only up to the printing date.

The purpose of this text is to educate, assist disabled workers, renew the spirit, and create new beginnings. The authors and Rehab Publications shall have neither liability nor responsibility to any person or entity with respect to any loss or damage caused or alleged to be caused directly or indirectly by the information contained in this book.

## CONTENTS

## SECTION III: The Business of Private Vocational Rehabilitation



## SECTION IV: Facts and Figures: Fantasy or Reality?

# PREFACE OF
# COUNSELING THE ABLE DISABLED

**What is new?**

We have purposely included the preface to our text **Vocational Rehabilitation of the Injured Worker** that was published in 1981. It is evident by reading that preface that the focus of the text was on Workers' Compensation.

Some of the material in this book is the same as that included in our prior text. Most of the information in this book is new. We have attempted to do more than simply update the previous text. We have added a number of chapters dealing with topics relevant to vocational rehabilitation practitioners and the recipients of their services. In our current book **Counseling The Able Disabled** we have 34 chapters, representing 16 new chapters and several major revisions.

Chapters discussing vocational rehabilitation in a variety of disability compensation systems are included. This includes: disability insurance income, Workers' Compensation, Federal Employee Compensation System, and Longshore and Harbor Workers' Compensation.

In addition, a published interview with Mr. Donald Gangemi, an applicant attorney, is included. How an attorney views rehabilitation is relevant since in many states 60% to 80% of cases are involved in litigation. The practical consequences of vocational rehabilitation as it affects disabled workers and as perceived by that worker's attorney is frequently an overlooked topic in books dealing with vocational rehabilitation.

A special chapter by Mr. Lawrence Kramer, a business consultant, discusses self-employment plans. Insights and suggestions as to how to make self-employment plans succeed is presented. Given the frequency that clients state an interest in being in their own business we think this chapter is particularly relevant. It should be read by counselor/consultants and clients.

Dr. Felton, a nationally known physician and clinical professor, gives a physician's perspective. This is a needed viewpoint when discussing vocational services. He spells out what physicians ought to expect and provide when working with a rehabilitation consultant.

Janette White, M.S., CRC describes how to provide services professional within the Longshore System. Her chapter is a blueprint for success.

Jan Lewis, M.S., CIRS, addresses a topic with an affirmative conclusion. Ethical standards do exist in private-for-profit setting. Her well-developed paper serves as an excellent rebuttal to those who "cry wolf" and who usually lack the experience as a consumer, provider, and/or manager of services. Ms. Lewis has performed all three roles.

Ms. Cindy White's, R.N., paper underscores the accountability requirement with special notice of a rehabilitation nurse perspective. Her observations as a rehabilitation nurse consultant adds breadth to the book.

The chapters published in Section IV enables you to study (and we mean study) for the first time in one source statistics across 14 states. We, as well as you the reader, are grateful to the California Workers' Compensation Institute, Mr. Alan Tebb, General Manager and the National Council on Compensation Insurance for giving us the chance to publish and disseminate their research.

We have expanded our discussion of vocational diagnosis, marketable transferable skills, and testing. The added information reflects our own learning as practitioners over the past five years.

Our discussion of the Rehabilitation Roadmap underscores the important role of a well-developed vocational plan. Without a good plan of action very few goals in life are reached. The same is true for rehabilitation goals.

We have experienced increased interaction with economists. As practitioners we rely on published labor market information prepared by economists. Therefore, we developed a common sense chapter dealing with economics for job seekers.

Information related to certification procedures is also included in the Appendix. The reason for this is simple: We advocate certification as a process of upgrading the professional skills and qualifications of people who provide services to the able disabled and various parties within a disability compensation system. The requirements of certification include corroboration of a person's academic achievements through the submission and review of a transcript. Corroboration of work experience is necessary. The passing of a full day objectively scored examination is necessary. Finally, in order to maintain a certification an individual must complete mandatory continued education requirements.

All of these requirements strengthens the identity of

professional service providers. More importantly they enhance the confidence that clients, customers, attorneys, insurance carriers, regulators, and judges have in the opinions and expertise of rehabilitation consultants.

This book was written from a practitioner's viewpoint. If rehabilitation consultants, whether they be counselors, nurses, evaluators, or placement specialists, can improve their understanding and ability to deal with the multiple problems confronted as a result of this book, then we have succeeded in our purpose.

This book is also written for the client, the disabled individual. Our previous text was given by many rehabilitation consultants throughout the country to recipients of those services, i.e., the consumer of rehabilitation services. This consumer included both insurance carriers and individual clients. This book in its entirety or selected chapters can be used the same way.

It is our belief that this book if read by clients, the injured persons, will enhance their involvement. It will expedite their rehabilitation. It will clarify the responsibilities they must take in order to rehabilitate themselves within a disability compensation system.

As a practical matter, most recipients of vocational rehabilitation services are not permanently totally disabled. Our research indicates across two studies, that of the clients receiving services, 67 to 82 percent have back disability problems. These disability problems are not considered by physicians or the compensation system as totally permanently disabling. This is reflected in the length of convalescence, the preclusions spelled out by physicians, and the permanent disability rating which is seldom greater than 50 percent. This is not intended to minimize the consequences of a partial disability on the economic livelihood of many individuals. Rather, it is to underscore a major theme throughout this book. Most rehabilitation consulting efforts within disability compensation systems are aimed at helping the **able disabled.**

**Changes of the Past Four Years**

When we wrote our text, **Vocational Rehabilitation of the Injured Worker,** in 1981 very little literature had been produced and widely disseminated on vocational rehabilitation from a private sector viewpoint or with attention to various disability compensation systems. This is no longer the case.

In 1981 the number of commissioners appointed to the

Commission for Rehabilitation Counselor Certification who made their livelihood by providing services in a private sector modality was a minority. Presently, a majority of commissioners engage in either full-time activities or part-time activities as private consultants with persons involved in a disability compensation system.

In 1981 if you were a counselor the credential that signified achievement of a particular standard was the CRC - Certified Rehabilitation Counselor. Now, there is an additional certification for individuals providing services to people within a disability compensation system; namely, Certified Insurance Rehabilitation Specialist. Professionals with either a nursing or counseling background are eligible.

Dr. Ralph Matkin, as part of his Doctorate dissertation and in a number of articles dealing with private sector rehabilitation, which are too numerous to list in this book, has studied the various roles and functions of rehabilitation practitioners. As recently as 1985, he reported that 61 percent of persons currently in private rehabilitation practice have at least a Master's degree, 25 percent are registered nurses, 37 percent are CRC, and 71 percent have between 1 and 5 years of work experience.

Through his research it is estimated that there are approximately 5300 personnel currently serving in a vocational rehabilitation capacity nationwide in the private sector. The private sector is the primary rehabilitation service providing agent for clients receiving disability compensation benefits.

In 1981 most clients receiving vocational rehabilitation benefits do so through a Workers' Compensation System. Today, however, a broader range of clients are served. Furthermore, the particular compensation system is more varied than that of a state Workers' Compensation benefit program. In some states the primary source of referrals because of a volunteer Workers' Compensation rehabilitation program is disability insurance income or long-term disability. In some regions of the country, particularly in the coastal areas, "longshore and harbor workers" is the primary source of referrals. And, for some practitioners the primary source of referrals is from a forensic environment in which a vocational expert evaluates the kinds of alternative occupations that an individual may or may not be able to return to and the wages that person can command.

The goal of this publication is to disseminate information provided by a variety of credible sources and respected rehabilitation practitioners. The practitioners include a physician, business consultant, attorney, rehabilitation nurse, and counselors. It is our belief that the body of knowledge contained within this book lays a solid foundation for being able to provide comprehensive vocational rehabilitation services on behalf of consumers of these services.

A secondary goal of this book is to help practitioners have a more successful business. We know that if you follow the suggestions in the chapters on Federal Employees Compensation System, Longshore and Harbor Workers' System, and Disability Insurance Income/LTD that you should be able to increase your business by $2,000 to $6,000, if not more, per year. Use the book as a practical business tool.

It is our premise that the more information given to all parties of disability compensation systems then the more expeditious will rehabilitation proceed. Misunderstandings, hidden agendas, and causes of frustration will be reduced. An individual receiving rehabilitation services needs to understand the system in which those services exist.

It has been said that "no man is an island." This is certainly true in provision of rehabilitation services. No benefit, such as the rehabilitation benefit, exists by itself. The understanding of how this benefit interacts with other benefits that an individual is receiving is critical.

L.J.D. and T.A.H. (April 1986)

## PREFACE of
## Vocational Rehabilitation of the Injured Worker
## (Prior Text)

Recent additions to Workers' Compensation laws in some states have established machinery for bringing the rehabilitation function directly into the Workers' Compensation system. This new machinery is intended to help injured workers return to suitable gainful employment. The worker is given the fullest opportunity to receive professional help to restore his earning capacity. Suitable gainful employment takes into consideration the worker's interest, work and educational history, transferable skills and abilities, preinjury earnings, and residual medical limitations.

This broadening of the scope of the Workers' Compensation principle to include full vocational rehabilitation marks a significant social and economic advance for all concerned. The individual worker is insured the right to restoration of some form of marketable work skills and a secure income. The business community and society as a whole are assured the economic advantage of a stable and trained work force in place of an ever growing number of injured ex-workers, either receiving direct compensation payments or some form of public assistance. With professional vocational rehabilitation services now an integral part of the Workers' Compensation system, more and more of the growing population of injured and unemployed ex-workers can be expected to return to the labor market as competent wage earners and taxpayers.

These improvements in the Workers' Compensation system are not yet fully known and understood. They are not yet operating at their fullest social and economic potential. As with any sociolegal change, this new aspect of Workers' Compensation has created its own bureaucratic problems. But it has also created a new type of vocational rehabilitation counselor who is learning to deal with the problems of this new approach to rehabilitation as a business as well as a social concern. This new rehab counselor has discovered that his role has been expanded. He is no longer **only** a client advocate. In this new system he is now accountable to professional insurance claims people, employers' representatives, medical and legal personnel from both sides of the case, and a sometimes bewildered and angry client who feels lost and hopeless in a bureaucratic, impersonal system.

The counselor working within the Workers' Compensation system is forced to look at his profession in a new light. He must develop new skills in order to deal effectively with this new delivery system. He must modify habits without losing sight of his main objective: helping his identified client, the injured worker, return to gainful employment.

The text will attempt to share some of the information and insights the authors have gained by working in this new and unique vocational rehabilitation situation. We hope to aid vocational counselors new to this field to better understand and deal with the problems of multiple accountability, and to gain a new view of the business aspects of a private vocational rehabilitation service. It is also hoped that some of the excitement and challenge of the work may be communicated to recent rehabilitation counselors just entering the field, and that some of them may be encouraged to consider a career in private vocational rehabilitation.

This book is also for the client, the injured worker. We hope that it may relieve some of the confusion he feels. It may serve as a guide to some of the options and services he has available to return him as quickly as possible to a feasible and satisfying work situation.

L.J.D. and T.A.H. (January, 1981)

To those who respond to the **NEW** challenge ...

## The Client

### The Able Disabled

Let us suppose for the moment that you are a work-injured husband and father, a good provider for your family for the past twenty years. Something has happened. An accident on the job. An illness connected with your work situation. You may be hospitalized for a period of time. But now you are not able to work. How long will it be before you are able to get back to work? You can't answer this question. Only your doctors may have ideas about when you can work again and what kind of work you may be capable of. At this point, the doctors themselves may not even have the answers.

Suddenly you have found yourself in the midst of the Workers' Compensation system, a state-mandated and supervised system of injury/illness insurance provided by your employer through an insurance carrier. Where can you find the information you need and want? Who is going to pay the bills, your mortgage payments, put the food on your family's table? After your injury, your employer probably gave you forms to fill out to file a claim with his insurance carrier. After he has mailed your last paycheck, however, he probably has no further contact with you. The boys in the shop may have sent you Get Well cards, but that's not much help. What do you do now?

Somewhere along the line you may receive a notice or phone call instructing you to get in touch with the insurance carrier's claims agent. You make the contact and are told that he will handle your medical expenses. He will also determine your temporary disability benefit. He may obtain expert medical opinions regarding your long-range prospects for returning to work. Meanwhile, you will be dependent on the insurance carrier's disability payments. The amount of these payments has no relationship to your normal family budget. You dip into savings. You seek help from relatives. You do whatever is necessary to make ends meet. Until your recovery is over, you are at the mercy of the medical establishment and the faceless insurance people with whom you deal by mail or phone.

If you are unable to return to your job, you may receive a referral from the insurance claims department to see a private vocational rehabilitation consultant. Who and what is a vocational rehabilitation consultant? What can he do for you in your present situation, unable to work and not knowing when, or if, you'll be able to work again? You're unable to meet financial obligations and to support your family properly. You feel discouraged and guilty about your failure to provide effectively. "I don't know what the future holds for me, and neither do any of the people I've talked to so far. Right now, I'm part of the Workers' Compensation system, an impersonal bureaucracy which seems to arbitrarily make decisions about my disability benefits, return to work and type of work. How can any part of this big system be aware of how helpless I feel and how angry I am growing?"

The appointment time arrives and you meet with our vocational rehabilitation counselor. He is probably the first person you've met in the system who seems truly interested in you. You can talk with him about your hopes and fears of returning to work, your near-desperate financial plight, the difficulties in your family situation, the concern you have about your future as a worker and provider. It makes you feel more confident and competent just to be able to let loose and talk about these things. Moreover, this rehab counselor is probably your first independent source of information you have had regarding your current status in the Workers' Compensation system. You won't get the insurance company's legalistic jargon of cautious ifs, buts, maybes and whereases. You won't get the medical establishment's obscure, technical and qualified assessments and prognoses. Here is a professional who can lay it on the line, tell you in terms meaningful to you just what is your likelihood of getting back to your regular job, or if your employer is seriously looking for another spot for you within the range of your postinjury limitations. He may even suggest that it is not too early for you to start giving some thought to job possibilities in another vocational area where you might be able to work more effectively in your present physical condition.

You begin to feel a sense of relief. Here is someone with whom you feel you can finally open up, voice your worst fears (they are not quite so fearful when you say them out loud), begin to take a realistic look at your situation, start to make plans for dealing with it, and maybe even dream up "impossible" future career possibilities.

The point is that there is now another human being in this system besides yourself, one who is interested in you and how you can move along toward making the most reasonable and profitable choices for your future. This is the private vocational rehabilitation consultant, retained for you and paid for by your former employer's insurance carrier. But his major concern, and only success in his job, lies in seeing you successfully back at work, employed at your highest and most feasible capacity and with a potential for future growth.

As an injured worker, your vocational rehabilitation consultant can be your best resource. He is the one who will work with you in formulating a realistic rehabilitation plan. He will support and defend this plan with the insurance representative who is primarily responsible to implement, finance and coordinate the plan. He will arrange whatever interest and aptitude testing he feels is needed to help you make the best possible vocational choices, and help you intelligently interpret the results of the testing. It's this rehab counselor who will eventually direct you into the right channels for getting straight information on job requirements in various fields. He will help you learn about the job market potential in the area you are ultimately interested in as a vocational goal. He's the one who can assist you when you're having vocationally relevant problems with insurance people, the medical team, attorneys and others whose support is needed to see you successfully return to work. The two of you are in the "trenches" together having the same goal ... a successful return to the job market.

## The Counselor - Consultant

The vocational rehabilitation counselor is the human element in the Workers' Compensation system. It is he who acts as the catalyst in bringing the client and the system together. It is his function to coordinate the work of insurance claims representatives, medical and legal teams on both sides of the case and many others in producing the real product of Workers' Compensation -- a restored and working ex-claimant, an independent and taxpaying member of the community.

The typical rehabilitation counselor working in the private sector has educational training similar to his peers working in other rehabilitation settings. He may have a nursing credential, a Bachelor's degree **plus** nurse credential, and/or graduate degrees related to counseling and rehabilitation. He may have experience in a variety of health and medical settings. He may have work experience as a nurse in private industry. The consultant may have achieved a nursing credential, such as R.N., and also qualified for and successfully passed the exam for Certified Insurance Rehabilitation Specialist (CIRS).

Many counselors are a product of a graduate school program in vocational rehabilitation counseling. He has a Master's degree that probably involved one and one-half years of full-time schooling beyond the Bachelor's degree, plus an additional three to six months of internship. Depending on his education and experience, he may have qualified for Certification examination and be a Certified Rehabilitation Counselor (CRC) and/or a Certified Insurance Rehabilitation Specialist (CIRS). He has studied counseling theory and occupational psychology. He has learned about the medical and psychological aspects of disability.

He has a fair command of medical terminology as it relates to disabling conditions. He is familiar with vocational and psychological testing procedures. He has interned or worked under supervision and applied his knowledge of counseling in a rehabilitation setting.

But, as a rehab consultant in the private sector dealing with Disability Compensation cases, he has limitations. He is handicapped by his traditional nursing or counseling training. Here his work requires a different perspective than that of his colleagues. He needs a broader view of the real world and the business of earning a living. Like his fellow professionals in other settings, he is concerned with the psychosocial aspects of rehabilitation and finding the right jobs for the right clients. But he must somewhere develop this broader view and learn the specific skills involved in the **business** of rehabilitation. He must learn to make accurate vocational diagnoses quickly and to formulate realistic vocational plans that will get his client back to work. Restoring injured workers to employment without unnecessary delay is the name of the game in private rehab. It's good economics as well as good vocational rehabilitation.

In accomplishing this end, the private vocational rehab consultant doesn't have to forget his individuality and become a cog in the huge rehab machinery. The person-to-person relationship that he builds with his clients is the most valuable tool of his trade. The client-counselor interaction can only be enhanced by this straightforward human approach. When the injured worker recognizes your sincerity, understands you are watching out for his or her welfare and knows that your major concern is to see him back to work, you have an involved, motivated client. Such openness solidifies the relationship.

But client-counselor relationship aside, the private rehab consultant is a businessperson, also. To effectively help his client, he must deal with and account to the cost-conscious businesspeople who are paying his and his client's bills. He must be in a position where he can defend his recommendation of, say a one-year training program in computer programming for a particular client as the most economical vocational program **in the long run**. As a businessperson working in the system, the rehab counselor must be able to see that the cheapest and quickest rehab plan, when it fails, is finally the most costly and wasteful. The conscientious consultant in this field comes to learn that there is no real conflict between good rehabilitation service and sound economic practice.

As some of the case histories in this book will show, the really effective private vocational rehab counselor **can** serve several masters. He can restore his client as a productive and reasonably satisfied wage earner while meeting the criteria of his cost-conscious, business-oriented customer, the insurance representative.

## Introduction

Up to the end of the nineteenth century, an accidental injury at work or an illness resulting from certain conditions on the job which disabled a worker and separated him from his usual work and source of income was viewed, by most, as a private affair between the injured worker and the employer. In those days of laissez-faire, the injured worker would generally find himself excessed, no longer part of the labor pool. If he was very lucky and had worked for a generous and humanitarian employer, other work at his place of employment might be found for him, work which he could handle in spite of his injury, at substantially reduced earnings. (The job of night watchman was one of the first of a long series of jobs for the handicapped.) However, most injured workers ended up dependent upon the generosity of relatives or as public charges for the rest of their lives.

It is here that the interests of the whole society became involved. With the growth of industry and the corresponding increase in the industrial accident rate, an economic drain on society became more prevalent. This economic drain, together with a growing social consciousness in certain sectors of society, resulted in government intervention on behalf of the injured worker.

Around the turn of the century, laws were formulated and enacted assigning some of the responsibility to the employer for his workers made unemployable by work-connected injury or illness. But just what this responsibility was to consist of, and who was to bear the brunt of the costs of a compensation system became the subject of a continuing debate through the first half of this century.

The first Workers' Compensation laws were enacted in this country in 1911 and spread slowly throughout the states over the next thirty years. Liability and payment amounts were continually debated issues. Over the years grossly inadequate disability payments gave way to more realistic consideration of the economic facts of life. A more generous social climate in the Thirties produced more liberal and comprehensive Workers' Compensation laws. The advances made by labor over these years contributed to the extension and elaboration of the principles of Workers' Compensation and the gradual improvement of benefits in both medical coverage and increased replacement income rate structures.

Early in the struggle for Workers' Compensation benefits, employers and the growing insurance business recognized a common concern in providing this coverage as dictated by state laws. The cost-conscious employer found insurance the soundest fiscal policy for handling his obligations to injured employees. More recently, larger employers meeting state requirements have become self-insured in providing Workers' Compensation benefits. Within the Workers' Compensation system it is the employer's responsibility to provide the benefits, either by contracting with an insurance company and paying premiums or by becoming self-insured as permitted in some states. In certain states there is only one carrier, usually designated as the State Fund. In other states there are State Funds, private carriers and self-insured employers.

Under the current expansion of Workers' Compensation benefits, the insurance carrier or self-insured employer is the usual retainer of a vocational rehabilitation counselor and the source for authorizing all vocational rehabilitation plans for individual injured workers. The carrier's decisions, however, are subject to approval by the State Bureau of Rehabilitation, a subdivision of the Workers' Compensation Board.

Dealing with these insurance and state offices is an important part of the work of the private vocational rehabilitation counselor in helping his client back to work. In this book, we shall clarify the sometimes complex accountability of the counselor to his client, the injured worker, and his customer, the insurance representative.

Richard Keane, in a chapter in the book **Handbook of Private Sector Rehabilitation**, discusses concisely and in sufficient detail the complexities of coordinating services on behalf of clients with insurance companies who are the "consumers" or payers of services. His chapter is one of the best discussions we have read. It enables a practitioner to have "empathy" with the primary funding source of vocational services in the private sector -- the insurance industry.

Throughout the text we refer to the state rehabilitation bureau. We have used this term to refer to an agency within a state's Workers' Compensation system that is responsible for regulating the delivery of vocational rehabilitation to the industrially injured worker. It does not refer to a state's agency responsible for the public state/federal vocational rehabilitation program.

California enacted one of the first mandatory vocational rehabilitation laws in 1975 as part of the regular Workers' Compensation benefits. Due to the size of California's labor force and mandatory rehabilitation, California has the greatest experience with private vocational rehabilitation of the industrially injured. Due to these facts and the locations of our own private rehabilitation services, we have referred in chapter one and throughout the text to selected State of California statistics. In Section IV national statistics are provided. These statistics are the most current available. In our opinion the methods of private vocational rehabilitation that we discuss are applicable in any state where the goal is quality services to return workers as soon as possible to suitable gainful employment.

# SECTION I

## Counseling Techniques

# CHAPTER 1

## Industrial Rehabilitation: Fundamentals

Each year there are millions of men and women who are injured at work or who become seriously ill due to a factor inherent in their work situation. In 1984 in the state of California alone, there were 373,600 disabling industrial injuries. Of these workers over 260,000 received temporary total disability payments.

Between September 1, 1975 and September 30, 1976, (according to the Rehabilitation Bureau, state of California), 3,713 injured workers received vocational evaluation and counseling services. For this particular thirteen-month period, 3,643 rehabilitation plans were approved.

By 1982, the Rehabilitation Bureau (California) had opened 29,211 new cases and approved 8,515 rehabilitation plans.

The California statistics are noteworthy for two reasons: 1) California was the first state to enact in 1975 a mandatory vocational rehabilitation law as part of Workers' Compensation (mandatory for the employer to offer it, voluntary for employee to accept it); and 2) The absolute number of cases underscores the need for effective vocational services. The incidence of vocational rehabilitation for disabling/indemnity cases is similar to that for the rest of the country. The incidence rate increases as claims files remain open for longer periods.

In a 1984 study by the National Council on Compensation Insurance, data for 13 states was examined. The states included Connecticut, Florida, Georgia, Illinois, Kentucky, Maine, Massachusetts, Michigan, Minnesota, New York, Pennsylvania, Virginia, and Wisconsin. This study is included in this book in Section IV. At this point it is important to note that among claims **closed** between 18 and 30 months, 4.07% of the injured workers received vocational rehabilitation benefits. Among those claims open after 30 months the rate is 11.08% receiving vocational services.

To say it another way, of the injured workers receiving temporary total disability payments and having the claim open between 18 to 30 months, 8.52% will receive and apparently need vocational rehabilitation services.

Among claims open after 30 months the total vocational rehabilitation cost averaged $4,387 with $2,012 spent for evaluation, $1,903 for indemnity, and $471 for education.

In California, a state **not** included in the above study, the average plan cost varies from $2,081 to $18,386. The average in all cases with rehabilitation expense (plan and non-plan) was nearly $9000. These amounts include temporary total disability payments which in 1985 were $224 per week. The average length of plans vary from 3.7 months to 8.9 months. This data is from a 1985 study (included in Section IV) by the California Workers' Compensation Institute.

In evaluative studies of state vocational rehabilitation services, benefit-cost ratios were demonstrated to have returned anywhere from $3.30 to $17 for every dollar spent on vocational rehabilitation. In a 1977 evaluative study done by a private vocational rehabilitation firm, the average earnings of clients at date of injury was $245.90 per week. The average earnings at closure of rehabilitation was $224.64 per week. Injured workers successfully rehabilitated following an industrial injury were earning 92% of their preinjury wage. In a recent repeat study of the clients successfully returned to work, the average weekly date-of-injury earnings was $281.62, and was, at completion of rehabilitation, $266.89. On the average, clients were earning 94.8% of their preinjury earnings. The client salaries varied form $693 to $2,575 per month at placement. These figures show how work as a private rehabilitation consultant in the Workers' Compensation system is not only a **helping** job, but is also good, sound business policy.

With competent medical help, many injured workers will be able to return to their previous jobs after a period of recuperation. These persons do not need vocational services. Your clients are those workers whose injuries have left them with a residual impairment, making it impossible for them to return to their former jobs or to seek work in allied fields. The nature of their disability prevents them from performing in their former jobs with industrially acceptable skill and speed. These are the workers who become candidates for vocational rehabilitation and, eventually, your clients.

Injured workers are entitled to professional assistance in returning to suitable gainful employment, as quickly as medical recovery permits. You are the provider of that assistance. Most of these former workers, your clients, have a substantial, well-paid, preinjury work history. They are anxious to return to work as quickly as possible. Most would like to return to their old jobs. They want to climb back to the same rung on the skill and earnings ladder they formerly occupied.

For many of your clients, this may be a realistic goal. Employers frequently find, with the help of a skilled vocational counselor, that with small changes in the design of the job or equipment to accommodate the injured worker's impairment, he can return to his former position. This is generally the most cost-effective and satisfactory form of vocational adjustment. In other cases a brief training program in a related skill, requiring less physical stress, will enable the worker to make a quick and satisfying vocational readjustment.

With some clients who cannot return to their previous job, the counselor may discover that the worker's educational background and his level of interest and skills open up vocational possibilities in a totally different occupational area. With proper counseling, the client may be able to match his previous skill and salary level in a relatively short period of time. These are clients the counselor finds easy to work with. Client and counselor share the same goal -- a quick return to gainful employment. Both must be realistic in their appraisal of the residual limitations of the worker's injury and be able to formulate reasonable vocational plans. These clients have a high level of motivation and can be expected to play an active role in their own rehabilitation from the start. Their chances of a successful vocational rehabilitation are good.

But your caseload is bound to include some unrealistic clients. These are the workers who (1) are unable to accept the severity of their disability and the occupational limitations it imposes, or (2) are unable, for whatever reasons, to accept their own preinjury vocational limitations -- those deficiencies in academic background, skill development, personal interests or characteristics which limit occupational choice. They are likely to have false expectations of what vocational rehabilitation means for them. They often expect the rehabilitation counselor to produce a magic wand and turn them into something they never could have been, injury or no injury.

There's the skilled mechanic, for instance, who has been accustomed to making an above-average income for many years.

He has little in the way of education, however, no real interests outside the immediate area of his previous mechanical trade and no observable, marketable, transferable skills. He will find it hard to accept the fact that his residual disability prevents his return to work on the complicated machinery with which he is familiar. Add to this his lack of formal education and generally low level of interest in other vocational areas and you have a problem client, one for whom it will take all the counselor's human interaction skills to promote a rehabilitation climate with some chance of successful outcome. The effective counselor must somehow get through to this client and encourage a realistic look at the client's vocational prospects. If he can crack through the shell of illusion the client has built up, the counselor may succeed in getting this formerly skilled mechanic to join actively in planning for a less physically demanding type of work. The fact that this client cannot reasonably expect the financial rewards of his previous job is a stumbling block. But an effective counselor can frequently help his client find other forms of compensation in a projected work situation. It is with these clients that the rehabilitation counselor must act as a therapist. He must help the worker face **and accept** his new vocational limitations and join him in actively designing realistic and rewarding vocational alternatives.

Where vocational options are very limited by the client's physical condition, the skilled counselor works creatively in uncovering skills and interests that may be converted into practical and realistic vocational goals. A serious, mutual exploration of the world of work may sometimes steer the client into a brand new and even more rewarding second career. But in embarking on these new and unfamiliar vocational roads, client and counselor must move carefully. Is the client really interested in a proposed new vocational field, or is he merely grasping at straws? Can he walk into a new learning situation and master a different set of occupational skills? Will the new field look as attractive in a daily work situation as it did during the training program? Does the client really have the abilities and skills -- intellectual, dexterity and personal -- required for success in the new area?

Finally, there are the clients who appear to have given up, people for whom their physical impairment triggers a sense of worthlessness. They perceive themselves as a burden to their families and the whole of society around them. These clients are likely to have had problems in defining their self-worth before their injury. The industrial accident has been the final blow. In a sense, it vindicates their own previous self-appraisal. Motivating these clients to return to work is difficult. It takes a formidable combination of understanding of where the client **is** psychologically at the moment and a real toughness on the part of the rehab counselor in demanding this "defeated" client to complete vocational assignments. Only in this way can success experiences be set up which can eventually motivate this person to full and active participation in his vocational rehabilitation.

The private vocational consultant will meet with a variety of individual clients, each bringing his own set of expectations, work attitudes, history, skill repertoire and personal traits into the counseling situation. The effective consultant soon learns he must wear a different hat with each of these clients. He must be aggressively realistic with the grandiose expectations of some, tender but demanding with the defeated-feeling client who needs a mild success in vocational exploration projects before he is even willing to try to invest himself in the vocational rehab process. He must be a store of vocational information for the client who knows little about employment options and direct this client into making his own vocational explorations. He must provide feedback every step of the way and be able to relate occupational needs to the client's own needs and specific limitations.

A skilled rehabilitation consultant is also able to sense where his client is on the road back to work. When is a client physically able to participate in his own rehab plan? When is a particular client ready to give up his vocational illusions and begin to explore and pursue realistic goals? When does the client have the attitudinal readiness to tackle intensive vocational exploration, planning and training programs? And, above all, when is the client's motivational level up to the emotional commitment necessary for the successful outcome of any vocational plan? Specific yes or no answers may not be available to all these questions, but the consultant should be aware of these factors in making his rehabilitation plan.

# CHAPTER 2

## Workers' Compensation Eligibility: Who Is a Qualified Injured Worker?

As a private vocational rehabilitation counselor working in the area of the Workers' Compensation system, you are dependent primarily on the claims representative for client referrals. This is usually done in consultation with the client's attorney, if there is one. Sometimes, however, an injured client may be referred directly by the worker's employer or by an attorney. To be eligible for your professional rehabilitation service, an individual must be determined to be what the state rehabilitation bureau defines as a Qualified Injured Worker. Specific guidelines for this classification are set by the bureau. The Qualified Injured Worker is one who meets these criteria: 1) When the effects of the injury, whether or not combined with the effects of a prior injury or disability, permanently prevent or are likely to prevent the worker from engaging in either a usual and customary occupation, or in engaging in the position in which he was employed at the time of the injury, and 2) if the injured worker can be reasonably expected to benefit from a rehabilitation program.

It is primarily your responsibility to determine if the client meets these criteria. You may assist physicians in determining criterion number 1. The client is then determined to be feasible or nonfeasible for vocational rehabilitation. The entire rehabilitation team bears a great responsibility in making this determination.

The first criterion is a medical/technical one and is most often determined on the basis of objective medical data, although even here, the subjective decision of what is a tolerable level of pain may enter.

The second criterion requires a determination on the part of the qualified vocational rehabilitation counselor based on a thorough diagnostic study of the client and his apparent motivation or lack thereof. Here too, however, objective referrants will be used: What is the client's stock of measurable skills? Does the client's educational achievement justify the pursuit of training programs? What kind of training programs are available and of what duration? Does the client's vocational and educational history indicate transferable skills? What are the job markets in the area of interest and transferable skills? Are there growing or shrinking employment opportunities in these fields?

Answers to these questions, together with your own observations about the client can help you determine reasonable expectations from your professional rehabilitation service.

Much of the information you will use in making this decision will come out of your initial interviews with the client, your personal impressions and observations. You will also find data in the client's file, his work history, special training, etc. More information may be added by requesting a testing program, if needed, and integrating test results with other information. But, largely, it will be a matter of the client's attitude toward being rehabilitated. And here, the counselor must rely on his skill in reading that attitude accurately. The really effective counselor will be able to detect a client's interest level in making serious vocational plans and to assess the strength of the client's motivational impetus to follow through into new vocational areas.

Before deciding on Qualified Injured Worker status for some clients, the counselor might want to take a closer look at the job the worker was doing before the injury, through what is known as a job analysis. Here he works carefully with the former employer. Together they take a closer look at the actual physical requirements of the job the worker had been doing. Sometimes a very minor modification in the job requirements will enable the worker to return to this job despite the limitations imposed by his injury. This is by far the most satisfactory form of rehabilitation for all concerned when it is economically feasible. The worker, using his acquired skills and earning his preinjury wage, goes back to his familiar work environment. The employer is spared the effort and time needed to train and fit a new worker into this slot. The insurance company has saved the cost of what might prove an expensive and lengthy retraining program with no guarantee of successful outcome.

Like most counseling decisions, the determination of the feasibility of rehabilitation for a particular client is more of an art than a science. After studying all the relevant information

-- client history, education, tested skills and interests -- the best of counselors must finally rely on his judgment of the client's motivation for return to work (and his experience with other clients) to justify his definition of a Qualified Injured Worker under state rehabilitation bureau guidelines. He must be prepared to substantiate this classification. It is part of the private rehabilitation counselor's total accountability -- accountability to employer, to insurance carrier, to the medical and legal establishments involved, as well as to the injured worker.

Clients can be determined not feasible for vocational rehabilitation for a variety of reasons. Most frequently these determinations are based on medical opinion, e.g., the client is in too much pain to participate in any type of full-time work or training program, or his postinjury recovery is too limited to consider any regular work situation. These are medical opinions and form the basis for the majority of determinations of nonfeasibility.

When nonfeasibility is determined by a rehab counselor, a smaller number of cases may be involved and certain familiar patterns recur. Normally, we might find a client who is medically released to participate in a rehabilitation plan. He is physically capable of going to appointments and of using mass transit to and from counseling and testing sessions. He is medically released to participate in on-the-job training (OJT). Yet, for some reason the client cannot or will not follow through. The counselor is thus faced with a pattern of broken appointments, no-shows on vocational testing, absences from school or OJT -- a client-aborted rehabilitation process. When this happens over a period of time, the counselor is forced to conclude that this client is not sufficiently motivated to benefit from rehab. The counselor would then determine such a client as nonfeasible.

All experience leads us to believe that, for any rehab plan to succeed, there must be a joint commitment by client and counselor. Only with this commitment can the counselor declare his plan has a reasonable chance of working out and thus be considered feasible.

In examining cases we have worked on, we find that 59% involve the lumbar region of the back, and 82% involve some part of the back -- lumbar, cervical or thoracic. That represents a large share of the total case load and indicates something special about back injuries and feasibility. On the other hand, of all successfully rehabilitated clients who have returned to gainful employment, 71% had suffered a disability of some part of the back. Rehab is possible with back-injured clients, but the chances of failure are always present.

It is important to remember that in all the research that has been done, physical and psychological, in a variety of medical centers, there seems to be a tremendous difficulty in assisting persons with low back pain, either before or after surgery. Helping them cope with pain, adjust to and complete vocational services and return to gainful employment presents a real challenge to the rehabilitation professional. This is where we see a blending of the medical and motivational backgrounds which frequently make it so difficult for the rehabilitation counselor to come to a decision on feasibility and what constitutes reasonable expectations.

On occasion, it is the client who makes his own choice about feasibility. Consider the man who has worked at the same job for eight years, making $15.00 per hour, enjoying four-week vacations and many other fringe benefits before his injury. During interest and aptitude testing, this client stated flatly that unless he could be guaranteed the same pay scale and all the other fringe benefits of his preinjury job, he had no interest in pursuing any rehabilitation plans. Here the client has determined his own nonfeasibility. No one could make such guarantees as the client insisted upon and there could be no reasonable expectation that the client could benefit from rehabilitation. It is certainly the client's right to say what kind of salary he expects after rehabilitation, but it is the counselor's duty to be realistic and to tell the client that in the present circumstances no such guarantees can be made.

There may be other times during the rehabilitation process when, for medical reasons, a client is deemed nonfeasible. For instance, his physical condition has not stabilized and his level of pain is preventing him from giving adequate attention and fully participating in a rehab plan. At this point the rehab plan may be temporarily suspended until the client's medical conditions have stabilized to a point where there is a reasonable chance of success for the rehab plan.

A client may also be declared nonfeasible for his refusal to cooperate with the efforts of the rehab team. The client's failure to keep appointments or to complete vocational assignments display insufficient incentive and throw serious doubt on the client's motivation to complete a rehab plan. Here the counselor must be open and aggressive with the client, demonstrating how his observed behavior makes the successful outcome of any rehabilitation plan doubtful, branding the client nonfeasible. In such a case, the counselor must be fully prepared to document all areas of noncooperation on which he is basing his judgment of nonfeasibility.

Lastly, the counselor, in making a determination of nonfeasibility, must look at his own attitudes objectively. Was he open-minded and unbiased with his client from the start? Or did he get negative vibrations when the client walked into his office and, on that basis, did he project negative expectations into his client's later behavior? A private rehabilitation counselor must be fully aware that the rehabilitation bureau will carefully scan a counselor's track record in feasibility determinations. A thorough evaluation and clear rationale are necessary to justify feasibility questions as well as a plan.

# CHAPTER 3

## What the Doctors Say ... and Don't Say
## A Rehabilitation Consultant's View

One of the most popular misconceptions in the field of rehabilitation is that the physician has all the answers. This is not true. In most cases, even with some of the answers, physicians have shown a peculiar reticence about expressing them. High malpractice lawsuit rates lend some support to a medical man's reluctance to be specific and to his penchant for broad, cautious terminology that allows plenty of room for interpretation. Definitive diagnoses and prognoses are sometimes lacking in the doctor's trade, particularly in the area of rehab medicine where almost anything can happen and often does. The variables are incalculable.

This is especially true when it comes to back injuries, a large share of the rehab counselor's case load. Almost never is there just one answer to resolving the question of a bad back. Physicians are keenly aware of this problem and are therefore expectedly cautious in describing the client's back condition. This caution, however, is of little use to the rehab counselor faced with a client and the question of rehabilitation feasibility. Physicians often leave the counselor on his own to make the decisive determinations regarding the employability potential of a client and the "safe" areas to consider vocationally.

The skillful vocational rehab counselor can, however, get much valuable information from the medical personnel involved in a case if he (1) knows how to go about it, and (2) knows how to use this medical information in making vocational determinations. First he must learn to use the original medical data which doubtless accompanies the referral of a client to his office. He must have familiarity with medical terminology so that he will be able to glean from these medical reports the information which is pertinent to his vocational explorations. He must recognize when medical reports fail to give vital information and must prepare himself to open lines of communication with the physicians to get all the data he needs. It is here that his training in medical terminology comes in handy.

It enables him to deal with physicians as peers. They are specialists in their own field and are able to contribute important information. This information will enable the rehabilitation counselor to steer the injured worker more effectively along a medically sound vocational path. The counselor does not have to be an expert in every field of medicine. He does need a list of the right questions to ask the physicians, questions relevant to the client's vocational interests and needs. The counselor must clarify the medical issues in his own mind and in the mind of the client before an intelligent rehabilitation plan can be formulated. The result of this clarification is a clear statement of physical capacities and limitations. This can then be translated by the counselor into vocational terms.

Once communication has been established with a physician, either by phone or mail, the counselor may find they have a common ground of interest. Both are eager to see the injured worker returned to some form of gainful employment. Other goals may vary. There may be disagreements about the extent and nature of the physical limitations as they relate to vocational planning. The shrewd counselor, however, will integrate, wherever possible, the physician's medical data into his vocational plans. He will cite specific medical evidence in his reports, involving doctors as fully as possible in his ongoing rehabilitation plans for the client. Soon he may see reference to himself and his ongoing rehabilitation effort noted in the medical reports. This will be valuable feedback for the counselor and will let him know whether or not the doctor really supports the vocational direction the counselor is moving in. This will also frequently clarify medical issues in terms of specific vocational goals under consideration.

Competent medical opinion is vital to the formulation of a rehabilitation plan that has a chance of real success. The effort to get this information will eventually pay off in terms of successful rehabilitation.

The physician is involved from the outset of the case. If the counselor is also involved early enough, he will find he is dependent on medical opinion to document whether or not a particular client can return to his original job, or whether his service as a vocational rehabilitation counselor will be required in directing the client into new vocational areas. As you recall, medical documentation is the first step in determining Qualified Injured Worker status. The physician must decide whether or not the client can return to his usual and customary occupation. The rehabilitation counselor does not make that decision. It has to be made by a physician before the counselor can even begin to consider other vocational options for the client.

The question of whether job modification by the employer may best serve the client's needs will also depend to a large extent on medical opinion. A thorough rehabilitation counselor will propose a job analysis at this point. Once completed, the job analysis is referred to the physician for review.

Certainly the question of new occupational opportunities for the client must be cleared with the doctor. For instance, suppose we have a documented medical report which states that the worker has a back injury which precludes work involving heavy lifting, bending or stooping. But the client wants to go into welding. Many types of welding involve this heavy lifting, bending and stooping which is precluded by the doctor's report. There are other, lighter types of welding, however, where there is some lifting, some bending, but these are not job constants. This is a gray area, and the effective counselor will certainly want a specific medical opinion on **how much** lifting, bending and stooping your client can tolerate without risk of reinjury. Here specific communication with the doctor is initiated. He must be informed of the client's interest in a welding program and the specific physical requirements of the type of welding job situation being considered. Medical approval is needed before enrolling the client in a welding school and making any further vocational plans.

To our knowledge, a malpractice suit against a rehabilitation counselor has never been upheld by any court. But if a counselor recommends a client for a specific type of training where there may be a chance of reinjury and that recommendation has not been cleared medically, the counselor has certainly left himself open for malpractice charges. The counselor must rely on medical opinion. That is an important part of his job in coordinating all the various elements involved in every rehabilitation case. It is frequently necessary to direct your medical inquiries to the doctor through the injured worker. Not many clients know how to communicate with physicians. There is an almost automatic assumption that the doctor will tell the patient whatever he should know. Here the client must be educated by the counselor. He must be taught to assume nothing, but to ask. His questions, however, must be specific.

The counselor can actually outline questions of concern with the client before his medical appointments. Such questions as:

What is objectively wrong with me?

How long will it be before I am fully recovered?

How long before I can expect to return to work?

If you cannot determine the exact nature of my injury, are there tests I can be given to make such a determination? What is the likelihood that surgery would improve my condition?

What kind of exercise or activity can I engage in on my own that would not hurt me but might allow me to exercise muscles that I am not now using? Are there certain types of pain that I can go through without causing further injury?

Are there other types of pain that I must pay attention to, or face possible further injury?

How much time can I spend standing, stooping, squatting, etc.?

Finally, the client can discuss with his doctor specifics of the job he intends to return to or the type of job for which he is considering training. He can be specific in describing the work, the amount of time spent standing, weights to be lifted and any other pertinent physical data on the occupation. After describing the job, the client can ask the doctor directly if he can handle this type of work without further injury.

However important the medical profession is in helping to formulate rehabilitation plans, the injured worker is sometimes exposed to too much of a good thing. The question of multiple medical opinions, particularly in cases which may be in litigation, is often a confusing one for the injured worker. He may be confronted with specialists of all sorts: from the general practitioner to the orthopedic surgeon; the rehabilitation nurse to an impressive bearded psychiatrist, complete with accent. The worker in these circumstances can sometimes be excused if he gets the notion that he must really be a sick person.

"What's wrong with me?" he begins to ask. "I have five doctors, but nobody tells me anything." Or, "I feel pain, but nobody can tell me exactly why. Maybe it's because there is nothing really wrong."

Sometimes the client feels that his physician wants to go ahead with surgery, but the insurance representative is just trying to save money by refusing to authorize the operation which could make a new man of him. He is rarely informed that the insurance representative's motive may be more than merely saving further hospitalization costs. They may feel another medical opinion is needed to determine the best long-term, overall treatment for the injured worker, to insure that surgical intervention **is** the treatment of choice.

The effective counselor will always keep in mind that he is the one who must translate and communicate what is happening on the medical scene into relevant vocational terms for the client and to relate this information to the client's ongoing rehabilitation plan.

Frequently the counselor's task of translating complex medical opinion into vocational options is complicated by the forensic rehab environment. Medical records and opinions of physicians representing both the insurance representative and the injured worker must be carefully reviewed and translated. In making this translation, the wise counselor will bear in mind that while both sides of an opposing medical argument may be seeking objectivity, subtle biases often creep into these objective judgments.

In the legal arena those physicians representing each side of the case have been selected by individuals who hope to have the case decided in a particular way. It is common to hear of certain physicians who are identified, correctly or incorrectly, as being "applicant doctors" and others who are called "defense doctors." According to this theory, applicant doctors seek to maximize the worker's disability and, subsequently, the amount of money he may receive as a permanent disability award. Defense doctors tend to represent the people who want to "wash out" the client, minimize disability and, subsequently, the permanent disability award. This is not to indicate that these physicians do anything other than offer their best consciously objective opinion on a particular case. Rather, it means that referral sources, applicant attorneys and defense attorneys select these physicians not only for their medical competency, but also because of certain attitudes and social values they may have. The vocational expert himself must finally select from these diverse medical opinions and reports the relevant information that is useful in developing the need for vocational rehabilitation and/or the degree of handicap.

# CHAPTER 4

## What The Doctors Say ... and Don't Say
## A Physician's Perspective

by

Jean Spencer Felton, M.D.*

Use strengthens, disuse debilitates. -- Hippocrates

**Introduction by Authors L. Deneen and T. Hessellund**

The following chapter by Dr. Jean Felton, Clinical Professor of Community and Environmental Medicine, University of California, is an opportunity to understand how a physician experienced in occupational medicine and vocational rehabilitation views the efforts of vocational rehabilitation consultants. His perspective is representative of many physicians involved in the vocational rehabilitation process.

He was specifically asked to address critical questions, such as:

1. As a medical practitioner what is important when working with a rehabilitation consultant?
2. What do you expect from a rehabilitation counselor in terms of communications?

Often a rehabilitation consultant must assert himself in order to secure communications whether in writing or verbally with treating and consulting physicians. To get through their efficient medical receptionist/secretaries takes persistence. Nevertheless, this activity is important. Dr. Felton underscores the importance of the rehabilitation counselor in assisting the impaired person back into the labor market. He "sets the stage" by taking us through a historical review.

**Dr. Felton's Introduction:**

While seasoned practitioners in today's sophisticated medical culture are modestly familiar with the concepts of rehabilitation, few are aware of the early and different meaning of the term. In the early years of the sixteenth century rehabilitation was the re-establishment or restoration of a person, degraded or disgraced, to his former rank and privilege, usually by formal declaration or decree. That contemporary usage is not too divergent and has been seen in society's perception of the physically impaired over past decades. Rehabilitation, for the impaired, has been, truly, a return to previous rank as gainfully employed members of the working world, from a position of second-class citizenship.

**A Matter of Definition**

Before addressing some of the issues of vocational rehabilitation, it would be helpful to seek definitions. Licht viewed rehabilitation as a synergy of medical arts and sciences by the use of which a patient strives to become as nearly normal as possible. And "normal," in this information/electronic age usually means belonging to the labor force. Note the frequent conversational opener of, "What do you do?"

Kessler, the late eminent voice of reconstructive surgery viewed rehabilitation as a creative process in which the remaining physical and mental capacities of the physically handicapped are utilized and developed to their highest efficacy, the powers of the individual being improved to the point where he can compete with equal opportunity with the so-called non-handicapped. Obermann sees rehabilitation simply as that activity required to assist an individual to move from a status of inadequacy to one of adequacy. But, in his perspective, it is a dynamic endeavor that changes in time. With each advance in the "rejection level" of the society in accommodating persons ill-equipped to cope with its more and more rigorous demands, rehabilitation takes on a new urgency. With each increase in the penalties for being unable to meet social-economic demands rehabilitation adds a new imperative.

While holy scripture cited early legal responsibilities placed on the employer when his servant was injured, the legal position was borrowed from the Code of King Hammurabi, dating back to 2000 B.C. In the growing American colonies, employers who released their servants were mandated to "see after their employment." In the eighteenth century, if a servant were injured, the master was responsible for his medical care. Marine hospitals were established to provide medical care for seamen.

Finally, in the early 1900's in the United States, when employers' liability laws failed to accrue benefits to the injured worker, and when the trio of intolerable defenses-assumption-of-risk rule, fellow-servant rule, and the contributory-negligence rule -- was replaced by State Workers' Compensation statutes, the injured employee began to receive medical care, partial wage-replacement, and other aid.

**World War I and Early Rehabilitation**

World War I saw the conscription of American youths aged 21 to 31, most of whom had no previous occupation. Prior to our entry into the war there had been almost no provision for rehabilitation of the disabled adult. In spite of good vocational education opportunities, no facilities were dedicated to re-educating the disabled. Through a private gift, the Red Cross Institute for Crippled and Disabled Men was created. Eventually, 14 months after the inception of war hostilities, legislation provided for the training of disabled soldiers. By June 27, 1918, Congressional action placed rehabilitative responsibilities of the disabled soldier and sailor on the Federal Board for Vocational Education.

**Maturation with World War II**

The war years of 1941 to 1945 saw the gradual increase in rehabilitative skills. In World War I the art and science of reparative maxillo-facial surgery was developed. In the second war lives previously lost to spinal cord injury were being saved, and amputees were undergoing appropriate preparation for the fitting of functional prosthetic devices. Kessler, who was mentioned earlier, initially performed amputations on the wounded coming out of the island conflicts in the South Pacific. Later he established a renowned amputee center at Mare Island in California where the rehabilitative program was being offered. He was instrumental in promoting the employment of impaired workers in war production plants and, subsequently, in encouraging placement of disabled veterans emerging from the armed services.

In the meantime, Dr. Howard Rusk was demonstrating the worth of the convalescent rehabilitation centers being established by the Army Air Force. Dr. Ludwig Gutman shortly thereafter began his eminent work in Great Britain with paraplegics. All of these activities marked the beginning of a convincing demonstration of the potential in restorative surgery, the patient conditioning and retraining undertaken in physical medicine, and the eventual return to the work force of persons able to be gainfully employed even though certain anatomic parts or senses had been lost.

Much publicity was given the returning veterans and nearly all social institutions -- the church, the government, business, and special community groups -- strove to publicize the need for an understanding acceptance. With the retrieval and reinstatement of the war-wounded, there began the correction of congenital anomalies. Persons with such invisible impairments as diabetes, convulsive disorders, and heart disease were included in the total rehabilitative effort.

Through the federal-state programs in vocational rehabilitation, counselors, mostly in the public agencies in the 1940's and 50's were making contact with employers so that clients who had undertaken a rehabilitation program could be placed in competitive jobs, along with the totally physically able. An early demonstration in the utilization of the physically impaired work applicant was conducted at a national atomic energy laboratory. Positions were held open while candidates would undergo the rehabilitative program needed to make them employable. Close cooperation between the vocational rehabilitation counselor and the medical director was required for such an effort to be successful.

Insurance companies hired rehabilitation nurses in the 1940's and 50's to assist in vocational rehabilitation of injured workers. Cost savings were recognized by offering early referral and prompt services.

The President's Committee on Employment of the Handicapped, created during the Truman Administration, gave support of the White House to the growing acceptance of the physically, and later the emotionally and mentally, impaired in commerce and industry.

With the years, the disease-specific voluntary health agencies -- heart disease, cancer, sickle-cell trait and disease, lung disorders, arthritis, and epilepsy among others -- added the push for employment to their preventive and direct service programs. Students in the various schools of medicine, nursing, and related caring professions began to rotate through, and receive some instruction in rehabilitation. Industry, in the form of their cardiac rehabilitation and wellness programs have joined the move in the conservation of human resources. Early writings in job placement have been replaced by scientifically tested systems of capacity analysis and the application of sound-non-discriminating medical standards.

**Role and Function of a Rehabilitation Consultant -- A Physician's Perspective**

While historically the great impetus to give employment to

and encourage acceptance and provide visibility of the impaired segment of our population came from a few far-seeing physicians, the weight of the task has been borne by the vocational rehabilitation consultant (VRC). Nearly all curricula leading to a Master's degree in rehabilitation counseling include instruction in the medical aspects of disability. There is an early contact and acquaintance between a physician and the VRC's to be. Such a relationship, nurtured seminally in the careers of both professionals, should grow into a highly productive partnership whose activities are targeted toward wider opportunities for the ability-restored worker.

The fact that the term "rehabilitation" is nearly always in today's conversation preceded by the modifier "vocational," provides the goal of nearly every rehabilitative effort except the programming solely toward independent living. Work is central to every person. But, unfortunately, in much of the health-care community work is a vague state to which a convalescing patient will one day return. Little is known by the treating practitioner of the work millieu, job demands, environmental constraints, or emotional stressors present as a living is earned.

Filling this gap is the VRC whose body of knowledge concerns not only a means of measuring the work capability of a client -- the physician's patient -- but a full understanding of the work world and its requirements of the job holder in thousands of occupations. Communication between the two professionals is mandatory, once an effective referral is made.

The physician's role is to aid and guide his patient in the return to maximum health. Yet, after reaching the point of greatest medical improvement, the injured worker may not return to work at his or her usual and customary job.

The reasons are many. In some instances, treatment can actually be anti-therapeutic and will fix "disability" in the mind of the patient. There may be no understanding on the physician's part of rehabilitation, let alone the role of a VRC. The patient, in turn, through a lack of insight into the emotional necessity of work and often as a result of litigation may visualize huge awards and a life of ease. The consequences of future inactivity is unknown during the long period of hope when the alleged or possibly real disability must be clung to in order to convince a jurist or a jury of the physical wrong which has resulted. There may be, in addition, a fear of resuming employment as a result of a rekindling of early behavioral deficits.

Such a person, seen early, and not after the usual 10 months' delay in referral for rehabilitation, can be evaluated, motivated, and returned to gainful employment. To effect a relationship between the physician and the VRC, it is necessary that the practitioner be informed of the functions and role of the VRC. Apart from those treating physicians engaged in a considerable amount of care involving Workers' Compensation, few have this awareness. Once known, the physician should apprise the VRC of the physical or emotional variants left as a result of the injury or illness. He should attempt to translate these anatomic or physiologic decriments into more meaningful phrases than "no heavy work" or "can only do sedentary work."

The physician's message is then incorporated into an evaluative study. This should eventuate into a matching of skills and behavioral capability with a potential job, customary or new. The physician, if concerned, dedicated, and desirous of providing care over a patient's lifetime, whenever needed, should expect progress reports at frequent, possibly semi-monthly, intervals. Such updatings are ideally made by telephone, but for purposes of record, should be supplemented by written reports every month and at the culmination of the rehabilitation plan. The most productive collaboration results from a personal knowledge of each of the working pair. Perhaps a shared lunch or a visit to the office, or in the case of a physician in industry, a visit and lunch at the company's and patient's plant site.

The physician who is exclusively oriented to diagnosis and treatment depends on the VRC, by virtue of training in behavioral science and with a sensitivity to a patient's need for motivation, to "take over" the recovering worker and prepare him or her, in all aspects, for a return to work. Practitioners, engaged as they are in meeting the demands of a heavy surgical practice, welcome the psychosocial restitution of their patients to the preinjury state.

The VRC has an educative role. It is only through apprising a physician of the patient's progress and the work done by the counselor that the practitioner will learn, thus benefitting future patients and the subsequent referrals. A VRC must be aggressive in the teaching process. He must not be the passive partner who feels disinterest on the part of the physician. Only through a persisting voice will there be movement in the effort to provide the continuum needed in the eventual return to work.

The mode of medical care is in transition. There is a dispiriting abroad occasioned by the introduction of regulations anathema to many accustomed to the power base of old. There is the emergence of much larger teams involved in patient care. The contribution of the VRC can be immeasurable in sharing the often difficult task of attaining the client's effective functioning after the point of maximum medical improvement. When the physician truly understands the role of the counselor/consultant, then will the patient's restoration be complete.

**Conclusion**

Up to the present from World War II saw the enactment of a law providing for rehabilitation of veterans. Slowly rehabilitative benefits were being built into the total benefit package of many State Workers' Compensation Acts, but on a voluntary basis. And, to bring us up to currency, California in 1975 was the first state to mandate vocational rehabilitation as a benefit under its Workers' Compensation law.

With this enactment, new disciplines were created to aid in the evaluation, counseling, physical restoration, adjustment, and placement of the rehabilitee. Specialists now appear in a private-practice mode and with corporate industry.

There is a legislative base for restitution of the impaired person. Yet, the rehabilitative process requires motivation of the affected individual and continued nurturing, leading eventually to a successful replacement in gainful employment.

While the law may bespeak simplicity in goal attainment, it may not be an easy road for either the rehabilitation professional or the returning employee. Vocational rehabilitation is a strict master and demands work from many participants. The struggle for a return to worth and dignity for every impaired person continues, and the years ahead will show eventually that physical and functional restoration and a return to the work site bring greater psychic reward than a litigious battle, a settlement, and a residual disability.

**References**

1. Licht, S. Rehabilitation Medicine: Definition and Origin. **Arch Phys Med Rehabil** 51:619, 1970.
2. Kessler, H.H., cited in Krusen, F.H. Physical Rehabilitation for Industrial Diseases.

**Br J Phys Med** 18:220, 1955.

3. Obermann, C.E. **A History of Vocational Rehabilitation in America.** Minneapolis, T.S. Denison & Company, Inc., 1965, p. 41.
4. Exodus 21:18-19, 26-27.
5. Obermann, **op. cit.,** p. 117.
6. McMurtie, D.C. **The Disabled Soldier.** New York, The MacMillan Company, 1919, p. 228.
7. Chuff, I.S. Rehabilitation for Industrial Cripples -- Federal-State Plan Adopted. **Am Labor Legislative Rev** 10:125, 1920.
8. Kessler, H.H. **The Knife Is Not Enough.** New York, W.W. Norton & Company, 1968, Chap. 6. The Early War Years, pp. 91-105.
9. **Ibid.,** Chap. 7, Mare Island, pp. 106-127.
10. Obermann, **op. cit.,** p. 306.
11. **Ibid.**
12. Felton, J.S. Job Performance of Physically Impaired Persons in Industry. **Occup Med** 5:466, 1946.
13. **Operations Manual for Placement of the Physically Handicapped,** ed. 3. Washington, DC, U.S. Civil Service Commission, (June) 1944.
14. Bridges, C.D. **Job Placement of the Physically Handicapped.** New York, McGraw-Hill Book Company, 1946.
15. Hanman, B. **Physical Abilities to Fit the Job.** Boston, American Mutual Liability Insurance Company, Engineering Department, 1956.
16. Nylander, S.W., and Carmean, G. **Medical Standards Project Final Report,** ed. 2, rev. San Bernardino, CA, County of San Bernardino, (Jan) 1983, Vols. I and II.
17. California Workers' Compensation Institute, personal communication, (April 18) 1985.

### Additional Readings

1. Return to Work -- Checkpoints Along the Rehabilitation Trail. **Occup Hazards** 46:43 (Jan), 1984.
2. Hanna, C.; Mullinax, J.; and Sadler, V. Rehabilitation Nurse or Vocational Rehabilitation Counselor: Competency Based Selection. **J Rehab** 49:75, (Oct/Nov/Dec), 1983.

3. Margolis, H., and Fiorelli, J.S. An Applied Approach to Facilitating Interdisciplinary Teamwork. **J Rehab** 50:13 (Jan/Feb/March), 1984.
4. Vocational Rehabilitation: Added Hope for Injured Workers. **Insurer** No. 83-A, 1983.
5. Spiegel, A.D., and Podair, S. **Rehabilitating People with Disabilities into the Mainstream of Society.** Park Ridge, N.J., Noyes Medical Publications, 1981.

# CHAPTER 5

## Job Analysis

The private vocational rehabilitation counselor working in the Workers' Compensation system needs relevant, accurate, specific and complete information about particular jobs. The physician needs this information when the eligibility of a client for rehabilitation services is being decided. What are the specific demands of the injured worker's previous job which make it impossible for him to return to this work, rather than go through a costly and time-consuming rehabilitation process? The counselor needs detailed job information while he is exploring vocational possibilities with a client. Are the physical demands of a particular job consistent with the client's postinjury limitations? Such information is based on good job analysis.

A job analysis performs these essential functions:

1. It describes objectively a job which the worker has done or is doing.
2. It describes objectively the worker's functions and the physical requirements of the job.
3. It describes objectively the individual worker's skills and abilities which are transferable to other jobs and work situations.

According to the Manpower Administration, U.S. Department of Labor, the following areas of use for job analysis are identified:

1. Recruitment and placement.
2. Better utilization of workers in terms of physical demands.
3. Job restructuring and engineering.
4. Vocational counseling.
5. Training programs.
6. Occupational health and safety.

Whether it is a physician using a job analysis to determine the injured worker's physical capacity to fulfill job demands, the counselor making use of it to include or exclude possible vocational regions of consideration for a client's rehab plan, or a placement officer using a job analysis to match up job with applicant capacities, it is an important tool when carefully used. Sometimes it can even help redesign a specific job to meet a specific client's needs by transfering job skills from one sphere to another. It is frequently essential in aiding clients to develop and accept realistic and objective vocational goals.

In talking about job analysis, the word "objective" has taken an enormous significance. As much as possible, a job analysis must be an impartial (and quantitatively measurable) description of the physical characteristics and energy expense involved in the job performance.

A thorough job analysis will include interviews with workers, supervisors and/or staff of the personnel department. Actual observation of a worker doing an explicit job, though sometimes difficult to get, is vital. Detailed factual reports of the performance of a job from several different points of view are desirable.

On many occasions photographs or video filming may be done. This is not necessary in all circumstances. When needed the cost will be more, particularly for videotape filming. This can be an excellent method of informing a physician of the work environment.

Once the data for the job analysis is gathered and a report is prepared it is desirable to have the injured worker and a job supervisor review it. If feasible the worker may be able to be present at the work site when the JA is being done.

Based on the expressed purpose of a job analysis, the use to be made of the analysis and the methods used to prepare it, a number of different abilities are needed to perform this technique. They are:

1. The ability to interview an employer and use nondirective communication techniques to gather the subtle aspects of job and worker functions.
2. The ability to accurately observe and record what is being done in a way that relates to vocational information, occupational resource information, rehabilitation counseling techniques, work adjustment theories and vocational decision-making research.
3. The ability to define a job by means of an acceptable model in regard to the nature of the

work, such as that of the Department of Labor in the **Dictionary of Occupational Titles** (DOT). This ability implies an understanding of the model.

4. The ability to classify work tasks in terms of aptitudes, interests, temperaments, physical demands and educational level needed to perform the job.

Thus, the truly effective vocational counselor must possess these specific job analysis abilities in order to adequately serve his client, the injured worker, as well as his customer, the insurance representative. When a job analysis is completed by a professional in the field of vocational rehabilitation, such an analysis bears weight and is given credence because:

1. A rehab counselor, thanks to his graduate school training, practicum supervision and internship, **perceives** a job and its context in a way that expedites the rehabilitation process.
2. There is less chance of missing important job modification possibilities, worker aptitude factors and personality indices, if a professional has done the job analysis.
3. A professional consultant executing a job analysis can use his expertise to document the mental pressures that do or do not exist on a job and the group pressures that may or may not prevail.
4. Employers, physicians and attorneys are more willing to utilize a job analysis to help in the rehabilitation of an injured person when they know it has been done by an expert with professional training in the use of occupational information, the physical demands of specific jobs and rehabilitation consulting.

The professionalism of the job analyses used in making vocational rehab plans is emphasized because the best of rehab plans may succeed or fail on the basis of the soundness of the job analysis. Satisfactory rehabilitation requires a thorough understanding of how workers satisfy their psychological and/or physical needs through work.

A counselor must be experienced and knowledgeable in how work environments, through technology, can be modified so that a disabled worker can fulfill his psychological needs through gainful employment. The counselor needs to understand work adjustment in terms of a worker being satisfied with his level of productivity, i.e., the degree of congruence between his abilities and those demanded by the job. The counselor needs a good knowledge of personality dynamics, decision making and work engineering to suit the worker to the job. He also needs the ability to translate one employer's job functions to the employment requirements of another job. The more training, skill and experience a rehab counselor can bring to his job analyses, the greater his rate of successful rehab outcomes.

As we have seen, these decisions based on job analysis make the difference between success or failure. A worker may be put through long, complicated training and eventually fail in a new vocational area when a specific and slight modification in his previous job (apparent in a good job analysis) could have put the worker happily and economically back at work in his old job. Or, on the basis of an inaccurate job analysis, a worker may be sent back to his old job and run into serious problems, be unable to handle the work pace or even reinjure himself. This is tragic for all concerned. The worker is that much further away from rehabilitation, has suffered additional pain, hospitalization and loss of income. The insurance representative is faced with additional costs for reopening the case and starting over with a new rehabilitation plan. Decisions like these must be based on the professional expertise of a conscientious and complete job analysis prepared by an experienced and trained rehabilitation counselor.

# CHAPTER 6

## Vocational Diagnosis

Once it has been determined that your client is physically incapable of returning to his previous job, the second question of feasibility enters the picture: Can the services of a professional rehabilitation counselor be reasonably expected to aid this injured worker in returning to another type of work situation? The first question of disability is primarily a medical one. Answering the second question involves receiving, digesting and integrating a wide variety of information before deciding on your client's chances of success in a new vocational area. Here it should be remembered that these are two separate and distinct questions. Because a machinist cannot return to his previous machine shop job does not mean he cannot be considered for any type of work with machinery. The transfer of existing skill development to a new work situation compatible with the client's disability is frequently a satisfying and economically sound form of rehabilitation.

Calculating an injured worker's likelihood of success in new work and/or vocational situations, and being restored to suitable gainful employment is perhaps the most important part of the vocational rehabilitation counselor's work. It is on the basis of the decisions he makes here that: 1) A determination is made by the counselor as to whether or not the client is likely to benefit from further rehabilitation services, or, 2) A specific vocational objective and rehabilitation plan is determined. The counselor's basic instrument in making these decisions rests mainly on a complete vocational diagnosis of his client.

The questions to be answered by a sound and accurate vocational diagnosis are twofold: What are the assets this injured worker can bring into a new vocational situation, and secondly, what are the specific limitations imposed by his disabling condition? In order to answer these questions as completely and accurately as possible the counselor must view his client in his total life space environment, past as well as present. Only with such a sweeping view can the counselor develop a picture of the total client, his strengths as well as his limitations. And only with such a total, unfragmented picture will the counselor be able to make a sound, realistic vocational plan and assist the client in circumventing the vocational limitations imposed by his injury.

The vocational diagnosis is thus an instrument involving all aspects of the client's life in its full specificity and uniqueness: his family, social and work history, his educational and experiential background. It is an assessment of his current family financial and sociocultural situation as well as updated psychometric data. Also included will be an analysis of specific physical limitations (**pre** and **post**injury as they relate to the world of work), and an assessment of special aptitudes, skills and occupational interests. In short, the good vocational diagnosis gives a reliable portrait of the client and his background in relation to his current and future work life.

If a vocational diagnosis is honestly, responsibly and effectively completed, it can form the basis for a sound and realistic vocational plan with a good chance of success. A haphazard or inaccurate vocational diagnosis can produce unrealistic vocational plans with little likelihood of successful outcome, another failure for the client and extra costs for the insurance carrier. After one or two of these failed vocational plans, the client begins to distrust himself, the rehabilitation counselor and the whole rehab process. He may be ready to throw in the towel. It is no exaggeration to say that producing a sound vocational diagnosis comprises half the work of an effective counselor.

Let's take a closer look at what's involved in an accurate, honest and complete vocational diagnosis.

### 1. Medical Assessment

This has already been discussed in the last section and is largely the product of the medical team working with a particular client. What is done with this medical information, how is it read and interpreted in terms of vocational options is the work of the vocational expert, the rehab counselor. In his meetings with the client, it is he who must assess the client's perception of his injury and how it relates to his chances of re-entering the world of work. A negative, "I can't do anything now" attitude on the part of the injured worker can defeat the soundest rehabilitation before it starts. The skilled rehabilitation counselor attempts to deal with the client's attitudinal problems regarding his physical status at the earliest possible moment. He must deal with these negative attitudes as key elements of the client's motivational structure and build realistic vocational goals around these difficulties, perhaps even "selling" certain goals to his defeatist client. The counselor is not concerned only with the residual limitations of his client's injury, however, and how these limitations affect work performance. He must also be aware of the client's ongoing medical treatment and prospects. Does the client's current level of physical functioning represent the best he can hope for, or is improvement over time a reasonable expectation? These factors must all be fed into a final determination of the type of work the client can be expected to perform.

### 2. Psychological/Vocational Assessment

Depending on the client and other information you have at hand, you may want to go through a complete psychological/vocational assessment before making your final vocational determination.

In private vocational rehabilitation, the counselor typically does his own testing depending on his qualifications and expertise. When selecting tests to aid in making the vocational diagnosis, the focus is in one or a combination of the following areas:

1. Vocational interests.
2. Aptitudes (verbal, numerical, mechanical, spatial, abstract reasoning, clerical).
3. Specific skill assessment (reading level, math level, clerical skills, bookkeeping skills) and temperament.
4. Personality assessment as it relates to vocational decision making.

Testing is discussed in greater detail in Chapter 8.

With some clients, you may rely on your own observations and information gleaned from the client file and the client himself during counseling sessions to determine his potential in specific areas of work under consideration. Whatever your choice, it is important that this psychometric and observational data be carefully screened and relevantly integrated into the overall vocational goals being discussed with the client. Pure psychological data out of the context of the injured worker's value system and expectations from his work is not applicable.

### 3. Educational Background

This area is important in judging not only where your client is on the academic ladder, but in attempting to assess what kind of success your client will have in a specific retraining program. What were his previous educational experiences? Does he have positive feelings about education, or was his previous experience in school distasteful to him? Are his reading and writing skills adequate for dealing with a formal education program which you might like to consider or in which the client has expressed interest? The answers to these questions can help you predict whether a client will stick with and complete a proposed retraining program, or whether he will drop out, costing him another defeat and creating an extra cost burden for the insurance carrier. For a client to see himself failing in a program because of inadequate reading or writing skills can be extremely destructive to his self-esteem and make him that much more wary of future retraining areas proposed.

When assessing the educational history, the categorical review should include:

1. Formal schooling.
2. Specific classes taken and grades earned.
3. Subjects enjoyed and disliked.
4. Technical courses completed in conjunction with a job.
5. Specialty training in the military.
6. Any other formal or informal education.
7. When a person's formal schooling includes college courses ask them to secure a copy of the transcript.

### 4. Social and Financial Support System

The primary focus in this area is generally the client's family and his financial budget. The immediate circle of wife and children may often be his entire social network. It is on them that he will depend for support and encouragement during his rehabilitation. Other significant relatives or friends may also be important in keeping your client's motivation alive but, in making your initial diagnosis, it is vital that you be familiar with the client's immediate social climate. If the client has a large and positive social support system, your job will be that much easier. It will do much of your work in keeping alive the client's interest and enthusiasm during the rehabilitation process. On the other hand, if your client is isolated and has no significant social network, the burden of keeping the client involved in the rehabilitation plan will be yours.

The client's budget cash flow and degree of indebtedness are important in understanding his current frustrations. It enables you to help identify a vocational objective that in the long run fits with the client's financial situation. Being skilled in financial planning is an asset in this area.

**5. Cultural and Environmental Factors**

Through both verbal and nonverbal clues you will be able to gather personal impressions of your client's sociocultural milieu. These impressions, together with the data you have from other professionals in the client's case record, should give you a fairly rounded view of the client's total living environment. Is he poor or is he moderately well-off? Does he live in a decent neighborhood or does he come from a bleak, impoverished area? What is his present economic status, and does this represent a lifetime pattern for this client, or is it the product of recent events?

Workers who have difficulty earning enough to meet only their basic needs of food, shelter and clothing will often have a different view of work than clients on a higher socioeconomic level. The poorer workers tend to view a job as only a means of making money. They have no idea that working can satisfy other needs, can give a sense of achievement or accomplishment, can give meaning to their lives. The personal satisfaction of meeting the challenge of certain work experiences means little to a worker who has trouble paying his rent and supplying adequate food and clothing for his family. The counselor will have to develop different occupational satisfiers with different clients. Many of the studies that have been made, however, indicate even the most culturally deprived individuals want satisfying as well as gainful employment and, given the opportunity to learn a higher level of vocational skill, they can succeed at more demanding occupations. Apparently, according to the literature on the subject, there is less variability in work motivators between the middle and lower classes than had been supposed. As a counselor, this means that you should be aware of your attitudes and not apply stereotypic labels to clients and make assumptions about client motivation based on these labels. An individual approach to assessing the client's work value system is more productive.

## 6. Vocational History

The single most important factor in making a vocational diagnosis is the client's work history. The analysis of the work history should be approached in the broadest sense. A systematic sequential analysis of the client's vocational background should be a part of every evaluation. The analysis includes the following steps:

1. Verbally question the client for his work history.
2. Have the client complete a Work Application Form which documents work history.
3. Have a second review of work history with the client following completion of the Work Application.
4. Identify and discuss a client's hobbies and leisure time activities.

Once the work history is thoroughly documented, the art of vocational diagnosis now comes into play. It is in this area that the counseling skills are either visibly present or clearly lacking. It is at this point that it becomes evident that either the client's past experience, skills and knowledge can be applied or cannot be applied in seeking re-entry into the competitive labor market. This is, of course, the important art of applying transferable skills.

When discussing a work history with the client, each job should be analyzed in detail. This detailed analysis includes:

1. Dates of employment (months and year).
2. Title of job.
3. Name of employer or supervisor.
4. Duties and responsibilities.
5. Types of tools and equipment used or manipulated.
6. Client's feelings about various duties.
7. Would the supervisor judge the client as a good worker?
8. Salary and pay.
9. Reason for leaving.

## 7. Transferable Skills

The injured worker should write down all the job titles, duties, and hobbies he has performed.

This information is next matched up with corresponding **Dictionary of Occupational Titles** or **Guide for Occupational Exploration** information.

The job titles that relate to the transferable skills and are physically appropriate are listed out.

Software programs are available to assist in this transferable skills analysis.

Dr. Botterbusch in his excellent review book titled **A Comparison of Computerized Job Matching Systems** enables you to easily compare the systems available. Dr. Field in his publication **Labor Market Access** discusses how percentage of labor market access and predisability/postdisability wages are computed using computers and software.

During a separate meeting with the client a thorough analysis of transferable skills is useful. The client in many instances can be taught to do his own **DOT** and **GOE** research. Then, the consultant can corroborate it. The process of transferable skills identification often enhances a client's confidence and self-esteem.

**8. The Vocational Synthesis**

Once you have gathered all the data you can on your client -- his history, physical tolerance, skills, attitudes, interests, social and cultural background, his postinjury assets and liabilities -- you are ready to contribute your own expertise as a vocational counselor. When blended with all the data you have gathered on the client's personal interests and qualifications -- your knowledge of the world of work, the physical, emotional and intellectual demands of various occupational areas and familiarity of the needs of the current labor market -- you will have the basis for a sound and reasonable vocational diagnosis for this particular client. Awareness of the client's current physical status and limitations helps narrow the focus, eliminating areas which must be ruled out on medical grounds. As more knowledge of the client's educational background, skill repertoire and interest level is acquired, however, you may open up new areas for exploration and give your client an even broader view of his vocational options. Your familiarity with the client's personal characteristics, the strength of his family and social support system and his attitudes toward work can furnish valuable clues as to the type and length of training program this client will be able to sustain. It is only this kind of solid fusion of your knowledge of what's in the client's life space with your knowledge of what's out in the world of work and training that can form the basis for a realistic vocational assessment. With such a solid vocational diagnosis, you and the client are in a much better position to formulate a sound rehabilitation plan with a good chance of a successful outcome.

It is frequently at this stage in the rehabilitation process that new counselors often fail. They do not take all the factors into account as they make their vocational plans. A clue missed in the client's background, his work or social history, may sometimes lead the counselor up a blind vocational alley, misusing some of the client's motivation as well as the insurance carrier's funding.

A competent vocational rehabilitation counselor does not have to be a crack psychometrician, a skilled physician or an astute psychologist to make a thorough vocational diagnosis. You can rely on the professional skills of other specialists in these areas. However, you must be able to read and interpret their reports. Your job is to bring all this information together, combine it with your personal awareness of the client's uniqueness and come up with a comprehensive portrait, complete with background. If you have read accurately all information from others and used some of your own gut-felt hunches about the client, you are about ready to recommend an informed and realistic vocational planning process.

# CHAPTER 7

## Marketable Transferable Skills

By
Lawrence J. Deneen, Ph.D. and
Colleen M. Deneen, M.Ed.

**What** are they, **Where** do you find them and **How** do they relate to vocational testing and counseling?

### Introduction

Transferable skills is one of the least understood methods of developing a Plan. If transferable skills are identified that render a person employable in the competitive labor market then it may not be necessary to proceed to more extensive vocational exploration or evaluation techniques as discussed in the next chapter.

The client must be agreeable to use his existing skills so as to return to work as soon as possible. **If not,** it is usually futile to try and "sell" those skills as a preferred rehabilitation plan. No employer will want to buy what an applicant **has** but does **not** want to sell. Frequently clients who are able disabled have skills that are marketable but they do not want to use them in pursuing occupations that require those skills.

If a client does want to use and sell his skills, it is important to assess the "marketability" of the transferable skills, i.e., will an employer pay money for those identified transferable skills and hire him.

John Crystal and Richard Bolles (1974) over the past decade have made a significant change for the better in the delivery of vocational services. In their publication, **Where Do I Go From Here With My Life?,** they present a systematic process for job changers and counselors to follow. This process maximizes client self-confidence, helps identify marketable transferable skills, and leads to job search success. Sidney Fine of the W.E. Upjohn Institute for Employment Research (1974) recommends this book for all helpers of those seeking career guidance (vocational rehabilitation). He feels it goes beyond the superficiality of most vocational counseling.

**Skills and Values Identification:** At the heart of Crystal's and Bolles' (1974) and Bolles' (1972) process is a thorough work autobiography that clients prepare on their own or with assistance. This autobiography or work history spells out the details of work achievements, duties, likes and dislikes, job satisfiers, responsibilities, and data-people-things knowledge. It includes educational accomplishments and other tasks the person has performed. It is the principal tool of skills and values identification. It goes beyond simply asking "what do you want to do?" or "what are you interested in doing?" It probes at the behaviors a person has done throughout his/her work/educational history. These are frequently more valid indicators of a person's true values and interests than simply asking a superficial question. This is especially true for individuals with limited education and few abilities in verbalizing their likes and dislikes.

Crystal and Bolles (1974) categorize skills as follows:

1. Skills which you do only with great difficulty **and** it looks difficult to others.
2. Skills which you do only with great difficulty, but it looks effortless to others.
3. Skills which you do effortlessly, and it looks effortless as well.
4. Talents that you were born with, which you have always been able to do effortlessly.

Crystal and Bolles (1974), as well as Louis Zinn of the Department of Health, Education and Welfare (1979), the Department of Labor in their **Dictionary of Occupational Titles** (1977) and, Drs. Field, Sink, and Harris of Vdare Service Bureau in their vocational diagnosis methodology (1979), purposefully refer to "skills" in a general sense. Clients are recommended to use as general a description as possible so that the transferability of the skills is obvious and easily recognized by themselves, counselors, and employers.

The entire systematic process for identifying skills, clarifying preferences, and succeeding in a job search strategy that is presented by Crystal and Bolles (1974) does not solely rely on a single source of data. It assumes candor and honest self-exploration on the part of the client. It relies on thorough data collection from as many sources as is practical including work autobiographies and selected vocational testing.

**The Real Truth: Vocational Tests Measure Behavior.** With persons less capable of verbalizing and writing their work/educational biographies, vocational testing and work evaluation helps "expose" and identify skills and interests. The words used to describe the results may include "achievements," "aptitudes," or "traits." These terms are traditional vocational testing terms and imply assumptions about what a performance on a particular test or task indicates. Across all of the theoretically based assumptions, the only truth is that the individual demonstrates behavior by doing something either physically or mentally.

If it was done physically, the behavior was timed, observed, and rated. If it was done mentally, the person probably manipulated paper, answer sheets, pencils, test booklets, and other such devices to tangibly record mental thoughts. Once recorded, the answers are rated or scored and the length it took to complete the process is timed.

Typically, the specific answers and results of vocational tests get clustered or grouped according to specific instructions of the test author. This is the scoring process. Once all the grouping of answers is done, generalized statements couched as "aptitudes" or "traits" are used to discuss the results.

The process of going from the specific to the general takes place in all methods of skills identification whether it is through vocational testing or work/educational histories. Frequently, both methods are helpful so as to correlate the results and develop greater validity. This is especially true in situations where litigation and secondary gains of a disability may exist.

**Definition of Marketable Transferable Skills (MTS):** In a recent survey, 12 professionals, including vocational counselors, job placement counselors, labor market analysts, and job developers, were asked to define the following:

1. Skill
2. Transferable
3. Labor Market
4. Marketable Transferable Skills (MTS)

These persons were all skilled professionals. Three (3) were Certified Counselors, one (1) had a Doctorate degree, seven (7) had a Master's degree, and four (4) had over 5 years' experience in placing persons in the competitive labor market.

Most of the definitions were different. Common elements existed across the persons surveyed. The results are as follows:

1. **Skills**
   - Talents used in an occupation or for recreational purposes
   - ability to perform a task
   - talents learned in performing a task
   - observable behavior that can be measured and used at will
   - learned experience and learned tasks
   - performance to accomplish a goal
   - behavior that is done or a thought process demon strated through words and paper
2. **Transferable**
   - application of one thing to another setting
   - move something from one place to another
   - the application of something to another area
   - can be moved from one place to another
   - used in a different setting with different criteria
   - movement, mobility
3. **Labor Market**
   - the place (usually a geographic area) where a combination of supply and demand exists for a particular type or group of skills or occupations
   - breakdown of supply and demand of the work force
   - availability of jobs based on samplings from employers
   - trends of job availability
   - existence of jobs where people are gainfully employed
   - samplings of job openings for a particular person and position
   - job openings specific to a particular date and geographic area
   - availability of jobs for particular types of or groups of skills

4. **Marketable Transferable Skills**
   - skills used in the labor market
   - abilities learned in performing tasks that are used in different work environments
   - abilities from education and work history that are used in new jobs
   - experience used in alternate employment that exists in the current labor market and that is marketable
   - skills that apply to another area of work with some similarities
   - performance of tasks that is applicable to duties of jobs and for which an employer will hire

As a result of this survey and rehabilitation counseling experience, the following definition is proposed:

> **Marketable Transferable skills (MTS)** are those behaviors which can be measured and used at will that are applicable to different situations and/or various job duties and for which an employer will pay.

**MTS, Case Management and Counseling:** The concept and above definition of marketable transferable skills should be at the heart of vocational counseling and job placement services. It is a necessary ingredient for enhancing a client's self-confidence, for efficiently utilizing a client's assets, and for achieving client success. The process is familiar, but the concepts and words to describe the process is different. First, you identify a worker's behaviors that can be measured and observed. You determine the applicability of these behaviors to alternative job situations. Secondly, you counsel and guide the worker in his own job search for a chosen vocational goal. You clarify his values and interests. Thirdly, you determine whether or not an employer wants to hire the worker due to his demonstrated behaviors and interests that apply to the job duties. You call employers to determine the marketability of the worker.

The above process gets results. It produces the desired end of injured workers **who have Marketable Transferable Skills:** a restoration of their earning capacity as soon as possible and as near as possible to their preinjury earnings.

The process requires interpersonal, motivational counseling on the part of the vocational and job placement counselor. It necessarily requires a decision to want to return to suitable work on the part of the injured worker. It provides structured activities that increase and sustain a client's motivation. The ongoing counseling and structured activities reinforce client behaviors that are associated with securing work. These behaviors include completing a work autobiography, selected interest and aptitude tests, informational interviews, job search skills training, self-directed labor market research, telephone calls to employers, and job interviews. For many clients, formal or on-the-job training is necessary.

If after calling employers, you determine that a person's skills are not marketable, then the individual will need to consider on-the-job or formal training. This training will give the person marketable skills.

The above process expects a lot from both client and counselor. Mediocrity will not help counselors effectively deal with client frustrations. Mediocrity does not help counselors confront the discrepancies between client verbalizations and client behaviors. Mediocrity does not foster the proper balance of toughness and tenderness. This balance is needed to inspire clients to believe in their own skills and to accept the objective appraisal of the counselor.

Mediocrity does not help a client sell himself to employers. Truly successful persons in all walks of life are not mediocre. They do what the average person does not like to do. Most people do not enjoy looking for work. When unemployed, they do not actively and daily look for work. They avoid their dislikes. However, successful job searchers who secure a job with a higher salary and/or greater opportunity are persons who ignore what average persons do. Successful persons do not like to look for work either. Yet, they do it. They do what they dislike. They do not settle for mediocrity in their vocational planning and job search efforts.

The greatest shortcoming of many clients is their unwillingness to do the behaviors that they know lead to employment but that they dislike to do. It is as if the dislike of looking for a suitable job is greater than the dislike of remaining unemployed. In some instances, there are financial reinforcements and contingencies for not pursuing gainful jobs. A person may believe he will lose something if he tries.

When both the financial disincentive exists and the greater dislike for seeking a job goal than remaining unemployed exists, the circumstance is ripe for a vocational rehabilitation failure. A mediocre counselor in such a case will not inspire a client to alternative behaviors. An exceptional counselor may not succeed either. Clients need counseling to help them understand the contingencies that exist. Then they must decide whether or not they are willing to do what leads to success in returning to work.

**Bottom Line Results:** The process of counseling and the use of a marketable transferable skills technology in a private rehabilitation counseling setting accomplished counselor goals and those of most clients who wanted to return to suitable work.

Success in accurately identifying transferable skills that are marketable for client-selected job objectives is evidenced by these recent case file review statistics, from a study of 87 job placement cases:

1. **Of the 87 cases:**
   - 25% were not fully active on their own behalf, did not attend all interviews, and were not available for daily job search
   - 7% were medically not able or eligible to participate
   - 1% declined further services
   - 10% were not placed and were further evaluated
   - 57% were placed.
2. **Of the 58 clients who participated fully:**
   - 86% WERE PLACED.
3. **Of the 49 placed clients:**
   - 31% earned salaries GREATER than date of injury (D/I) earnings.
   - 67% earned salaries less than D/I earnings.
   - 2% earned salaries equal to D/I earnings.
   - 72% who had received schooling earned less than D/I earnings.
   - 78% were placed on transferable skills.

The ultimate intent of effective vocational rehabilitation with the industrially injured is to restore a person's earning capacity. Case management and counseling that thoroughly and objectively helps clients realize their transferable skills will lead to greater success. Clients need help in identifying their skills and in translating them to other occupations. If their skills are not marketable, they need training.

Rehabilitation professionals working with clients who were substantial wage earners prior to disability will increase the probability of these clients remaining substantial wage earners after disability if, when possible, they identify and use the client's Marketable Transferable Skills.

## REFERENCES

** Bolles, R.N. **What Color Is Your Parachute?** Berkeley: Ten Speed Press, 1972, 1979.

** Mischel, W. **Personality and Assessment.** New York: John Wiley, 1968.

** Crystal, John C. and Bolles, Richard N. **Where Do I Go From Here With My Life?** Berkeley: Ten Speed Press, 1974.

** Deneen, L. "Results of Private Vocational Rehabilitation Services: Length, Costs, Success." Paper presented at American Personnel and Guidance Association National Convention, American Rehabilitation Counseling Association Division, Las Vegas, April 5, 1979.

** Field, T., Harris, S., and Sink, J. **Vocational Diagnosis and Assessment of Residual Employability.** Vdare Service Bureau, Roswell, GA 1979.

** Fine, Sidney A. **Where Do I Go From Here With My Life?**, Foreword, Berkeley: Ten Speed Press, 1974.

** U.S. Department of Labor, **Dictionary of Occupational Titles.** Fourth Edition, U.S.Employment Service, 1977.

** Zinn, L. **Department of Health, Education, and Welfare,** Social Security Administration, Vocational Consultant program, Lecture presented at a vocational expert conference in Los Angeles on May 24, 1979.

## RESOURCE TEXT

** Deneen, L. and Hessellund, T. **Vocational Rehabilitation of the Injured Worker.** Rehabilitation Publications, P.O. Box 22606, San Francisco, CA 94122, 1981.

# CHAPTER 8

## Testing In Career and Vocational Counseling
## Why use tests, what are tests, when to use tests.

By

Lawrence J. Deneen, Ph.D.

In our data gathering process we each demonstrate different degrees of orderliness, organization, structure, and sensitivity to the disabled person. In professional offices there are often very precise and detailed manuals that describe what, how, when, and why certain things are done with clients or patients. These procedures reduce individual staff variations and flexibility. These same procedures maintain uniformity and high quality of services.

Standardized testing is based on a similar idea. The what, how, when, and why are spelled out for the tester by means of the test manual and answer sheet directions. Informal testing approaches do not clearly state how to administer or score a particular test. Consequently, the test results are influenced to a biased degree by the ability of the "tester."

**Advantages and Disadvantages of a Standardized Approach**

The advantages of a standardized testing approach versus a more informal testing approach may be obvious. They are the same as for standardization of any process or procedure. Needless to say, the disadvantages are also the same. First, the advantages:

1. A standardized approach increases the consistency for all clients, patients, students, etc. It reduces and controls for individual differences which are demonstrated on the part of the rehabilitation helper.
2. If an error or mistake in the procedure occurs, it is easier to locate the area of difficulty with standardized testing.

3. If normative data is gathered, which is a reference group to compare a client's score, then it is necessary to make sure that the clients undergo the same tests as the reference group. Otherwise, any comparison is meaningless. Standardized testing insures the meaningfulness of comparing a norm group with a client.
4. A standardized approach in testing usually results in clearer directions for a task and increases the efficiency of the task.

The disadvantages of standardized testing may be sensed by you. Terms like "consistency," "standardization," "systematic," "efficient," "error reduction," and "accountability," which often accompany standardized tests and procedures, connote a coldness and a mechanized approach. This is the major drawback of standardized testing in the helping professions. In the name of standardization more patients and clients in medical centers, dental clinics, and vocational evaluation units have been processed like numbers and "turned off" to the services they were receiving.

To effectively use standardized testing, the subjective and personal touch, the human sensitivity that must prevail in all human service enterprises, is necessary. It is essential. A combination of standardization and human sensitivity is needed for a vocational evaluation and planning process to truly assess and direct a person's vocational potential.

**Selection and Purpose of Tests**

Vocational tests are selected to help with the decision making process of vocational rehabilitation. However, many test developers and users define the purpose of testing differently. Their choice of words and circular definitions make testing seem mysterious. They state that the purpose of using an aptitude test is to estimate an injured's aptitudes in relation to jobs or training. This type of description of the purpose of testing is from textbooks. It is circular and does not give any clear functional purpose.

The primary and critical basis for using a test in vocational rehabilitation is how it will aid in the decision making process of a specific client and of a specific referring source. Practically all testing methods measure a person's past performance and abilities. In order to get a client to seek the acquisition of new work skills, motivation through personal interaction and counseling is needed. The relationship of the rehabilitation consultant to the client determines whether or not testing has moved a client towards a specific vocational objective. There is no magic in the testing.

Adequate test result feedback and interpretation for clients is important. This takes time and depends on the client's ability to understand the results. A vocational evaluation report may help you justify a rehabilitation plan and document a referral to a rehabilitation service provider, but only the feedback of the test results will move a client toward a specific vocational goal. Many testers do not give adequate attention to the feedback process in rehabilitation counseling. If they do not, the referring source and the injured person are short-changed.

**Terminology in Vocational Testing**

Certain terms are important in testing. It is advantageous to become as comfortable with them as with medical terminology. The knowledge of this terminology facilitates efforts in dealing with rehabilitation cases effectively and ensures the highest quality of vocational services.

**Validity:** The validity of a test refers to the validity of a test result rather than the instrument itself. It is the results which are or are not valid. If the test results measure what the test says they do then it is considered valid. Typically, the longer a test then the greater its validity.

The validity of a test is affected by a tester's skills. Consequently, if the test is standardized and the scoring and administration is the same regardless of who the rehabilitation counselor is, then greater validity usually results. Validity of test results is always specific to the particular purpose and use of the testing. No test is valid for all decision-making and all purposes.

For example, a well-constructed math test that requires computational and arithmetic skills may not be valid for predicting a client's success in a modern math class that emphasizes sets and whole integers.

**Reliability:** The reliability of a test refers to the consistency of the test scores. If you were to test the person on January 2nd and again on February 2nd, and he scored the same on a verbal ability test, then the test scores are considered reliable. Another example may help. If you were to interview an injured worker and I was to interview the same worker but we gathered different information about his work history, vocational interest, and vocational plans, then our interviewing would not be considered reliable.

Usually, the longer the test the more reliable it is. This is because changes made from one testing situation to the next testing situation tend to cancel each other out with a test that has a lot of questions.

**Validity and Reliability: The Difference**

An example for differentiating between validity and reliability may be helpful. When a witness is testifying in a courtroom trial, the fact that he consistently tells the same story does not mean that he is telling the truth. The truthfulness of his statement demands a comparison with other facts just like the validity of a test requires the comparison of the scores with other data. The truthfulness of a test relates to its validity.

It is because of the critical importance of validity that care and attention must be taken in the proper selection and interpretation of tests. Unfortunately, when it comes to test selection, not all rehabilitation consultants and vocational evaluation specialists continue to keep abreast of the research published in professional journals. Standards for test selection and interpretation are available but not always followed.

**The Problem for Test Selection**

Let me give you a feel for the magnitude of the problem of proper vocational test selection for a particular client. Note these figures which are provided by the **7th Mental Measurements Yearbook** published in 1972. There were over 1,152 tests identified, including 147 personality tests, 121 intelligence tests, and 181 vocational tests. Totally there are over 3,000 tests in print and over 500 personality tests alone.

**Types of Testing**

1. **Paper and Pencil Tests:** Paper and pencil tests are often referred to as psychometric tests and they require the materials of paper, pencil, and a test booklet. They are largely screening devices developed by psychologists in industry and education for the purpose of screening out applicants. A book published by the American Psychological Association titled **Rehabilitation Psychology** describes these tests as only marginally useful for purposes of vocational potential assessment with the disabled. Most studies show these tests to have high levels of objectivity, standardization, efficiency in administration, and reliability,

but low predictive validity for worker success.

2. **Job Analysis:** Job analysis assessment focuses on the work which was or will be performed by the worker. While the characteristics of the worker may be assessed by observations, interviews, and paper and pencil testing, the work task to be performed is systematically described in job analysis. This field has been developed by industrial engineers and efficiency experts. It is useful in letting physicians get a thorough picture of a job before deciding if a person with a specific disability can return to the work.

3. **Work Samples:** Work samples take the strengths of both paper and pencil testing and job analysis. From paper and pencil testing the qualities of the standardization and objectivity are retained. From job analysis the notion that the most realistic way to evaluate work behavior is to observe people at work is retained. By observing people doing tasks that look like work and simulate work situations, their potential to master specific job skills such as eye-hand-foot coordination, hand dexterity, whole body range of motion, hand strength, and spatial and size discrimination is assessed. The primary advantage to work samples is that they are less influenced by cultural differences, reading skills, and educational attainment than psychometric tests. Typically, they hold a client's interest and they get him/her more actively involved in the vocational rehabilitation and evaluation process. They are extremely useful in developing and assessing client's motivation towards returning to work.

Work Samples' chief disadvantage is that they are more time-consuming for an evaluator since his presence is required. In paper and pencil testing this is not so. Consequently, the cost of this type of assessment is greater in terms of the time required. The greater increase in cost is offset by the increased information and motivation that usually results from work sample evaluations.

4. **Situations/Adjustment Assessment:** While work samples assess a client's potential for mastering specific skills, situational assessment evaluates work behavior in general. It is typically done in work adjustment centers and sheltered workshops. In industry, the same thing is accomplished by means of on-the-job training. Situational assessment typically gets a person totally involved if the job he is doing seems relevant and is of some interest. It helps determine if a person can work at

all; what his work personality is; and how he relates to supervisors, co-workers, and the organizational structure. It is extremely useful in determining work endurance, stamina, and tolerance to pain in a functional capacity that goes beyond what can be assessed with work samples. For the handicapped person, on-the-job training may be the most appropriate form of situational assessment if workshops are not available.

**Need for Specific Questions in Testing**

Specific questions that need answering set the stage for what a rehabilitation consultant will do with testing. The more specific the questions the better for the client and for the referral source. In all vocational testing the client is the key for letting a rehabilitation consultant interpret tests accurately. A relationship is necessary before a valid evaluation program can begin. Typically, two to three hours of counseling with an injured person is necessary in order to convey interest in his vocational exploration needs and to select appropriate tests that answer the specific questions being asked. This initial interview time in which rapport is established assists the injured person to move towards a vocational goal through the testing process.

Tests are imperfect. They are ultimately as good as the tester, as the counselor, or as the vocational rehabilitation specialist who uses them. Success as a draftsman or electronics technician cannot be predicted from one test or from one interview. Motivation cannot be assessed by a single instrument. To the degree that tests help a person become more equipped to sell himself to an employer, is the degree of their utility in vocational rehabilitation. Of secondary importance, yet essential, is the use of testing to support a vocational rehabilitation plan. Testing helps take the justification of a rehabilitation plan out of the arena of opinion and into the arena of documented evidence.

Vocational testing, if properly used, can be invaluable in the motivation of a client towards returning to work. It can help concretize and specify his aptitudes, interests, temperament, and personality characteristics that converge into a single occupational choice. It can shed light on difficulties that a client is having in vocational decision making and help him progress in the counseling process. All of this is possible if vocational testing is done in conjunction with sensitivity and high levels of facilitative counseling skills on the part of the vocational rehabilitation consultant.

## INDICATIONS FOR VOCATIONAL TESTING & WORK SAMPLE EVALUATION

**Principles**

A frequent question that arises with vocational rehabilitation consultants and consumers of vocational or career services is whether or not testing is needed to help a particular client. Or is testing merely a means of charging more fees? Private clients, as well as insurance-referred clients, ask this same question.

Richard N. Bolles, author of **What Color Is Your Parachute?**, and Richard K. Irish, author of **Go Hire Yourself an Employer**, represent a conservative and cautionary view regarding vocational evaluation and testing. From a different perspective The Vocational Evaluation and Work Adjustment Association of the National Rehabilitation Association has encouraged the professional preparation of graduate trained vocational evaluators. These evaluators recognize how the selective and appropriate use of tests and work samples can enhance a client's self-exploration and understanding of his abilities, interests, values, temperament, and work stamina.

**Principle One:**
Vocational tests and work samples should be administered and interpreted to clients when reason for testing is indicated.

**Principle Two:**
If no reason exists or if no question can be answered by testing, then clients will not benefit from the testing.

**Principle Three:**
If a client has a vocational problem that is diagnosed, and if the problem matches with the purpose of testing, then tests or work samples are indicated.

**Reasons for Testing - A Check List**

1. To provide information about a person's interests, mental and physical abilities, and temperament with respect to work.
2. To support, clarify, and document impressions gained during interviews of a client's interests and abilities.
3. To discover job interests and potential vocational objectives when neither the counselor or client can verbally state a client's job interests, likes, or dislikes.

4. To more objectively and accurately describe a person's likes, dislikes, needs, and abilities, than can be inferred from verbalized interview statements.
5. To individualize a client's reasons for choosing and being motivated towards a particular occupation. People choose occupations for a variety of reasons, such as due to needs, interests, money, family influence, physical demands, geographical location, self-fulfillment, and personal achievement. The specific reasons for a particular client can be identified through testing.
6. To match and compare tested abilities with stated abilities and tested interests with stated interests.
7. To motivate and stimulate vocational decisions into a realistic direction.
8. To support and enhance a person's self-esteem and self-concept as related to job seeking.
9. To document and validate the reasonableness and feasibility of a Rehabilitation Plan for the Rehabilitation Bureau or other regulatory agency.
10. To compare the tested aptitudes of a person with the necessary level to perform various jobs as specified in the **Dictionary of Occupational Titles** (DOT) or Occupational Aptitude Profiles of the General Aptitude Test Battery (GATB).
11. To observe and evaluate the physical stamina, endurance, agility, and range of motion that a person possesses in relationship to industrial performance requirements.
12. To evaluate the degree that a particular impairment is a physical disability or handicap.

**Why Two or More Similar Tests**

Frequently a vocational rehabilitation consultant or evaluator will select, administer, and interpret two or more tests that "appear" to be for the same purpose. A private paying client or a third-party referral source may feel that excessive testing is being done. Before this conclusion is reached, a good understanding of test construction and test validity is necessary.

Sometimes a test is administered, and due to factors beyond the control of the evaluator, the results are invalid or questionable. A client may be on medication that affects his attention, mental alertness, and agility. A client may be hostile or uncooperative. The testing environment may contain uncontrollable distractions. The test form may have a printing error. The evaluator may overestimate a person's reading ability. A client may use aids, such as encyclopedias, to answer aptitude questions on a self-administered inventory. For any of these reasons the results of a particular test or work sample may not be valid. If so, then alternate forms of the same test will have to be administered. If alternate forms are not available, then a similar test, one that measures the same thing and is intended for the same purpose, should be administered. An uninformed cost-conscious private client or referral source may interpret the retesting as excessive, when in fact, good professional judgment and concern for validity warranted the additional testing.

Another professional and meaningful reason for administering tests or work samples that "appear" similar is that appearances deceive. Two tests may state in their titles that they each evaluate a person's vocational interests. Therefore, they are repetitive. WRONG!

The construction of vocational tests, whether they measure interest, aptitudes, achievements, temperament, personality, values, needs, or physical capacity -- vary according to the instrument. Each test author operationally defines his concept of interest, aptitudes, personality, etc., differently to meet his purpose. Different validation and reliability criteria are selected for different interest tests, aptitude tests, work samples, personality tests, etc. Some operational definitions may be more appropriate for some clients than others. Typically, no single instrument is a perfect match for a particular client's educational background, age, sex, stated interests, or vocational testing needs. Consequently, a knowledgeable evaluator may administer two interest tests, each with a different operational definition of interest, to a client. Or, he may administer two reading tests because one operationally measures pronunciation (i.e., WRAT) and the other measures speed and comprehension (GATES). Or, he may administer two multiple aptitude tests because each has a different norm group that is relevant to a particular client's expressed and tested interests.

Before assuming that testing is not necessary or was excessive, contact the evaluator and ask the reasons for the test selection. If a reasonable explanation is provided that you understand, then you are working with a concerned and informed rehabilitation service provider.

# CHAPTER 9

## The Situational Assessment: Work Samples, Habits, Attitudes Versus Work Skills

We have talked about making a vocational diagnosis of the individual client in order to examine thoroughly his remaining capacities, skills and interests in light of the limitations created by a handicap resulting from an industrial injury. We will use this information to develop a vocational rehabilitation plan for the client. But first there is another area which must be looked at before we are able to come up with a viable plan for returning the worker to gainful employment. This is the client's current ability actually to perform in a work situation.

For many of your clients who have a long work history and who appear to be strongly motivated to return quickly to the labor market, it is only necessary to find an occupational area where their previous skills may be successfully transferred to a new job situation not precluded by their present physical limitations. For other clients, however, whose work history may be spotty, who may never have achieved a very high level of skill development, or whose work attitudes and motivation for speedy return to work may be open to question, special work evaluation procedures may be advisable. Such procedure is also applicable when physical tolerances are in question. As the coordinator of rehabilitation services, you may want to see a particular client in a more realistic work situation before recommending a rehabilitation plan or committing yourself to a specific training program. You may want to send your client to a vocational evaluation center where his actual work habits, attitudes and use of his residual skills may be observed over time in a more or less realistic work setting. In such a situation, specially trained vocational evaluators can observe and report to you on all work behavior and attitudes of your client:

> Is he sufficiently mobile for certain types of employment, or must you look at more sedentary areas for vocational possibilities?

> Are your client's work attitudes and relationships to supervisors and peers such that he can work effectively in a group setting?
>
> Does he demonstrate physical stamina adequate for eventual employment in competitive industry?
>
> And, most importantly, does he display the motivation and interest necessary to sustain him through a training or job search program?

The success or failure of your rehabilitation plan may well depend on attitudes and observable behavior before committing a client to a vocational plan. If the client's attitude and motivation is in question, it is the counselor's responsibility to assess this prior to enrollment in a vocational plan.

A second important contribution made by this type of realistic vocational evaluation is the work sample approach. As the evaluators observe your client actually producing work samples, they can note his postinjury level of skill at various types of mechanical tasks. Working with this kind of data the counselor is able to discuss the specific skills the client brings to a vocational plan. The counselor helps him realistically appraise his chances of success in different vocational areas. Suppose, for instance, that your client has worked on machines all his adult life but his postinjury capacity for long periods of standing is limited. If the machine shop job under consideration requires long periods of being on one's feet, you and the client may decide that such a vocational alternative is not possible. You will agree on the basis of his tryout and proceed with exploration in other job areas where the client can function more easily and with less discomfort.

Suppose, on the other hand, that the client's level of usable skills remains what it was at pre-injury, but that there have been subtle changes in his work attitudes. He seems less willing to work at expected levels of production over a long period of time. This is vital information for the rehabilitation counselor. Work attitudes and interest are much better faced before a formal program is undertaken and both money and time are invested.

A counselor may have doubts about a client's stamina and ability to function physically. He may be concerned about a client's motivation to search for employment. In such instances, a work evaluation is necessary. A work evaluation of one to two weeks enables a counselor to determine a client's probable adjustment to a new job or training situation. It will greatly increase the validity of any predictions of a client's work behavior since it is based on actual work experience.

## Services of Vocational Evaluation Center

1. 1 to 2 day assessment

2. 5 day evaluation for skills, stamina, work habits, attitude.

3. 10 day evaluation or longer such as progressive work tolerance.

4. Work Hardening: Developing a gradually more time-consuming and regular series of work tasks, may cover 2 to 8 weeks.

**Vocational evaluation centers answer questions related to:**

1. Is the client interested?

2. Does the client behave in a manner consistent with returning to work, either full-time or part-time?

3. What are the client's strengths and weaknesses in terms of skills, aptitudes, achievements, interests, work habits, and work attitudes?

4. What are possible vocational goals that match with worker traits based on: (**a**) work/educational history; (**b**) based on testing results; (**c**) based on computerized job matching systems.

# CHAPTER 10

## Vocational Exploration: The Client's Role

It has been observed that rehabilitation is an ongoing and dynamic process. If we view the process as it has been presented thus far, it seems to be a fairly static and objective look (a catalogue, if you will) of the client's existing vocational liabilities and assets. Our medical, social, psychological and vocational evaluations, the determination of feasibility versus nonfeasibility, are all events that happen to a client. He has submitted to the scrutiny of professionals of various disciplines. The more actively a client participates in these "rites of evaluation," the greater the likelihood of drawing an accurate vocational portrait of him at this existing moment of his life.

The rehabilitation process is an ongoing interaction of three closely related activities: the evaluative stage; the development and application of a plan or strategy for the client's return to work; the implemented expectations of both client and counselor for a successful outcome. We are now at the second stage where, based on the accumulated evaluative data, we can begin to look at the world of work for the most rewarding and realistic vocational options. This is not a job for the outside experts, however. The client has much at stake in decisions made here. To relinquish here may prevent the victory of returning to work. So has the counselor, the insurance carrier and all others concerned with the case. Success or failure of the plan is directly related to how closely the client himself is involved in creating that plan. Here something is not happening to a client. With his vocational rehabilitation counselor and all the accumulated data on his vocational assets and liabilities, client and counselor must formulate realistic goals. These goals need to be approved and implemented to get the client returned to suitable productive work compatible with his limitations.

At this stage the skilled vocational counselor has already won the confidence of his client. He can now encourage him to step out on his own to explore the world of work, to identify and define his transferable skills, to discover where his vocational interests will lead him, and to examine the requirements for various occupations. Finally he must take a look at the opportunities for employment and advancement in various fields.

The client should not be allowed to sit back in the counselor's office and merely have these options described for him, or simply take a quick look through the **Occupational Outlook Handbook** or the **Dictionary of Occupational Titles** as though he were reading some kind of a vocational menu. With the counselor's guidance, the client can do his own leg work. He can check out the public libraries, looking up information on various occupations under discussion. He can complete informational interviews with employers. He can call and schedule his own job interviews as well as have some scheduled for him by the counselor. He can visit training schools, find out what courses of study are involved and learn the requirements for admission. He should also learn what employment opportunities exist in diverse fields and what help the school is prepared to offer in placing him when he completes his training program. The more exploration the client does on his own, the more he will become aware of the suitability of any particular occupation for him. The more time he has expended in these investigations, the greater stake he will have in the successful outcome of his rehabilitation plan once it is initiated.

Many clients find it hard to go out and make these explorations. They feel that this is the counselor's job. Sometimes they look upon the idea of a second career as "unlikely at my age." They begin the process feeling defeated. It is here the good counselor brings all his human interaction skills into play. He finds ways of moving the client onto the path of vocational discovery. He makes appointments at schools or union training programs for the client and insists that the client keep these appointments. Arrangements are made for informational interviews with employers. It is crucial, at this stage, for the client to develop an interest and enthusiasm in his own vocational rehabilitation process. A few early successes in job explorations are also crucial in order to keep the client involved. Counselor encouragement at each step is important in keeping the ball rolling. But the counselor, as total coordinator, must keep in mind all the facts of the case -- medical, psychological, social and vocational. The client's realistic explorations are encouraged. Unrealistic job areas are carefully examined by client and counselor before being determined impractical at this time. Client impact is extremely important.

Out of all this exploration and discussion will come an emerging sense of direction for the client, and the beginnings of a commitment to a sound rehabilitation plan with a good chance of successful outcome.

### The Case of Mr. R. -- Vocational Explorer

This case illustrates the importance of client involvement. Mr. R. was 33 years of age when his back was injured on a moving job. He had been a truck driver and furniture mover for the previous eight years. It was a low back injury which was treated with lumbosacral surgery; a disc protruding into a nerve root was removed. Since heavy lifting and strenuous activity were against all medical opinions in this case, he was precluded from returning to his usual occupation.

At the time of his injury, Mr. R. had been married for twelve years and had two children. Though he had been earning a good wage ($1,100-$1,200 per month), the couple was having financial problems. They did not own their home, and had a tough time making ends meet. His indebtedness at this time amounted to approximately $2,000. His wife had recently enrolled in a nurse's training program to go to work and help restore the family to solvency.

At the time of his referral for vocational rehabilitation, Mr. R. expressed feelings of discouragement and depression. He seemed lost in terms of the vocational direction he wanted to pursue. He was unable to look at job alternatives creatively and could only restate his interest in returning, in some capacity, to his previous job. It was the only job he had performed in any regular fashion for the past eight years and the wages seemed better than he would be able to earn by entering a new field. He knew that with his bad back there was little likelihood he would return to being a trucker or a mover. It was a difficult fact for him to accept.

After about eight weeks of involvement in vocational services (intensive counseling and an exhaustive diagnosis), a tentative goal of travel consultant was identified and agreed upon. Such work was not ruled out by his physical limitations and it was consistent with an interest pattern in the field of travel Mr. R. had maintained over the past ten years. It was also consistent with the traveling he had done and enjoyed while in the military.

Once this tentative goal was identified and considered to be a realistic one, Mr. R.'s counselor arranged a number of vocational assignments, such as interviews with people in the travel business, travel bureaus, consultants and workers in the bus, railroad and airline industries. This proposed a wealth of data on the duties, responsibilities and training involved in this field. Mr. R. also visited and spoke with instructors from three schools offering training programs in this industry. He also sought out data on the labor market, availability of job openings and starting salary levels in various segments of the travel field.

With all this information in hand, it was fairly easy for Mr. R. to decide that he was interested in this field. He believed he had a fairly good chance of success in completing the training program and eventually finding a job as a travel consultant. He selected one of the three schools he had visited, one whose program sounded realistic. A full-time nine-week program was involved, which was consistent with Mr. R.'s interest and need for getting back to paid work as quickly as possible. A rehab plan was drawn up and approved by the insurance carrier and the state rehabilitation bureau.

One month before Mr. R.'s training program was scheduled to begin, he was told by his wife that she was leaving him and would ask for a divorce. This new and unexpected crisis was as much of a surprise to the client as it was to the counselor. The exact reasons for his wife's decision and subsequent actions were not clear to the client.

With the counselor's help, Mr. R. decided the best thing he could do in the face of this new crisis was to get really involved in the structured learning program he had planned. In this way his feelings of accomplishment in a new vocational area might tend to neutralize or counterbalance his reduced sense of confidence and self-esteem after the breakup of a twelve-year marriage and the loss, through divorce, of his two children.

He threw himself into his training program, received excellent grades and graduated top in his class. The counselor arranged additional training for Mr. R. in resume preparation and job-seeking skills to help prepare him for effectively handling interviews with prospective employers. Though Mr. R. had previous experience in making presentations in front of large groups on topics dealing with religious and marital values, when it came to job interviews his sense of diminished self-confidence prevented him from really selling himself. He was given additional training in specific job-seeking skills to enable him to translate his basically positive personality traits and temperament into a successful job interview situation. The counselor urged him to gain interviewing practice by going on more informational interviews with travel people so that he could build his self-confidence in these face-to-face situations.

Eventually he was sent on selected interviews with travel agencies and cruise lines where he was given positive feedback from prospective employers. Five weeks after completing his training program, Mr. R. was offered a job arranging cruises with a steamship line. He accepted the job at a starting salary of approximately $800 monthly, plus benefits.

In spite of this reduction in his earnings, Mr. R. was excited with the new position and felt that it was like a dream coming true. For years he had wanted to be a part of the travel industry but had never had the opportunity or drive or initiative to pursue it on his own. It took an industrial injury, a broken marriage and the desperate need of finding a new vocation to spur him into realizing this lifetime dream. It also provided a rewarding career that met his deep personal needs and provided more than just an income.

The rehabilitation counselor for Mr. R. was a guest of his former client at a bon voyage party aboard a cruise ship a year after the completion of his rehabilitation plan. Mr. R. was a different person. He exuded self-confidence and self-esteem. He was well-respected in his new position and his talent for relating tactfully and personally with the cruise passengers was evident. He himself commented that probably one of the best things that ever happened to him was his industrial injury. It had forced him, while he was still a young man, to reexamine his whole system of work values and to select a new career objective that met more of his needs than just a paycheck. Because of his age and the good response to the surgery he had received, he was now symptom-free. With the receipt of the remaining permanent disability settlement, he was now able to get himself out of debt and was currently confident he could succeed in his new career and eventually equal or surpass his previous earnings.

More than once during the bon voyage party he expressed

thanks and appreciation for the rehab services he had received. The important lesson for the counselor in this case, however, is that he is merely the catalyst. It is the client's role as active vocational explorer and activator of a new career which finally makes the difference. Without client participation and motivation, the best of rehabilitation plans can fail.

With Mr. R., his domestic, financial and personal problems (over and above his physical vocational limitations) had all the makings of a failed case. Low back injury, surgery and subsequent physical limitations, lack of identifiable skills, concurrent domestic crisis, lack of self-esteem and confidence -- all these had to be confronted, accepted and overcome before Mr. R. could face the future and take the necessary steps in building the career he wanted, instead of taking the job that paid the best wage.

Adapting from Richard Bolles, author of the best seller, **What Color Is Your Parachute?**, Mr. R. was not only unmindful that he was responsible for coloring his parachute, but, at the beginning of vocational planning, he was not aware he was also responsible for packing it. Once he accepted this responsibility, he was able to make his visions become reality.

# CHAPTER 11

## The Vocational Plan -- A Rehabilitation Road Map

Once the vocational research is completed by the client and counselor, the next step is to make use of this information to drawing up a vocational plan. The formal and finalized rehabilitation plan spells out in detail the steps that will be taken in returning the injured worker to the competitive job market. This formal document, which is essentially the client's own brainchild, is formulated through the guidance of his professional counselor. It is considered the most practical and efficient way of surmounting the injured worker's limitation and putting him quickly and satisfactorily back into a job situation.

The results of hours of counseling, testing, evaluation, labor market research, and related vocational exploration, must first be submitted to the scrutiny of others for approval. Once the client and counselor have obtained agreement, it is the counselor's task to convince the insurance claims representative that given the client's work limitations, prior earnings, interests, and incentives, this is the best route for a return to the competitive labor market. Then, in interest of protecting the worker's rights under a Workers' Compensation law, it is also discussed with the client's attorney.

Once all parties have agreed to the rehabilitation plan, it is then submitted to the state or regulatory agency for review and approval. The experienced vocational counselor will already have an understanding of the requirements of the regulatory body prior to submitting the plan. Therefore few plans are rejected by the regulatory body.

The counselor will have weighed the time and cost factors and will be prepared to defend the plan if necessary. There should be an ability to demonstrate the cost-effectiveness and worker satisfaction of the plan to a cost-conscious insurance representative as well as the ability to explain how the plan is best suited to returning the client to work, given his interests. Once this point on a case is reached, the counselor must be confident that the plan is both objective and realistic.

## The Vocational Plan

A vocational plan may take one of the following several forms:

A. Return to modified work with the same employer
B. Straight job placement using existing work skills in searching for modified position or position other than held at the time of injury
C. Enrollment in on-the-job training program
D. Enrollment in a formal training program, or
E. Consideration of self-employment

At a minimum, the description of the vocational rehabilitation plan should include the following items. In most states, these basic areas, along with descriptive information regarding the responsible employer, insurance carrier, and the injured worker, are included on the state or federal form.

The following are the minimum items to be included:

1. How the employee is going to prepare for entry into the new occupation.
2. If it is straight job placement, who is going to provide the job placement services, how they are going to be provided, how often, and the responsibilities of each participating party (job placement agent, counselor, and the injured worker).
3. If it is a training program, to list the name, address, and location of training institution.
4. The tuition cost or training fee and how this is to be paid.
5. The length of the plan, plan commencement date, and plan completion date.
6. How often the plan will be monitored by the vocational counselor.
7. The attendance requirements of the injured worker.
8. How long a period of time is allowed for job placement upon completion of the program.
9. A place for the client, responsible insurance carrier, and the counselor to sign and that they all agree with the rehabilitation plan.

## Plan Rationale Statement

The plan rationale statement provides a summary of information that led to the plan decision. At a minimum, this will include the following data:

A. The review of the client's transferable skills, work history, and educational background.

B. Vocational testing data. This would demonstrate how the new vocational aptitude objective is compatible with the client's vocational interest, aptitudes, and incentives.

C. Demonstration of how the vocational objective is compatible with the client's physical limitations. The client's physical limitations have previously been described in medical records and should be documented, including statement received specifically from treating or consulting physician regarding client's physical limitations. These limitations are related to the physical requirements of the new job and/or vocational objective. In a modified work plan or straight job placement plan, reference would be made to the job analysis/job description that has been documented and is in the record.

D. Labor market and earning potential. Labor market information is extremely important to the success of a plan. If adequate labor market data is not included in the plan rationale statement and there are no jobs found upon completion of the training program, the responsible employer/insurance carrier could be liable for further rehabilitation.

E. Listing of prior vocational objectives that have been considered. Statements as to why other plans were rejected.

In other words, within the Workers' Compensation rehabilitation benefit every attempt is made to assist the injured worker (client) back in to the labor market as soon as practicable but through a means which is reasonably attainable. Thus, if on-the-job training is shorter than a formal training program and still would accomplish the same end result, then this would be definitely considered "as practicable." Also, if enrollment in a technical school is quicker than say enrollment in a city college, then the former is once again considered the preferred avenue.

**Potential Problems**

In some settings, it is appropriate to also have a separate heading that outlines potential problems and accompanies the vocational plan and plan rationale statement. The purpose is not to call attention or to create any potential problems. Rather, it is to call attention to the problems that the counselor and client have both established through the evaluation process and should be paid attention to throughout the course of the vocational program. Such areas would require extra support by the counselor throughout the course of the plan.

For example, if a client has a limited reading ability or marginal reading ability and is entering a program where reading comprehension and verbal skills are required, tutoring may be required. Other example areas that could present potential problems if not addressed prior to commencing the vocational program could include the following: babysitting problems, other domestic issues, alcohol or drug problems which would require ongoing counseling by a support agency, a change in financial status sometime during the plan, anticipated financial problems if the training program is lengthy, automobile or transportation problems, and a limited labor market.

By calling attention to these areas prior to actually entering a vocational plan, an anticipatory game plan can be established to provide support for these problem areas, therefore maximizing the likelihood of successful completion of the rehabilitation program.

**Types of Plans**

Each of the following "plan types" have their own unique attributes. In addition to the items outlined above, the following factors are to be taken into consideration in each of the specific vocational plans. There are other factors that you may deem important. However, these are seen as a minimum to include with each of the respective vocational plans.

1. **Return to modified work with the employer:**

   **(a)** A Job Analysis of the modified work position (it has been reviewed by the client) and is submitted to the treating physician for review and release to modified work.

   **(b)** How much does the modified work position pay in relation to the original job?

   **(c)** The availability of this particular job in the general labor market. In other words, the Rehabilitation Bureau is going to be looking at this job. If it is so specialized that there are very few or practically no other similar jobs in the labor market, then it is not as likely to be deemed as a suitable plan or, if the plan does not work out down the road, the individual is more likely to be entitled to further vocational rehabilitation benefits. Thus, they require labor market surveys or other labor market information to document the general availability of that job in the open labor market.

**(d)** To monitor the individual return to modified work for a minimum of 60 days.

2. **Straight job placement:**

**(a)** Labor market research justifying moving into a straight job placement plan.

**(b)** Clear time perameters. Will proceed with 30, 45, 60 days job placement.

**(c)** Clear delineation of geographical areas of job search.

**(d)** Note that there may be the necessity to modify the plan following 30, 45 days. For example, if the individual is not placed following 45 days of job placement, then either (a) plan will be extended, (b) modified for on-the-job training, (c) new vocational objective. The only way such a plan can be terminated and the statement made that the carrier has fulfilled their obligation is if the client is noncooperative during the period of job placement.

**(e)** Clear outline of responsibilities of each individual:

1. Counseling firm:
   Who provides job placement
   How the job search will take place
   Consideration of OJT negotiation if feasible
   Considering use of private placement agency (for fee)
   Documentation of whether or not job-seeking skills, resume preparation, job application review, etc. will be provided.
2. Client:
   To be accessible at all times during the period of job placement (available and accessible).
   The client is expected to make contacts on his or her own. If possible, put in number of expected contacts.
   That the client will document all job contacts (keep a diary).
   Also, will be active in looking for jobs through

reviewing want ads, Employment Development Department, etc.

Will also be active in own job search through keeping in contact with counseling firm a minimum of three times per week and, if possible, and has the ability, to come in and use the counseling firm's telephone and make telephone contact on own.

3. **On-the-Job Training Programs:**

1. If a plan began as a search for job placement or on-the-job training and results in straight job placement, then the client's progress back on the job will be monitored from 30-60 days. If, however, the search resulted in an on-the-job training program this will necessitate a modified RB-2 (vocational plan). This modified plan will include the following factors.
2. The specific employer with whom the on-the-job training will take placee as well as documentation of who the trainer with the employer will be.
3. The skill acquisition schedule by weeks if possible and certainly by months. In other words, in month one in a cabinet making on-the-job training program, the individual will learn the basic use of handtools, saws, types of woods and types of finish. In month, two, etc.
4. Documentation as to how problems will be handled after they arise.
5. Documentation of the on-the-job training agreement including fees, reimbursements, when the check is to be mailed from the insurance carrier to the trainer, who completes the progress reports, and the monthly follow-ups by the counselor (more often if problems arise).

4. **Formal Training Programs:**

Formal technical training programs are considered appropriate as a vocational alternative when there are:

(a) Limited transferable skills
(b) Poor labor market for existing skills
(c) Severe physical limitations
(d) Test results support successful completion of technical training

(e) Labor market is excellent for that particular vocational objective

(f) There are factors which show extreme limitations in reentering the labor market such as: age, increased disability, obesity and other factors.

(g) When there needs a tighter monitoring of the client's participation in rehabilitation (a more highly structured rehabilitation program).

**The documentation of a formal training program would include:**

(a) Why this particular training institution was chosen over others as well as over on-the-job training and straight job placement.

(b) Documentation of the track record of this particular training institution, specifically as it relates to their job placement success (preferably, having contacted graduates of that school).

(c) Documentation of tools, supplies needed in addition to the tuition cost required for the training institution.

(d) Documentation of attendance requirements and noting that the client must comply with those same attendance requirements.

(e) Documentation of how often a program will be monitored by the counselor and who the contact person is at the training institution.

(f) Documentation of who is responsible for job placement and when that begins.

**5. Self-Employment:**

Self-employment is a final alternative that on rare occasions may be considered. Due to the failure rate of small businesses, self-employment is considered the least attractive of all the vocational alternatives. The following factors may add to the potential of considering self-employment as a realistic alternative.

1. Other vocational alternatives have already been evaluated (job placement, on-the-job training, formal training).
2. That the client is so physically limited that he cannot work a regular 40-hour work week and the self-employment alternative allows for more control over

his own work schedule. Credence is added to this particular alternative if a spouse or some other family member can also be active in the business.

3. That labor market is extremely limited and self-employment offers a means to at least provide an alternative to earning an income. This typically is the case in the more rural environments.

## Summary

In summary, a document entitled, The Vocational Rehabilitation Plan or Vocational Rehabilitation Program should be a stand-alone report that A) clearly defines the method through which the client will gain reentry into the labor market; B) clearly documents the objective data that led to the finalization of the program.

It is important in the Plan Rationale statement to reflect the other alternatives reviewed and reasons rejected. The standard reasons that other plans are rejected are physical limitations, potential earnings too low, not interested, and/or insufficient qualifications, skills, or aptitudes for a certain area.

It is also important in the Plan Rationale to document that all parties know and are aware of the earnings potential as well as advancement potential. There should not be any argument at the time of job placement regarding the acceptance of what is described as a "reasonable job offer," if the acceptable wage level has been addressed prior to entering into the vocational plan.

The labor market research that was conducted and led to the vocational plan decision is an extremely important factor to include in the Plan Rationale statement. The labor market research is typically documented onto a labor Market Survey which addresses such items as A) wages, entry-level; B) potential wages; C) training requirements for entering into the occupation; D) physical demands of the occupation; E) job duties; F) specific statement of how and from where the information is used in the Labor Market Survey was obtained.

The Rehabilitation Road Map is probably the most important document in a Worker's Compensation vocational rehabilitation file. The documented plan becomes the combination of the thorough vocational exploration that has taken place on the part of the client and counselor. It also becomes the "contract" which the counselor, client, claims representative, and attorney all sign. The "contract" expresses the intent of the client and claims person and delineates the agreements he/she made in terms of level of participation in the rehabilitation program. The "contract" holds the counselor responsible to provide supportive counseling services throughout the course of the vocational plan to maximize the likelihood of successful completion.

## CHAPTER 12

### Client Motivation: The Key to Successful Rehabilitation

A client's motivation is frequently mentioned as one of the most important factors in the rehabilitation process. Motivation, however, is not just something that is present or absent in the client. Any good counselor knows motivation can be generated or dampened by counselor attitudes.

As a counselor, your attitudes toward your client are expressed in your expectations of him. These expectations may be communicated either verbally or nonverbally. To the client, they convey your belief in his ability to return to work. If he suspects you have any doubts about his ability, he will probably have great trouble convincing himself. Your expectations of the client have a tremendous impact on his feelings of self-worth and therefore on his own expectations of successful re-employment. Once you communicate doubt to a client, that doubt becomes contagious. The client begins to question his ability to "come back." This questioning dampens the enthusiasm so important to getting through training and job hunting. With doubt replacing enthusiastic pursuit of his new goal, there is a good chance the client will have a harder time completing training and getting a job.

At this stage the counselor's position must be that of a convinced advocate. Once you come across to the overly sensitive client as an adversary, his defenses are raised. He picked up your cues of doubt and translated them into expectations of defeat. Rather than face another defeat, he lowers his expectations. His efforts diminish with his chances of successful rehabilitation.

The twin issues of motivation and expectations are extremely important when it comes to providing service to clients who are often group-stereotyped. "Poor people" are often perceived by middle class counselors as not sufficiently motivated toward work. This is not always an accurate stereotype; not all poor people are poorly motivated toward work. Even if it were true, the intimation of failure that follows from this perception is no help in trying to encourage a return to work. The contagion of your implied prognosis of failure infects him even more with doubt and lower expectations.

If, on the other hand, the counselor is able to demonstrate his faith in a client's potential, that, too is contagious. It isn't long before the client **believes** he can complete his rehab plan successfully, with his counselor/advocate. He has become the motivated client with reasonable, realistic expectations.

**Motivation, Lost and Found: The Case of Mr. J.**

This case example illustrates the importance of positive counselor expectation and expertise in communication skills. In December of 1980 Mr. J., age 40, a warehouse partsman, twisted his back while trying to prevent a crate from falling. He was given appropriate and conservative medical treatment and, in April of 1982, the doctors suggested that he was able to return to his former job. Mr. J. returned to his job and remained until November of 1982 when, according to the company records, he was let go because of a reduction in the work force.

Complaining of increased symptoms and pain in his back, Mr. J. immediately went to see his physician. He made no attempt to return to work between November, 1982 and December, 1983. During this period his medical condition appeared to worsen. He complained of increasing severity and frequency of pains in his back. Throughout 1983 Mr. J. spent several periods of time in the hospital receiving conservative treatment for his back. The final medical evaluation, however, prepared by orthopedic and neurological experts, concluded that Mr. J.'s current medical condition did not preclude his return to the type of warehouse work he had been doing prior to his injury. The psychiatrist, the social worker, a vocational evaluation and a job analysis all supported this medical finding. Technically, therefore, Mr. J. did not qualify for vocational rehabilitation service; there was no evidence he had a handicap interfering with a return to his customary occupation.

Since the client had been loudly expressing interest in returning to work he could handle, however, a fresh look was taken at Mr. J.'s background. He had successfully completed two years of college and had earlier in his career been employed in supervisory positions. Thus, as a warehouse partsman at the time of his injury, Mr. J. was probably accurately categorized as underemployed, not working to his full potential. An experienced counselor can recognize that such underemployed persons frequently have less motivation after an injury, to return to the same line of work. And, in Mr. J.'s case, because of a reduction in the work force, it was impossible for him to return to his former job. Though he could have looked elsewhere for this type of work, Mr. J. appeared to be unmotivated, complaining of his back condition, while at the same time insisting he was anxious to return to work.

In the face of this contradiction, the physician wisely recommended vocational rehabilitation services. The insurance carrier went along with the plan and authorized the service.

Mr. J. began seeing a vocational rehabilitation counselor in early December, 1983, two years after his injury. During the first meetings with the counselor, Mr. J. focused on his sense of pain and discomfort. The vocational counselor noted the discrepancy between Mr. J.'s insistence upon his desire to return to work and his constant complaints of pain and discomfort. This confrontation -- of pointing out to the client the contradiction between what he was saying he wanted and the roadblocks he seemed to be throwing in his way -- was precisely what he needed. He came to see how he actually felt underemployed in his last job and, limitation or no, he was not eager to return to strenuous physical labor.

With the help of the vocational counselor, Mr. J. was able to look into other job areas more consistent with his education and previous work experience. By looking in new vocational directions, Mr. J.'s lack of motivation was reversed. Working in tandem, counselor and client developed a new vocational objective, solidly based on the client's previous achievements in sales, supervision and management. It was decided he should look for work as a salesperson and/or management trainee. Mr. J. was given training in job-seeking skills, had a resume developed for him by a professional job placement counselor and was referred to selected employers by his vocational counselor. Very quickly, the newly motivated Mr. J. developed a capacity to sell himself. Once he was headed in the direction that was right for him, he was able to muster enthusiasm and motivation.

A few weeks later, in January, 1984, Mr. J. accepted a position as a management trainee in an auto paint shop. After a three-month training period, Mr. J. would be earning $200 a month more than he had been making at the time of his injury, and he would be managing the franchise, selling to customers and supervising four or more employees.

Because of the conflicting signals Mr. J. originally put out to the counselor -- at one moment saying how much he wanted to return to work, and the next moment complaining of how much his back hurt him -- it was felt that this client was not adequately motivated for successful rehabilitation. He has expressed much anger with the insurance carrier, the physician and the counselor. He approached the entire rehab process as though the rehab team were his enemy. Through skillful counseling, however, and with the development of a new vocational plan, Mr. J. began to lose some of his hostility. Involving him in specific job-seeking skills training, and eventually sending him on job interviews, changed this "unmotivated" into a successful rehabilitation in less than 45 days after he was referred for services.

Once he was hired, Mr. J. stated he was very pleased with his new career and felt growth possibilities with his new employers were "fantastic." He was convinced he would exceed the estimated $1,500 per month earnings he had been promised at the end of three months on the job.

The experience with Mr. J. taught the counselor that motivation is not an abstract quality found in some people and not in others. It is an attitude that can be developed and nurtured along specific lines directly connected with a client's needs and capacities.

**Commitment to Success: The Case of Mr. B.**

Mr. B. was a 39-year-old male whose last employment was 12 years as a truck driver for an oil transporting firm. His earnings were in the neighborhood of $30,000 per year. He was a high school graduate and had a few college units completed at the community college level, his grade point average was a 1.8 on a 4.0 scale, (with 4.0 being an A). He was a Vietnam-era veteran.

The industrial disability was injury to his back which eventually required surgery. This was a result of a trucking accident. He was released to go back to truck driving, but was unable to continue the job due to a combination of residuals from his back injury and a psychological component.

The psychological component was partially related to his having been a Vietnam-era veteran. Ever since having the accident, whenever he drove on the freeways, he had flashbacks to the war time and envisioned himself as being in a war zone. In his mind, he was at war between his truck and all those around him.

When entering vocational rehabilitation, as many injured workers who have had high prior earnings, he had high wage expectations. His aptitudes and learning ability were below average. He did not qualify for the fields that require stronger reading, writing, and math aptitudes necessary for becoming an electronics technician, accountant/bookkeeper, or similar occupations. However, he did have relatively high spacial relations. Because of the potential of earning a decent wage ($9 - $10 per hour to start), he agreed to enroll in a 25-week training program to become employed in the field of printed circuit design.

Throughout the course of the training program, Mr. B. had a difficult time with applying the mental discipline required to acquire the skills in the relatively short period of time that is required by a high-powered technical school. He definitely was detail-oriented and the instructors continued advising both the client and counselor that he had the ability to do this job.

On three separate occasions throughout the course of the program, Mr. B. threatened to quit. Each time, the counselor met with his instructors and Mr. B.; the instructors would reassure both that he had the skills and ability to do the work. His low tolerance for frustration and at times verbal explosiveness was disruptive in the classroom. However, the constant reassurance and support did bring him to the point of successfully completing the program.

During the final three weeks of school his motivation and attitude had declined. Even during the first half of the 60-day period of job placement allowed at the end of the plan, he was only marginally cooperative. To his surprise, the employment specialist working in conjunction with the school did land him two or three solid job interviews. To his surprise, he was offered and did begin a job in the field of printed circuit design.

He was hired as a trainee, with the insurance carrier agreeing to an additional 90 days of OJT reimbursement during the training period on the job. At the end of the 90-day OJT extension, the case was closed as being successfully employed.

After six months on the job, Mr. B. called the counselor stating that he was sure he was going to be terminated. He didn't feel he was able to perform at a level required by the employer and that the employer was about to let him go. Though the insurance carrier's obligation was finished, the counselor continued to work with Mr. B. to make this a permanent placement.

The employer was contacted and areas of skill deficit were learned. Mr. B. was referred back to this instructor who provided the training. The instructor agreed to work with Mr. B. for as long as it would take to bring him up to a skill level if the employer would give him the time off. The additional training would be required at no cost. Thus, for the next four months, Mr. B. would work three days a week with the employer and attend school two days a week with the goal of bringing his skill level up to a point that was acceptable to the employer.

After the four months, Mr. B. was able to return to work on a full-time basis and the successful return to work was finally implemented a little over 9 months after he actually returned to work in the new occupation.

This was a case of a) client motivation and wanting to make it in his newly chosen profession, b) motivation on the part of the training instructor and institution to have a rehabilitation client successfully employed in the field, c) an employer who had a worker who had a good attitude, was responsible, but was short in terms of skill and not what one would describe as being a quick learner. Because of these other attributes held by the client, they were willing to go with the extended schooling.

All of this took place without the insurance carrier ever knowing what had taken place after they had closed their file. The counselor was willing to continue monitoring this result without pay, knowing that it would require time to maintain communication with the client, the school, and the employer. Also, the motivation on the part of the counselor was knowing that it would be much better to stick with this placement and continue to work on making it successful, rather than take the risk of having the client come back into the insurance rehabilitation system stating that he was not adequately trained for the job or job market.

## CHAPTER 13

### People-to-People Interaction: The Basic Counseling Tool

When a person is injured and finds himself unable to work, enmeshed in the Workers' Compensation system, he often becomes confused and frustrated; he experiences disgust with his inadequacy, self-pity, is resentful, discouraged, angry and helpless. His entire lifestyle is disrupted. If this continues long enough, he gives up hope of changing his situation. This particularly dangerous combination of emotional situational factors blunts whatever problem-solving abilities the client has shown in other life situations. He is unable to make plans, to make intelligent choices among options, to act in a way to alter his present intolerable position.

While it is true that a person's way out of any unhappy situation lies in his own actions, a crisis such as the injured worker experiences when he finds himself unable to earn his living in his usual way blunts his awareness of this fact. He tends to become immobilized; action of any kind often seems impossible to him. He feels that he has lost control over his life, that circumstances are moving him. Any action he might take would prove either useless or counterproductive.

At this crucial point, human interaction is needed before the injured worker can begin to believe in his own power to do something about his situation. This can be viewed as crisis intervention and is the main work of the vocational counselor. Regardless of the array of services provided by the technology and machinery of the rehabilitation system, it is person-to-person interaction, counselor-to-client exchange that starts the ball rolling. Such exchanges help the client gain a realistic understanding of his situation and what coping strategies are required. The counselor helps the client climb back into the driver's seat and experience some feeling of control over his life. Such exchanges help the client to start making reasonable plans for getting out of the negative emotional/situational morass in which he finds himself as a disabled worker.

In a very real sense, the client's disability ends when he

discovers, during counseling interviews and the completion of the counselor's assignments, that he is able to think clearly and unemotionally about his situation and begins to act to change it. He begins to realize that, despite his injury, he is able to make decisions about his life and follow through on them. He rediscovers his problem-solving ability and with the help of the counselor, is able to put it to work for him. Talking frankly and openly with someone who understands his total situation, he begins to accept his limitations and capabilities. He starts the process of making reasonable plans for getting himself out of the Workers' Compensation system and back into the productive and profitable labor market.

Human interaction is the key to change in the vocational rehabilitation area as it is in most other areas of our lives. Let's take a look at people interaction and see how much a part of our lives it is ...

**How** many of your working hours involve interaction with others?

**How** do you respond to people with emotional or physical hurts?

**How** frequently and how effectively do you interact with your peers?

**How** often do you provide understanding and assistance to people working with you?

**How** much of your nonworking day is spent with your family, spouse, a close friend?

**How** much of your time is spent in providing some kind of help for others?

**How** often have you experienced problems and sought the help of another?

**How** many times have you been bursting with good news and looked for someone to share it with?

**How** many times have you just needed someone else to listen to your hopes and dreams?

**What** kind of a response did you get the last time you sought help from another for home or auto repair, financial assistance, medical or personal advice?

It seems obvious: people need people in crisis as well as noncrisis situations in life. Yet how little most of us ever bother to look at people interaction, this most significant part of our lives. We seldom examine our performance to see how effective we are at it. We don't look at it as a skill that can be systematically developed and sharpened to make us more effective people-movers.

For the vocational rehabilitation counselor, his success or failure depends on these skills of interpersonal effectiveness. Whether a client is ever going to get moving by and for himself is to a large extent due to how effective a people-mover his counselor is.

When an injured worker appears in your office for an interview, when you confer with a claims examiner, or a rehabilitation nurse, when an employer is asked to approve a rehab plan, when you deal with the rehabilitation bureau, when you are asked to intervene in your client's family situation, all of your people interaction skills are needed. Any meeting of two or more people for a purpose -- to acquire information, to give information, to solve a problem -- requires the ability to interact skillfully and to communicate effectively. Your level of accomplishment in any interpersonal activity can be enhanced or hindered by the level of your interaction skills.

# CHAPTER 14

## Communication, Crisis Intervention and Rehabilitation

The central theme we have emphasized about the disabled worker throughout this book is that he is in a state of crisis, his response to a stressful event. The injured worker's reaction to loss of job and income is generally to become immobilized attitudinally as well as physically. He is stunned, overwhelmed, unable to make plans for changing an unliveable situation. He is in need of crisis intervention. This is a form of people interaction in which a skilled vocational counselor helps the injured client regain his coping strategies, return to productive employment, and, as nearly as possible, to his previous lifestyle. Most of all, the injured client must regain a belief in his ability to act to change his current situation.

The vocational counselor is the central figure in this crisis intervention. Because he has direct face-to-face contact with the injured worker and has available to him all the relevant information on the case from doctors, nurses, and insurance claims people, he is in a position to communicate intelligently with the client. He can coordinate all this information and give the client, perhaps for the first time, a realistic view of his actual and legitimate expectations.

In this role, the counselor is primarily a communicator. Eventually he must help his client organize and structure these communications regarding current status and prognoses for future changes in that status. For the moment, it is enough if the counselor can bring his client to a point where he can view his present situation rationally, without anger, resentment, hopelessness. Only then can the client begin to recover his own problem-solving ability and begin to take an active part in plans for his rehabilitation. The counselor here is the facilitator, the human contact who has opened the client's eyes to the full nature of his condition and prospects.

The next stage of crisis intervention requires teamwork -- the client and counselor working together. He must be open enough with the client to establish a climate of faith and trust. He must sometimes penetrate a wall of apathy and resentment built up by the client as he slowly recovers from the effects of his injury. It will take all the counselor's skill to breach this wall and inspire the client to participate in his own recovery. Here's where the counselor begins to provide a structure: tentative rehabilitation plans which may rouse the injured client's interest and start him thinking of his own options.

With his access to information that the client does not have, the counselor provides the initial structure in the case. With his medical knowledge, familiarity with insurance carriers' policies, vocational training information, labor market information, etc., he is an invaluable resource for the client. He begins to bring structure into the client's thinking, and with structure comes a rediscovery of the client's coping strategies, the beginning of client involvement in his own rehabilitation. Hopefully, when this stage is reached, most of the negative thinking has been replaced by the client's active participation in formulating a rehabilitation plan that he believes will work for him. Client and counselor have evolved a joint commitment.

The following formulas may help in illustrating the relationship between crisis and intervention:

Industrial Accident + Job Loss = Crisis

Communication + Structure = Crisis Intervention

The rehabilitation counselor himself becomes a part of the client's response to his injury. Through your communication skills and ability to supply input for a new structuring of the client's life, you become actively involved with the client's efforts to overcome the negative aspects of his experience and begin to create a more positive, problem-solving approach to his rehabilitation plan. You do not create a rehab plan for the client but aid him with your encouragement and your exploratory work assignments to evolve his own realistic vocational goals. This approach, using communication and people interaction skills in restructuring the crisis situation, results in more cost-effective rehabilitation because the Plan is basically the client's. He is more likely to finish it successfully. No matter how rational, a rehab plan which the client has had no part in formulating is more often uncompleted. Then, new vocational alternatives are sought, adding considerably to rehabilitation costs.

Successful crisis intervention requires all the informational input from every side of the case, from the medical team, the insurance people, employer, even family. Gathering all this information and using it effectively in working with your client requires a high level of facilitative interviewing skill on the part of the counselor. You must not only know the events of the case, but must understand fully how your client feels about these events. To help your client understand and act upon those feelings is perhaps more important than the objective history of the events themselves.

How the injured person responds to his disability eventually determines his future expectations on which you, as the counselor, must build. Your success or failure in the rehab process ultimately depends on your client's feelings and attitudes toward his disability. By helping him identify those feelings, venting his anger, frustration, or hope, you help him constructively build toward a restored future in the labor market. Your interviewing skills are your basic tools in this process.

# CHAPTER 15

## The Interview: Formalized Interaction

Interviewing is a form of people-to-people interaction, generally formalized by a particular setting, aim and expected outcome. It encompasses all the forms of communication expertise and interpersonal effectiveness. It demands a degree of sensitivity to the needs, language and expectations of people from all walks of life.

More specifically, an interview is a social situation where one person is in need of help (social, interpersonal, vocational, financial) and has requested service from another who is presumed to have the expertise, resources or experience needed for providing that help. Not the least of the expertise provided by the interviewer is a particular skill in the art of interviewing.

Rehabilitation counselors use these skills when they intervene in the crisis situation of the injured and disabled worker, when they determine how best to provide the benefits and when they deliver the services of the rehabilitation system. Competent interviewing skills help enhance the injured person's satisfaction with the quality of care he is receiving and more quickly enable him to develop a belief in his own recuperative powers.

### What Are Effective Interviewing Skills?

During the late 1950's psychologists, social workers, personnel experts and medical educators were investigating the basic ingredients that go into any really effective helping situation. They came up with a number of such ingredients, qualities or conditions that seemed to be always involved in effective helping interactions.

In the 60's and early 70's adequate research evidence was provided that substantiated the crucial role of a limited number of core conditions for the helping situation to be successful. These core conditions were identified by most researchers as empathy, respect, genuineness, self-disclosure and concreteness. (Some researchers used slightly different terms, but their meanings were practically identical.) The evidence of these research teams showed that the presence of these core conditions in a helping relationship significantly enhanced the outcome, while the absence of these core conditions significantly led to a deterioration in the situation the helpee had brought into the relationship. In short, there is positive evidence that suggests **how** helpers must act with helpees if growth and improvement are to be expected.

For the vocational rehabilitation counselor, this means that if he wants to increase the rate and speed of the recovery and rehabilitation of injured persons, he must include these core conditions when working with his clients. These conditions are required in all types of two-way communication, whether only factual information is sought or emotional and affective states are to be identified and dealt with.

Let's look at these **core conditions** as they apply to the helper/helpee interview.

**Empathy:** The ability to adopt another person's frame of reference, to participate in his thoughts and feelings, and to see things through his eyes. The ability to "walk in another person's shoes" and to know and feel how his shoes fit. To be understanding and compassionate is to be empathetic. Most importantly, it is the ability to communicate this understanding to the helpee so that he feels understood.

**Respect:** The ability to accept another person as he is with his own set of values, to actively listen to what he has to say, and to show concern and consideration. It does not mean that you fake agreement with a person. It does mean that you avoid putting him down. You treat him as an equal and avoid being judgmental. Most importantly, it is the ability to communicate concern and interest to a helpee so that he feels respected as a person.

**Genuineness:** The ability to convey honesty and commitment toward a person, to be sincere, straight and trustworthy, and to respond to a person in a consistent manner. It is the opposite of phoniness. It is showing enthusiasm and being spontaneous. Most importantly, it is the ability to communicate and show a real interest in a helpee so that he feels you are being honest and fair with him.

**Self-disclosure:** The ability to be open and talkative with another person but not in an overbearing way. It is talking about yourself and your own experiences as they relate to those feelings, thoughts and experiences of the person you are helping. It is sharing your outlook on a problem with a helpee in a personal way. Most importantly, it is the ability to discuss your thoughts about a person's problems so that he feels you are really involved in helping him.

**Concreteness:** The ability to interact and suggest positive actions to a person needing help in a specific, candid and down-to-earth way. It means you are precise in what you say, yet not short and quick with a person. You are able to back up your impressions and suggestions with hard, observable data. Most importantly, it is the ability to communicate in a specific and meaningful way when helping a person so he feels you have given him useful suggestions and plans of action.

The importance of these five core conditions in the helping situation cannot be overstressed. They are the ingredients that prepare the human climate for change. But they are not only theories that the counselor has about the helping situation. They must be demonstrated to the helpee. Only when the helper shows those qualities in his relationship with the helpee, will that person be able to see and feel them. And only as he experiences them in the interaction will the helpee be open to the changes necessary to successfully alter his present situation. It is the doing that counts, not just the intention.

The core conditions of empathy, respect, genuineness, self-disclosure and concreteness are the basis of the effective client-counselor relationship. They are the means of assuring your client that he is listened to, understood and that someone is sincerely trying to help. As their use encourages your client to open up, tell about his feelings, his expectations, hopes and fears, to identify and label his emotions, they cannot help but move the rehabilitation process forward and improve your overall performance as a counselor. Your client will come to realize that he is being helped by a competent professional and his expectations for his own improved performance will almost surely follow. The use of these skills emphasizes your important role in actively intervening and providing your client with the best professional services when he needs them most.

### Counselor-Client Rapport

In describing the factors involved in effective interviewing, what we have in fact been talking about is the creation of the helper-helpee relationship as discussed by Carkhuff and Berenson. This very special interaction of a person needing some kind of service and another person providing that service is the crux of any constructive change on the part of the help-seeker. All of us may have, at one time or another and in different settings, been both helper and help-seeker. We have known both roles. But what is important here is to be fully conscious of our helping role and use all the helping tools at our command.

Your task is to help another human being through a life crisis, the loss of some degree of his work ability, and to aid that person in compensating, making the best vocation adjustment possible, given the residual effects of his injury. But how do you know when you have been helpful rather than harmful? What assurance can you have that our efforts have left the client better rather than worse? Is he improving, constructively responding to your crisis management? Have you been able to help him in expressing and coping with his feelings of frustration, confusion and anxiety? Have you been able to help him halt the disorganization of his lifestyle, restore some of his problem-solving skills after the initial shock of his injury and unemployment? Is he satisfied with the care he is receiving, accepting and adjusting to his disability, actively involved and participating in his rehabilitation plan? Or, do you find an uncooperative, self-pitying, defensive and angry person, not involved or concerned with his medical and vocational services, not improving physically or psychologically and making little or no effort to return to a productive work situation? Does he vent his feelings destructively on family, friends, physicians, counselors, anyone within reach, complaining of the care and service he has received?

To find out what effects your efforts are bringing in a counselor-client relationship, the only place to look is at the behavior and attitudes of the client. The only meaningful index of your progress as a people-mover is the self-starting motion you have initiated in your client and observed in his changed behavior. The relevance of this index is clear from your characterizations of the helped and nonhelped expressed in the questions above. This judgment may seem obvious, yet research from the fields of rehabilitation, nursing, medicine, dentistry, teaching, counseling, psychology and personnel indicates that the helper does not spend enough time observing and attending to how the helpee is feeling, acting, talking and working. In many cases, it has been observed that helping is not intended to improve the condition of the helpee. Rather, the helping process seems aimed at making the helper feel better, getting his thoughts and feelings expressed, helping him complete his reports on schedule, etc. In these nonproductive situations it is obvious that the helper-helpee relationship is characterized by very low levels of the core interpersonal conditions. Hence, there is no effective interpersonal relationship and the client seems to get worse instead of better according to all relevant criteria.

Another indication of the effectiveness of a helping relationship is, Who does most of the talking? When the client does not have sufficient chance to talk and be listened to attentively, then his needs are not being met. If he is not allowed to freely express his feelings, explore his problems, consider all the options, no matter how far-fetched, it is hard to locate the problem areas and deal with them. Here the helping is not for the helpee and cannot create the desired change.

To be truly helpful and change-producing, this interpersonal relationship between counselor and client must include high levels of the interpersonal core conditions, as described earlier. These core conditions facilitate attending and observing actions on the part of the counselor. They "keep his eye on the ball" which, in this case, is creating change in the client.

### Helping Behavior in the Face-to-Face Interview

The people-to-people approach is, of course, most effective in the face-to-face interview. Here all the core conditions combine to aid the counselor's focus on the client's feelings and experiences. The counselor's empathy, respect, genuineness, self-disclosure and concreteness are his route to building client confidence and accomplishing the purpose of the interview. Whether a rehab counselor wants to solicit information, to clarify behavior patterns, to give the client an opportunity to vent anger and frustration or to explore a client's possible vocational interests, the surest way to an inside track on the client's views is through effective interaction promoted by these factors. If the counselor is truly interested in producing constructive change by maximizing the client's participation in his own rehabilitation, he will master these facilitating behaviors. They will become automatic in his client contacts.

Whatever the counseling problem, it will become that much easier to solve by a counselor skilled in the core conditions of human interaction. When he successfully communicates his genuine interest in the client, the information he is seeking flows from the client. It is valid, factual information. When he needs to know how a client really feels about a proposed rehab plan, the client's confidence in an empathetic counselor brings out the client's real feelings, not what he thinks the counselor wants to hear. Accurate information about the client's true state of mind is essential for making sound vocational plans and managing the client's life crisis wisely and economically.

These interpersonal conditions can be learned and developed to make your counseling work easier, more effective. They are conveyed by specific behaviors on your part, behaviors that not only ensure that you look at, listen to and understand what your client is saying, but also how he **feels** about what he is saying.

Here are some of the attending behaviors that will facilitate your client interviews and make them more productive:

1. Comfortable eye contact.
2. Appropriate head nodding and facial gestures to show attention.
3. Relaxed and attentive physical posture.
4. Verbal following or verbal reflection.

To feel at ease and open, your client needs to know that you are paying attention to him. Without staring directly at him, you can watch him as he speaks. Give **him** your attention rather than the reports before you. Don't constantly take notes as he speaks. The client wants and deserves your full attention. Nodding your head at certain points and smiling tells the client that you are following what he is saying and that he is getting through to you. Your own physical posture and relaxed attitude set the tone for a free-moving interview in which your client may relax also. He will not feel rushed and anxious to blurt everything out at once. When you follow your client verbally and reflect back some of the feelings he is expressing, you establish a rapport that deepens the level at which the client is talking. He knows he is being understood and will perhaps go deeper into his feelings than he thought possible. Essentially, to verbally follow another person is to continue the conversation on the same subject rather than switching around to matters you may think to be important. In verbally reflecting what a client says about his feelings you are assuring him that you have received his message, that you know how he feels about the matter under discussion. It reduces defensiveness, facilitates the counseling process, creates a warm, accepting, supportive atmosphere where the client will feel freer, and goes more deeply into the matters which are troubling him.

Counseling at this level will help you identify your client's feelings and attitudes which may be impeding his rehabilitation progress. Your ability to see and identify these problem areas enables your client to see them also, but in a new light. They are no longer just dark areas in his mind. If he can air his negative feelings, he can take a constructive new look at them, understand what is producing them and how they may be preventing him from realizing his goals. He becomes more able to cope with the stress of his situation and his anxiety level drops so that he can regain his problem-solving skills and attack a rehab plan positively and constructively. In short, these counseling behaviors help the person in crisis get a better hold on himself, organize his thoughts and expressions clearly, and finally start making moves on his own.

Each of these four attending behaviors on the part of the counselor complement and enhance each other. To fully communicate his understanding and concern for the client's future, the counselor needs to demonstrate all of them in every contact with his client. The more the counselor uses these behaviors, the more spontaneous they will become. And the more spontaneous they appear to the client, the more genuine and sincere the helper will come across to the injured helpee. When the helper is not consistent with these behaviors, if he does not maintain casual eye contact, does not maintain a relaxed and attentive posture, but **does** verbally reflect a helpee's feelings and words, a mixed message is conveyed. The injured client is left wondering if you really care and are interested, or whether he is just seeing your professional facade.

The rationale for including an overview of basic communication skills in this book is obvious to some yet does deserve specific emphasis. It is a special blend of a counselor's interpersonal skills with systematic, thorough evaluative procedures and techniques that leads to sound, feasible vocational plans. One without the other leads to ineffectiveness and a high failure rate.

### Who Helped Mr. L.?

This case illustrates the importance of financial incentive on reducing subjective discomfort. The counselor's impact on the client is often perceived as being negative while the client is in the Workers' Compensation system. It is only after completing case closure that an accurate assessment of counselor impact is possible.

At the age of 45, Mr. L., a bartender in a cocktail lounge adjacent to a family-style restaurant, slipped and sprained his back while working. He was given conservative treatment. All physicians involved -- those selected by his attorney, those picked by the client himself as well as the medical team from the insurance company -- agreed that surgery was not required.

Mr. L. remained out of work for one and a half years. He continued to experience symptoms that made him feel that he had to get off his feet and stay in bed for excessive amounts of time.

Mr. L. was a high school graduate and had served in the military. While in the service he had been trained and gained some experience as a chef. His entire post-military work history, however, had been as bartender or manager in small bars and cocktail lounges, though in some jobs he had supervised up to twelve employees. His work had taken him up and down the West Coast, including Alaska and Canada.

Mr. L. was married at the time of his injury, but from the start of counseling he indicated that the marriage was breaking up and he and his wife were planning to get a divorce.

Mr. L.'s subjective sense of physical limitations was inconsistent with the pooled medical opinion in this case. However, with his feeling of being limited physically, his prospects for returning to work seemed remote at best. At the beginning, he participated in vocational testing and evaluation and was about to undergo a workshop training situation which would involve his regular attendance for ten consecutive days. It was hoped that this direct work adjustment evaluation would enable Mr. L. to increase his stamina, and perhaps come to realize that he was capable of more physical activity than he believed. At this point he had been involved in vocational rehabilitation services for about six months with several interruptions because of hospital admissions for rest and traction.

The prospect of ten days in a workshop training situation apparently discouraged Mr. L. He seemed to feel it was beyond his power of endurance. At this point, through his attorney, he officially informed all concerned parties that he was no longer interested in receiving vocational rehabilitation services. Family and personal factors entered into this decision, but it was clear that Mr. L.'s self-doubt played an important part.

Mr. L. wrote a personal letter to the rehabilitation counselor explaining why he had dropped out of the rehabilitation program. His son had been in an auto accident in Oregon and Mr. L. wanted to relocate immediately. Thus, he was no longer interested in looking for reemployment in his home area. He also was not interested in having his case transferred to Oregon. In simplest terms, Mr. L. wanted his disability settlement and he wanted to get out of the Workers' Compensation system entirely. He did not want to account for himself to physicians, attorneys, rehabilitation regulators, nor to the rehab counselor himself. Mr. L. did, however, add a special note of thanks to the counselor for the service he had received. He felt that their counseling sessions had helped him realize that he was going to have to push himself harder than he had been doing if he wanted to reestablish himself vocationally and get back to work.

Case Closed. Did the counseling fail?

About one year later, Mr. L.'s counselor received a two-page handwritten letter from his former client. In this letter Mr. L. told how the counseling services he had received had been of help to him. He thanked the counselor for the encouragement and support he had received, even though he hadn't been able to make use of it at that time. What he had particularly appreciated was the counselor's emphasis on Mr. L.'s own capacity to cope. His capacity to cope was greater than the client had been able to experience at that time. He also felt that their counseling sessions had enhanced his self-esteem and that the completion of the informational interviews assigned to him had given him the beginning of a feeling of accomplishment.

Mr. L. also wrote that his son had recovered from the auto accident and that he, Mr. L., had moved on to Alaska. Here he had gotten a job as chief chef working in a facility connected with the Alaska pipeline. He said that the physical demands of the job were still great and that he experienced the same level of discomfort and pain that he had known before leaving his home. However, he succinctly clarified his motivation and new-found ability to cope by saying, "The fact that I'm being paid $1,200 a week enables me to do a lot of coping and stay on the job in spite of the physical duties and discomfort."

In a strange way, he was a successfully rehabilitated client even though no official closure or formal plan was ever submitted. Ultimately, the success or failure of any injured client lies within his own state of mind and sense of commitment. Nor were the counseling sessions wasted on Mr. L. He got the message in his own time and place. He found that he could accomplish more than he had believed when the stakes were right.

Some clients make a success of themselves in or out of the disability compensation system. A counselor, however, doesn't often discover when his work has paid off in such an unexpected way. Mr. L.'s case represents a long-distance tribute to the art of people-to-people interaction.

# CHAPTER 16

## Job Placement: Back to Work

Once our injured client has come this far, we know him quite well. We know his specific vocational needs, his level of motivation and the particular motivators that improve his physical functioning on a day-to-day basis.

We are now in a position to search out the labor market for specific job referrals, or to turn this client over to a professional job developer for the final phase of his rehabilitation. For most clients, however, there are a few additional steps to be taken before turning them loose into the job interview situation.

For many individuals, job hunting is a new and foreign experience. They may have worked in their last job situation for many years and forgotten what particular skills are involved in getting a job. They will need help and support. But more importantly, they will need involvement. A good rehabilitation counselor works by a rule of thumb: "If a client can do it for himself, let him." In other words, the more of the actual legwork completed by the client in seeking out job and employer information, the better. The consultant can tell him where to find the information he needs. He can introduce the client to his local public library, a great source of all kinds of job data, such as the **Dictionary of Occupational Titles** (DOT) published by the Department of Labor, the latest issue of the **Occupational Outlook Handbook** containing up-to-the-minute data on a wide variety of jobs, and all the many listings of different types of employers in his area (Chamber of Commerce Directories, etc.). Activity like this on the part of the client can often build up a real enthusiasm and optimism that carries over into his initial job interview.

The client may need specialized training in job-seeking skills, interviewing techniques, resume preparation, application forms, paperwork, etc. The counselor may be able to direct him to local community resources offering several day seminars or training courses in these skills. The more thoroughly prepared the client is, the more confidence he will be able to muster for his job hunt. And the more confidently he approaches this task, the greater the likelihood of early success and job placement. Too long a period spent at this phase of rehabilitation can be discouraging for the client, and perhaps lead to a growing feeling of hopelessness.

If this phase is too long, intervention on the part of the counselor to rebuild client confidence and move him back into the job mainstream is necessary. It must be done before a client begins to accept vocational defeat and sit back to wait for his disability settlement and/or some kind of disability income. Arranging a few positive information-gathering interviews can frequently reverse the client's negative attitudes. New job interviews are arranged. The client becomes more hopeful. He is able to get back on the job-hunting track.

There is one particular area of job-hunting preparation where our clients may need special help. If we have taken the time to sit down and role-play a job interview situation with our clients, we may see that many of them become almost tongue-tied when the subject of their disability and limitations is brought up. This is a subject which needs open and frank discussion on the part of employer and employee. We can help our clients in this area by coaching them in stressing the positive assets they are bringing to their jobs, their long experience in a closely-related job field or perhaps their very recent training and familiarity with the newest occupational information in a new vocational situation. Our clients at this stage in the rehabilitation process **do** have skills and work habits to sell an employer. They need help in presenting these vocational talents in the job interview situation.

A structured job placement program to secure a position for a client, either directly once transferable skills are identified or at the completion of formal training, is a necessary service in a private rehabilitation setting. It is frequently this service that determines the difference between success and failure and identifies a quality rehabilitation process.

A structured job placement program is necessary when the following criteria are met:

1. Client is medically stable.
2. Client has job skills and appropriate work attitudes.
3. Client has mastered effective job search techniques including proper completion of job applications, developed resume, and interview skills.
4. Client has a specific vocational objective that is

realistic and feasible.

The structured job placement services need to spell out the responsibilities on the part of the client and the counselor. It is helpful if a specific number of calls to employers per day or per week are expected on the part of both the client and the counselor. Structured time where the client may utilize the counselor's office in order to receive ongoing coaching while contacting employers may be implemented. The counselor should identify specific job openings or positions compatible with the client's skill level, experience, and physical abilities. Once these job openings are identified, the counselor should schedule interviews for the client. Once the interviews have been completed, follow-up contacts with the prospective employer should be done. This follow-up contact helps identify strengths and weaknesses of the client's job search skills and provides further information to document the feasibility or nonfeasibility of the vocational objective.

## Components of Job Placement

Excellent texts devoted entirely to "job placement strategies" are available. John Crystal and Richard Bolles in **Where Do I Go From Here With My Life?** discuss in a workbook format a variety of practical techniques. This book has sections geared for professional consultants and for individuals seeking work.

Richard Bolles in **What Color Is My Parachute?** has demonstrated how an easily read, popular paperback can help people out of work or planning to make a job change. This book continually goes through revisions. It inspires the job changer, regardless of the reason for the change, to take responsibility for his or her own success.

Dr. Azrin, the father of "job club" technology discusses in **Finding a Job** how job-seekers who give persistent and consistent effort are able to secure work quickly.

We recommend that these tests or comparable ones be purchased and studied by counselor/consultants. The techniques, strategies, and structures for successful job placement should be adapted for use with the "able disabled."

Consumers of vocational services, whether they be individuals or insurance carrier representatives, by studying these or comparable tests are able to develop benchmarks for judging quality services. Rehabilitation providers that implement many or all of the strategies discussed in the above tests and briefly noted below are probably more thorough. They may be more expensive due to additional overhead costs associated with video camera and playback equipment, phone stations, multiple phone lines, a group meeting room, and a job search monitor. However, you pay for what you get -- greater quality, greater placements.

What are some of these success-oriented strategies? What components of job placement technology should the able disabled, insurance carriers, self-insured employers, and attorneys expect? What would the job placement process and environment look like?

First, resumes (preferably the functional variety and not the chronological variety) will be done. A person with marketable transferable skills to several job goals may need several functional one-page resumes. Remember, the one-page resume is **not** a job application or curriculum vitae. It serves the purpose of a marketing flier or business card. It is an attention getter.

Second, a structured Job Search Skills Workshop should be provided. If not feasible, then individual job search coaching is necessary. The Workshop takes advantage of group processes which help change job search attitudes and enhance self-confidence. Videotaping of mock interviews and playback with suggestions overcomes the "denial" attitudes so frequently observed. The Workshop will cover topics such as: informational interviews, job applications, phone calls to prospects, job interviewing, how to handle the question of "Why did you leave your last job," follow-up with prospective employers, time management and job hunting.

Third, logs for recording one's job search activities should be maintained. Who you called, when you called, what was the result of the call, plans for future calls, results of job interviews, etc. need to be recorded. Such a log is similar to a journal maintained by a successful sales representative. It helps a person plan his time and analyze his results. It documents the effort a person spends seeking work.

Fourth, phone stations or work areas with phones enhance the seriousness of job placement. It integrates within vocational rehabilitation a technology considered effective in outplacement services for discharged employees. It allows counselors to schedule clients anywhere from 4 to 40 hours per week for phone calls to set up interviews. It is the persistent, consistent effort that secures positive results.

Fifth, coordination and joint meetings of counselor/consultant, client, and job placement specialist helps ensure consistent expectations. It enables all parties to develop and negotiate on-the-job training (OJT) when appropriate. It reinforces a client's active involvement on his own behalf. It documents a lack of participation if it occurs. It enables an ongoing quality decision regarding labor market feasibility.

Some of the above components are available by state employment service offices. Selected components can be implemented by a person without the assistance of a counselor. The above components, regardless of how they are set up, increase the effectiveness of job placement for the able disabled.

### Mr. B.: A Rehabilitation Failure

This case illustrates that even after doing a thorough job, a case may fail due to factors beyond the control of the consultant/-counselor. There are times in the work of every counselor in this field when, for one reason or another, his efforts fail. The client is not rehabilitated. It is not important who gets the blame for the failure. What is important is the counselor can learn about rehabilitation work from this failure.

Mr. B. at the time of his injury was working as an electrician. Due to an on-the-job accident, he suffered left leg sensory impairment and lumbosacral problems. According to the medical reports dated May, 1983, Mr. B. would be unable to return to any form of work until May, 1984. It was predicted that he might continue to experience weakness, sensory impairment and pain in the left lower extremity.

Mr. B. was a high school graduate who, during his last two years in high school, had worked as a TV technician in a neighborhood TV repair shop. He went on and successfully completed engineering preparation courses at a junior college. However, he did not complete the necessary two-year program. Mr. B. had been employed for 19 years as a TV repairman. At one point, he had even gone into business for himself doing electrical installation, carpentry, plumbing and light TV repair work.

Since he was considered a journeyman electrician at the time of his injury, it was decided that, medically, Mr. B. was not precluded from returning to his usual occupation. He was referred for vocational rehabilitation plan development in

October, 1983.

From his initial interviews with the vocational rehabilitation counselor, Mr. B. expressed interest in pursuing training as an electronic technician. This goal appeared consistent with his previous junior college training and his experience as a TV repairman and electrician. It was further supported by vocational interest and aptitude testing.

At the time of his injury, Mr. B. was married, but had no children. Mr. B. had been earning $14.80 hourly and his wife had recently gone to work. Financially, he was not experiencing any serious problems. Between his disability payments and his wife's income he was able to manage his house and other loan payments. However, even in initial vocational counseling sessions, Mr. B. was expressing some resentment that he had been turned down twice on his application for Social Security disability payments.

When he was referred for vocational service in late 1983, Mr. B. had been off work for one and a half years. He had been completely inactive up until the time of his referral. Medical reports indicated that he would be able to return to work by the summer of 1984.

After eight weeks of vocational counseling and testing sessions, a rehabilitation plan was developed that enabled him to participate in formal schooling concurrent with his medical recovery. A vocational objective of electronics technician was recommended involving a one-year training program at a school located in nearby San Francisco. Mr. B. seemed very interested in pursuing this plan and it was signed by both him and the insurance carrier.

Three months into this training program, Mr. B. experienced a seizure of unknown origin. Because the physician had reported this seizure, Mr. B. was informed by the State Department of Motor Vehicles that he was about to lose his driver's license. This produced extreme anxiety and concern and seriously jeopardized his ability to drive back and forth to school in the city. Alternate public means of transportation were arranged and financed by the insurance carrier as an additional living expense connected with his rehabilitation plan.

Early reports from the school indicated that Mr. B. was maintaining a solid "B" average and was attending regularly. There were no problems at that time. In April, 1984 the client seemed to be enthusiastically and successfully involved with his rehabilitation plan. He was coping well with the stress caused by his recent seizure disorder, the loss of his driver's license and the adjustment to new instructors at the school.

Problems began developing in the middle of May. The counselor was informed in early June that Mr. B. had not attended school for the past three weeks. The school was informed that a death in Mr. B.'s family forced him to leave town for a period of time. Because of the school's requirement that students keep the school informed of continuing absence in order to maintain official enrollment, Mr. B. was in danger of being dropped. Quick intervention on the part of the counselor, the school and the insurance carrier was required to keep the client's rehab plan alive. Arrangements were made with the school to work out alternate schedules and coursework so that he could graduate as projected in his rehab plan. While Mr. B. still maintained his "B" average, he missed another week of classes and the school was forced to drop him from enrollment. He would have to wait until the beginning of the next quarter before resuming his studies. The counselor arranged a means for Mr. B. to maintain contact with the school by attending lecture classes in the interim. At that time, the client agreed with this plan.

In mid-July, 1984, Mr. B. informed his counselor he had decided not to attend the lecture classes, and that he did not want to continue with his rehabilitation plan. He intended to inform all concerned parties, including the insurance carrier and his attorney, of this decision. Moreover, Mr. B. told the counselor that he had lied about the trips out of the state and the deaths in his family which he had given as reasons for his absences. He had just been sitting at home. No further vocational services were recommended. Mr. B. had withdrawn himself from this rehabilitation plan.

Mr. B.'s failure in a seemingly sound and reasonable vocational plan shows many of the frustrations a counselor can experience in this work. The counselor is forced to look at his work carefully and ask where **he** has failed. Did he help the client select a logical vocational area? On the basis of the educational and work history, yes. Did he properly assess the client's medical ability to complete training and return to work? Again, on the basis of all medical evidence, he did. How about that intangible, client motivation? All early evidence, including the client's grades in the training program, indicated that the client was seriously working at the rehabilitation plan. The client's words indicated that he was convinced he was moving in the proper vocational direction and was eager to get there.

When and where did the failure of Mr. B. occur? Early medical reports had mentioned that the client appeared intoxicated at times and showed some symptoms of being an alcoholic. To the counselor, he denied these allegations, claiming that he had been overdrugged from the prescribed medications. Should the counselor have become a detective and sought to verify these statements?

Again, with the client's explanation of his absences from school, was the counselor to accept these explanations, or do some investigating on his own?

The vocational counselor is particularly valuable in some areas of a client's rehabilitation progress. He can validate a client's progress in a training program by remaining in touch with the training facility. He can maintain an ongoing scrutiny of the client's medical progress as it relates to training and work situations. But attempts to go further and to validate every statement made by a client are beyond the counselor's duties. Any attempts to police the activities of the client and check out his every statement cast the counselor in a different role, that of detective or investigator. Such a role would invalidate his ability to help his client as a counselor. The openness and trust so vital to effective counseling would be lost in a mass of detailed accusations and denials.

The failure, in this case, was finally the client's. The counselor is dependent on the client for full and open communication. He cannot read minds or motives. All he can effectively do is to observe client behavior in his presence and listen to the client's hopes and fears on the path to rehabilitation.

# CHAPTER 17

## Economics For Job Seekers And Job Changers

by

Lawrence J. Deneen, Ph.D. and Colleen M. Deneen, M.Ed.

We are not economists. We know how to **spell** macroeconomics and microeconomics. But, do not ask us for definitions.

Most of our clients, people seeking work or planning a career change, do not care about academic debates regarding the latest theory of economics. They want to know **where** a job opening is likely to exist. "How do I find out about openings, duties, wages, etc.?"

As consultants we too want answers to the practical questions of our clients and referral sources.

Through various legal proceedings, the following questions are frequently asked:

1. What percent of the open labor market is he/she precluded from?
2. What wages/earnings is he/she able to command given current skills and abilities **AND**, secondly, given additional training?
3. With the high rate of unemployment, won't it be difficult for **this person** to secure a job in a reasonable period of time?
4. How long should it take him/her to find a job, assuming "diligence" in a job search?

These questions and others are answered based on our experience of over 10 years, hundreds of labor market surveys, hundreds of job analyses, thousands of interviews, and thousands of employer contacts. We use the **results** of research and labor market analyses as published by economists. We may not understand their methodologies, **but so what! We understand** their conclusions. It is the conclusions that our clients need and we use.

This discussion is intended to inform you of **some** of these results and conclusions. We discuss this information with clients, customers, and referral sources. It helps motivate job-seekers and elicits cooperation from other concerned parties.

We hope that this information, adapted to your situation, will enhance your success rate.

**Understanding Unemployment, Employment -- Digging Beneath The Statistics:**

There are three types of **Unemployment:**

1. Frictional: People are qualified but not matched with a job. To solve this type of unemployment a person must **want to work** and **job search skills must be used.**
2. Cyclical: Boom versus recession type of unemployment, i.e. layoffs when GNP declines and recession occurs. **Temporary** job creation by government is a solution.
3. Structural: People looking for work are not qualified for available jobs. **Training is a solution** for this type of unemployment.

According to a U.S. Department of Labor study, 42% of unemployment is **frictional** and **58%** is **cyclical and/or structural.** In terms of Vocational Plans, returning to school **assumes** a structural problem and direct placement assumes a frictional problem.

The **size** of the labor force **changes slowly.** However, large groups of the population **move into and out of the labor force** and are between jobs at any point in time. **This labor force "flow" is approximately ten times the labor force growth rate.**

The greater the turnover rate or "flow rate," which may be caused by a person quitting, layoff, or a hiring process, and the greater the number of new job-seekers and new job vacancies each week, **then the more difficult** it is to match jobs and workers. In such a circumstance unemployment rates will go up.

From a text **Labor Economics** published in the mid 1970's, there is an interesting observation. It relates to understanding employment and unemployment figures. In a 100 million labor force, there are 15 to 20 million job changes per week. **During a particular census sample,** these **people in the process of a job change and not employed,** would be **categorized as unemployed.** Granted, while these persons are properly considered unemployed, close to one-half of these individuals may only experience a one or two week gap between jobs. Based on historical data, the proportion of unemployed individuals out of work a **long time** (15 weeks or more) rarely exceeds 25% of the unemployed. This means that if the unemployment rate is 7%, only 1.75% is long-term unemployment.

It is an accurate understanding of the **causes of unemployment** that enables vocational counseling and job placement services to be effective. Through a vocational evaluation and counseling process, quickly identify **structural** unemployment problems and recommend training or schooling so that an individual becomes qualified. Likewise, quickly identify skills and abilities that are transferable from one job to another or from one occupation to another. This helps match a person with a job **and** this in turn solves the **frictional unemployment problem.**

As a single firm and as individuals, we are **helpless in solving cyclical unemployment** since these **causes relate more to** politics, deficits, money market trends, and those esoteric subjects described by politicians as **"fiscal and monetary policies."**

**Job Search Statistics:**

According to Mr. David Roberts, a consultant with the U.S. Department of Labor:

1. 65% of the unemployed (according to a 1976 labor statistic study) spend 5 hours or less per week seeking work.
2. The unemployed on an average contact 6 employers per month.

Consider for a moment **the view that looking for a job is a self-employment venture** in which **your business** is selling yourself to an employer. It is no wonder there is such a "business" failure rate, described as "Plans Completed - Not Return to Work." Individuals do not take themselves seriously. They usually do not spend the time in their own job search that they would **if** they were in another business venture.

**Looking for a job must become a full-time job.** It must be treated as a serious business venture by the individual job seeker. To put in 5 hours per week and to claim you cannot find work is not an accurate portrayal.

**Seeds of Success:**

There are popular books with programs spelled out in which individuals develop their own job search program without the guidance of an outside professional. Such home remedies are often quite effective. A book titled **Twelve Steps to Finding a Job Under $30,000 in Four Weeks,** by Mr. Marcon and Ms. Worthington, is such an example. Their statistics are consistent with those published in professional journals by such authors as Nathan Azrin, Ph.D., the developer of the well-known Job Club approach to job search.

According to these researchers and authors, **over 65%** of individuals with varying experience and backgrounds **who seriously participated** in their own job search efforts **as if it was a full-time job** and **as if it was their own business secured work in less than four weeks.**

These individuals spent considerably more time than 5 hours or less per week. They contacted by means of phone calls, resumes, informational interviews, job applications, and interviews, many more than 6 employers per month.

As is true in any endeavor, the key to success is once again confirmed as being "hard work, persistent and consistent effort."

In our experience, we have found on the average that **individuals who have marketable skills** either **as a result of** their prior **qualification and experience OR recent education** and who pursue a job search effort in **a structured and systematic manner will usually secure a job offer within 5 to 8 weeks.** This experience is consistent with that of others.

**Where To Look:**

Some additional statistics that point the direction toward successful job search efforts are the following:

1. 66% of new jobs are created in firms of 1 to 20 employees.
2. Only 1% of job growth occurs by Fortune 500 companies.
3. 31% of job growth occurs by government.
4. 68% of job growth occurs by small business.

The answer to the question: **"Where should I look for work?"** is obvious. **Focus your attention on that part of the economy in which most new jobs occur.** While many jobs may appear "juicy" with the large employers that employ thousands of workers and while the benefits may appear more desirable, the prospects of securing a job are less likely than with firms employing under 20 employees. Across all industries the job growth was 29.3% from 1976 - 1982 in businesses with 20 or less employees. On the other hand, across **all firm sizes** the employment growth was only 15.6%.

Here is another interesting statistic. Soon, according to Dr. Thomas Stanley, a marketing professor at Georgia State

University, **the nation will have 1 million millionaires.** California has more millionaires than any other state with 114,427 and Vermont has the fewest with only 1,031. Approximately **80% of the surveyed millionaires are self-employed** and are **first generation wealth.** They are disciplined, have limited cash, and the households are composed primarily of married couples with children living near or in a metropolitan area. The **average age of a millionaire is 57-years-old.**

The full significance of this **final statistic** is difficult to appreciate and it is with tongue in cheek humor that it is included. However, it does underscore a direction to pursue if you want to become a millionaire. The best opportunity appears to be in California. Avoid Vermont. Be married. Have children, and, if you are not disciplined, forget it.

# SECTION II

## Areas of Special Interest

# CHAPTER 18

## The Longshore and Harbor Workers' Act

Janette White, M.S., C.R.C.

### Introduction

In 1917, a longshoreman was injured on navigable waters off the New England coast. When he tried to receive compensation for his injuries, he found that neither the state that he had left, nor the state for which he was destined, were liable for compensating his injuries or paying the medical bills he incurred. He found that he had no coverage even though each state had Workers' Compensation systems which insure that workers are provided benefits when injured on the job. This circumstance laid the foundation for the development of the Longshore and Harbor Workers' Act.

There seems to be a prevailing myth that these employees, longshore and harbor workers, are a unique breed of client, different from those employees covered under state compensation. It is thought that, as counselor/consultants providing rehabilitation services to workers covered by this act, we are faced with a whole different ball game than that of providing services under the state system. It is, however, **not the clients who differ, but the systems** through which each program is administered.

In looking into the Longshore Act, this chapter will be divided into six sections: Program Goal; Program Administration; Employees Covered; Basic Benefits; Rehabilitation Benefit; and Rehabilitation Process.

### Program Goal

The Longshore and Harbor Workers' Compensation Act is administered by the Department of Labor through the Office of Workers' Compensation Programs (OWCP). Financial benefits are provided by insurance carriers retained by each company. It is mandatory for each company to carry Workers' Compensation insurance. When an employee is injured, the primary goal of the OWCP is to insure that medical and financial benefits are provided while the employee is unable to work. Once the employee is medically able to work, the emphasis of the OWCP shifts to either modifying the preinjury job or providing training in an area where the injury or disability will be vocationally irrelevant.

Under the Longshore Act, disability is an **economic**, not a physical concept. It is defined as the "incapacity because of injury to earn the wages which the employee was receiving at the time of injury, in the same, or any other employment." (1) Take for example, a longshoreman who must lift 50-75 pound boxes on a daily basis in his job. Due to daily lifting, this worker's back is injured and his doctor determines that he is permanently restricted from lifting over twenty pounds. This is a vocational handicap or "disadvantage that makes success difficult" if it restricts him from earning the same salary he earned before the injury.

It is the goal of the OWCP to remove that vocational handicap by modifying the existing job or identifying a job within this worker's skills and medical abilities. A job modification could involve eliminating duties that require lifting by the use of an assistive device or exchanging them for job duties that do not require lifting. A job modification is the most desirable choice and is the first avenue pursued by the OWCP. It is often the least expensive plan for the insurance carrier and allows the employee to remain at a job he knows with an employer with whom he is familiar.

If a job modification is not possible, reemployment with the same employer is the next most desirable choice. Of all workers injured in 1984, 20% returned to alternate work with the same employer. Again, reemployment with the same employer means a quicker return to work and therefore less of a salary loss for the employee as well as being of minimum cost to the employer. If neither of the above two options are possible, more extensive rehabilitation services may be necessary.

In summary then, it is the objective of the OWCP to provide financial, medical and rehabilitation benefits to an employee injured on the job that will enable him to return to a job where his disability is not a vocational handicap.

**Administration**

The Longshore and Harbor Workers' Compensation Act is administered by the Department of Labor through regional offices of the Office of Workers' Compensation Programs (OWCP). There are a number of people involved on each case -- primarily the Claims Examiner and the Rehabilitation Specialist, both employed by the Department of Labor. Outside of the Department of Labor, defense and applicant attorneys, employers, doctors, and private rehabilitation consultants are also involved.

Under this compensation act, it is the Claims Examiner who acts as case manager. The Claims Examiner is responsible for: determining whether an employee is eligible for benefits; recommending medical treatment; and insuring that disability payments are paid by the insurance carrier. (Keep in mind that this Claims Examiner is employed by the Department of Labor and works in conjunction with the claims representative from individual insurance companies representing each employer.)

The Claims Examiner is also responsible for referring the injured worker to the Rehabilitation Specialist should it look like rehabilitation will be necessary. This determination is made based on medical information and a job analysis. The job analysis is usually completed by a private rehabilitation consultant and is a detailed description of the physical demands of the job. This analysis is sent to the injured worker's treating physician who determines, based on the employee's medical condition, whether or not he is able to return to the job. Many employees are able to return to work after a recovery period and rehabilitation is not needed. If rehabilitation is indicated, the case is referred to the Rehabilitation Specialist.

The Rehabilitation Specialist is responsible for further screening of the injured worker and establishing 1) whether or not he would benefit from rehabilitation services and, if so, 2) what services would help him to return to work. That is, is the individual's medical condition such that he will, in the future, be able to return to gainful employment with rehabilitation services or is the medical condition of such a nature that he is not able to return to employment? If rehabilitation is indicated, the Rehabilitation Specialist coordinates services in order that the employee is enabled to return to a job where his injury is vocationally irrelevant.

The OWCP Rehabilitation Specialist is responsible for insuring that proper rehabilitation services are provided to the injured worker. The OWCP Rehabilitation Specialist can direct which benefits and services can be provided. The Specialist has the ability to directly authorize monies for services not paid for by the carrier. These services may include rehabilitation counseling, training and job placement.

Under the Longshore Act, it is an administrative law judge (employed by the Department of Labor) who can order that compensation be paid.

To summarize, the Longshore Act is administered by a division of the Federal Department of Labor. The primary personnel involved on each case are the OWCP Claims Examiner and the Rehabilitation Specialist. In the next section, we will look at exactly which workers are covered by this act.

**Employees Covered**

While the name of the Longshore and Harbor Workers' Act reveals in part which employees are covered, it does not tell the whole story. The act has grown from the original 1928 legislation to cover a wide variety of longshoring employees. In 1928, the act covered those employees working on navigable waters and dry docks. Navigable waters are those that are deep enough and wide enough to be used for navigation, trade and travel or those that are located in adjoining states. Lake Tahoe, located between California and Nevada, for example, is considered to be navigable water.

The 1972 amendments added any person engaged in maritime employment: longshoremen, ship builders, ship repairmen, stevadores, ship painters, freight handlers, ship breakers, and individuals working on areas adjoining navigable waters where ships are loaded and unloaded. Casual visitors to areas where longshoring is done may also be included. Such visitors would include, for example, representatives of Longshore and Harbor Workers' Unions, insurance claims personnel, employees of steamship companies and cargo handlers. Approximately 525,000 nonfederal employees fall under this compensation act. Of this number, 53% are ship builders, 10% are longshoremen, and the others work in the variety of areas described above.

Four additional acts have been legislated since 1928 to provide a host of other workers with the same coverage provided to longshoremen and harbor workers. In 1928, the District of Columbia Workers' Compensation Act was legislated to cover employees working in Washington, D.C. In 1941, the Defense Base Act covered all civilian employees of military, air and naval bases. This act was expanded in 1942 to add contract employees working on these bases. Two more acts were passed in 1952 and 1953. These were the Non-Appropriated Fund Institute Act and the Outer-Continental Shelf Lands Act to cover, respectively, civilians in the Armed Forces and employees working on the outer-continental shelf in developing natural resources.

As one can easily see, the Longshore Act covers a very wide variety of workers. This broad coverage makes it possible for some people to be covered by more than one act. A claims representative, for example, injured while visiting a dock may be covered by state Workers' Compensation through his company as well as by the Longshore Act. One is not entitled to receive benefits from both sources, but is able to choose to apply for disability with the most comprehensive benefits plan -- usually the Longshore Act.

Claims involving intoxication or willful misconduct on the part of the employee are not covered under this act. The burden, however, is on the employer to prove that an accident was caused by an employee for these reasons. Also not covered by this act are the master of a crew and those he employs (cooks, pursers, deck hands and repairmen) to work on a ship of under 18 tons.

In the next section, we will look at the benefits that you would be entitled to receive if you were an employee injured and covered by this legislation.

**Basic Benefits**

Workers covered by this act are entitled to a wide variety of generous compensatory benefits. This compensation act is considered to be the most generous of all -- a fact which has brought it under attack by many critics who feel it to be an unnecessarily expensive piece of legislation.

When an injury occurs, medical attention is usually required. Under this act, medical expenses, including hospital care and prosthetic devices are completely paid for by the insurance carrier. The injured worker is initially allowed to choose his own physician but may be asked at a later time to go to a doctor selected by the OWCP for an additional evaluation.

Many injuries are serious enough to require medical care but do not involve missing more than three days of work. The employee, after missing three days of work, is entitled to receive temporary disability indemnity payments. These payments are equal to two-thirds of the employee's salary with a maximum benefit of 200% of the national average weekly wage. In 1985, the average weekly wage is $298.87 making the maximum allowable temporary disability payment $579.74 per week. As these payments are tax-free, many employees receive benefits that come close to or equal their regular take-home pay.

The minimum allowable payment for temporary disability is one-half of the average weekly wage. Using 1985 figures again, this minimum would be $144.94 per week. Any worker who makes less than $214.74 per week will receive the minimum weekly benefit of $144.94. **The average disability payment is $500.00 per week.**

This high rate for the temporary disability benefit has been greatly criticized as having an adverse effect on an injured worker's desire to go back to work. Employees are given little incentive to return to their old job or find a new one, when they can receive almost the same money by not working. This problem is taken into consideration however, with the use of a wage earning capacity evaluation. (This will be discussed below in the Rehabilitation Benefit section.)

That the injury needs to be reported in order for benefits to be provided, seems unnecessary to point out. Yet, this often causes delays in a worker receiving compensation. It is the responsibility of the employee to report the injury to his supervisor and the responsibility of the supervisor to report it to the insurance examiner. (They will then report it to the Claims Examiner of the OWCP). While some injuries occur that are visible and obvious, many occur in such a way that if not verbally explained, may go unnoticed. Take again, the example of the longshoreman who injured his back. Perhaps toward the end of a long day of loading and unloading heavy boxes, he feels a little sore but continues to work. The next day, he is in too much pain to work and calls in sick. Unless he tells his supervisor that he is out for work-related reasons, the employer does not know to file an injury claim.

The language of the act specifies that benefits are to begin retroactively from the time that the employer knew or **should** have known that the injury occurred. It is therefore, to the benefit of all involved, particularly the injured worker, to never assume that because **you** know that you have sustained a work-related injury, that the proper benefits personnel will know.

Temporary disability benefits continue until a permanent disability settlement is reached between the employer, the injured worker and, if applicable, the worker's representative. Permanent disability sums are made in either lump-sum or life-time payments. A lump-sum payment is for "scheduled injuries." This schedule is similar to insurance companies' schedules for claims under an Accidental Death and Dismemberment policy. For example, if an injury caused a worker to lose the use of his dominant hand, he would be given a total disability rating of approximately 50 per cent. This figure would then be adjusted according to the worker's age and occupation. That is, a young laborer would be rated at a higher percentage than an older worker if both lost the use of their dominant hand in an accident.

Unscheduled injuries are injuries that do not involve the extremities -- most commonly, the back. These settlements are more flexible as they are agreed upon between employer and employee. These payments can be either in a lump-sum or divided into a series of payments. If spread out, the payments are subject to an annual 8% cost-of-living increase.

In the event that an employee is killed in an industrial accident, the benefit goes to the surviving spouse and children. These benefits will continue until the spouse dies or remarries. This death benefit is equal to one-half of the employee's weekly salary and is subject to no maximum. If a young employee is killed, this benefit can be very costly to an employer. For example, if a 35-year-old longshoreman, making $450 per week, is killed and the spouse does not remarry for 15 years, the total compensation paid is $175,500. Comparatively, under most state systems, the maximum for a death benefit is $95,000 (for a worker who has one or more partial dependents) or less.

It is also interesting to note, that the death benefit under the Longshore Act, is for **any** worker who dies, of any cause, while out of work for a work-related disability. This is one provision of the bill which has drawn much criticism. Critics say that this aspect is not appropriate, especially if the death is not due to a work-related accident, and unnecessarily raises administrative costs.

As described above, most of the basic benefits provided by the bill involve disability payments and coverage for all medical costs. For many workers, these basic benefits are all that is needed and after a period of recovery, they are able to return to their job. For some, however, the injury prevents them from returning to their job and rehabilitation services are needed. In the next section, the rehabilitation benefit will be explained in greater detail.

**The Rehabilitation Benefit**

If an employee is injured and cannot return to his former position, he may be entitled to vocational rehabilitation at the employer's expense. Returning the employee to work may be as simple as modifying the job through a change of job duties or by means of an assistive device. For those who are more seriously injured relative to the physical demands of the job, rehabilitation may involve direct placement using skills the employee already has, or retraining into an entirely new field.

It is not mandatory for an employee to participate in vocational rehabilitation. He may feel that he is too disabled for rehabilitation to be beneficial or he may just not be interested. If an employee does not want to participate, he may or may not continue to receive his weekly disability payments. An employee's benefits may be adjusted with the use of the "loss of wage earning capacity" evaluation. If the employer can show that 1) there is a job that the employee can do physically and 2) the job exists readily enough in the general labor market, the weekly benefit can be adjusted accordingly.

Take for example, the case of an injured ship builder who was making $600 per week. After his injury, he received $400 per week in disability benefits (2/3 of his average weekly wage). A vocational evaluation and labor market analysis showed that with his previous experience and current medical condition, he could be employed as an electronics technician making $250 per week. According to the loss of wage earning capacity formula, he had lost 58% of his wage earning capacity due to the injury. ($600 per week minus $250 per week equals $350). If he does not participate in rehabilitation, his disability benefit will be 66 2/3% of his actual loss of earning capacity or approximately $233.35 each week for the rest of his life (66 2/3% times $350).

If the evaluation shows that there are no appropriate jobs, the employee will continue to get lifetime benefits based on 2/3 of $600 or $400 per week. If the injured worker were to die, his spouse would continue receiving these benefits until she died or remarried.

Rehabilitation services may include any of the following: vocational testing, counseling and evaluation; prevocational and vocational training; work evaluations; and labor market studies. Until January of 1985, rehabilitation services were provided by a wide variety of private rehabilitation counselors. In January, however, the first Department of Labor counselor training was held. This three-day workshop outlined the policies and procedures of the OWCP. In the west, 119 counselors from California, Arizona, and Nevada were certified to provide services. These are the only counselors to whom Longshore and Harbor Workers' cases will be referred by the Department of Labor until more counselors are certified at the next training session. This session is to be held in 1987 or 1988. Cases may be referred by parties other than the DOL, such as attorneys or carriers, to counselors not certified by OWCP.

During rehabilitation, the employee will receive a maintenance allowance of $25.00 per week. This is to cover daily expenses like transportation costs. This is different from many state Workers' Compensation systems which does not put a ceiling on mileage and transportation expenses. Under the state system, employees are frequently reimbursed for mileage, for parking, or for public transportation, if the proper receipts are submitted.

When providing rehabilitation to a longshoreman or harbor worker, the limit for daily expenses must be considered when developing a plan. If he is not going to be reimbursed for expenses above $25.00 per week, an employee will probably not be as willing to travel long distances for evaluations and/or school. A careful calculation should be made of transportation costs before school or training is begun, so that the employee knows how much he will have to contribute to transportation costs. A decision can then be made as to whether he is willing to begin the plan.

While the rehabilitation benefit is only a part of the benefits that an industrially injured worker has available to him, it is a vital one. In the typical case, the injury is to a worker in a physical job -- most commonly, an injury to the back. If rehabilitation is necessary, it means that the worker has not been able to return to his former position. The monetary benefits are meant to alleviate the financial burden. The rehabilitation counselor can help with the emotional impact by providing support and help as the employee refocuses his energies and talents in a new vocational area. In the next section, we will examine in more detail how the rehabilitation process is developed.

**The Rehabilitation Process -- Referral By Dept. of Labor:**

Rehabilitation services are initiated when the Claims Examiner refers the injured worker to the Rehabilitation

Specialist. As discussed above, this referral is made based on medical information (i.e. a report from the treating physician indicating that rehabilitation will be necessary), or a request from the employer, applicant attorney, insurance representative or injured worker. Under the Longshore Act, with the use of the loss of wage earning capacity evaluation, only one-third of the injured workers screened for rehabilitation are referred for full vocational services. Of these, 55% were back injured, 25% had injuries to the lower extremities, and the remaining 30% consisted of disabilities involving the lungs, heart and skin.

Under the Longshore Act, the rehabilitation process is carefully mapped out in terms of time and money allowances. The Rehabilitation Specialist refers the case to a counselor by submitting a referral/authorization form (OWCP Form 35A). This form indicates the benefits that are being requested and is valid for one year. This form also authorizes the counselor to provide services costing up to, but not exceeding, $2000. If charges are going to exceed this amount, the funds must be requested and approved in advance. When received, the counselor contacts the Rehabilitation Specialist to discuss the case. The counselor then contacts the applicant attorney to obtain permission to work with the client. Finally, the client is contacted.

The vocational rehabilitation process proceeds in a series of set stages once the initial contacts have been made. Services provided to an employee may encompass all or a portion of the following "stages." The first stage is the "plan development stage." This is different than what is considered the "vocational exploration stage" under many state systems. Under the Longshore Act, the plan development stage is designed for a counselor to meet the injured worker and assess his vocational potential and **determine if he is eligible for rehabilitation services.**

The plan development stage encompasses ten counseling, guidance and contact hours within a two-month time period. The counselor assesses the client's vocational potential in terms of skills, aptitudes and physical abilities. Similar to the idea behind the loss of wage earning capacity, an employee's vocational potential is defined as the salary that he **could** be earning given his existing skills and physical condition. Remember, under the Longshore Act, disability is seen in economic, not medical, terms.

To assess vocational potential, the counselor considers the employee's work history, transferable skills, desire to return to work, previous earnings, and medical condition. A job (or jobs) is then pinpointed, based on the above information, for which the employee is qualified. The job must actually exist in the local labor market, but does not have to be currently available for it to be considered an appropriate job. If the wages paid by the above job are higher than the employee previously earned, he is not eligible for rehabilitation services for "only employees ... who have permanent, compensable disabilities resulting ... in a significant vocational handicap and loss of wage earning capacity" are eligible for services.

The counselor must provide specific information regarding the results of such an evaluation. In addition to documenting the factors considered in the assessment (i.e. medical reports, work history, etc.), jobs located for which the employee qualifies, must be described in the following manner:

1) Job Title
2) Dictionary of Occupational Titles #
3) Estimated Salary
4) Physical Requirements
5) Availability in the local labor market

There are three possible outcomes once the assessment has been completed. If it is determined that the employee did not, as a result of the injury, lose any capacity to earn the same amount as his previous salary, rehabilitation services will not be provided. If, on the other hand, he is determined to have lost earning potential because of the injury, then rehabilitation services will continue if the employee is interested. If not, the employee's disability payments will, as discussed above, be adjusted accordingly.

If the employee is eligible for services, the case will progress to the training or placement status. When it is determined what course vocational services will take, the plan is outlined on the OWCP Form #16. If it is determined that an employee will only be employable after a period of schooling, a training program will be set up. Training may be in prevocational or vocational areas. Prevocational training may involve the employee returning to earn a high school equivalency degree or attending brush-up classes at a local junior college in math and English. Prevocational training may last up to 1-1/2 years and be followed by ten counseling hours devoted to job-seeking skills.

Vocational training may involve a school program to develop a particular skill. For example, an employee may take a series of courses in data processing which will make him employable as a data processor. Like prevocational training, vocational training may be followed by ten counseling hours in job-seeking skills.

Once training is completed, or if it is not necessary, the next stage is placement. There are three possible statuses in placement: placement with the same employer, placement with a new employer, or self-employment. No placement will be considered without labor market documentation citing at least two titles of jobs that the injured worker is qualified for and medically able to do.

If the worker is to be placed with the same employer (this should be considered first), the counselor is allowed 25 counseling hours within four months to locate alternate work that the worker is able and qualified to do. This includes five hours of follow-up services after placement is made to insure that the new job is successfully working out.

If placement involves a new employer, the counselor is authorized to spend 50 counseling hours (40 job-seeking and 10 follow-up) within a four-month time period. New employer placement **requires** that vocational testing be done to confirm that the person's aptitudes and interests are consistent with the requirements of the job. Once placement is secured, the counselor is to follow-up with the worker at the end of the first day, the end of the first month, and the end of the second month. The meeting at the end of the second month includes the employer. Follow-up services are designed to help alleviate any performance or vocational difficulties that the new employee might have. These services are very important as a means to overcome any problems that may develop and cause the placement to fail.

The final placement possibility is self-employment. This is always a risky venture and should be considered only if it is truly in the worker's best interest and not as a "last ditch effort." A business plan is to be developed in conjunction with the Small Business Administration. A full battery of tests is to be administered to confirm that the employee's aptitudes are in keeping with those required by the business. The tests given are to include the Wide Range Achievement Test (WRAT), the

Wechsler Adult Intelligence Scales (WAIS) and the Strong-Campbell Interest Inventory.

Each month during rehabilitation, the counselor submits a report to the Rehabilitation Specialist documenting the status of the case. This report is submitted in duplicate and contains ten sections detailing the services provided over the last month. These ten sections are: 1) information identifying the case; 2) status; 3) job development contacts, including employer name, job title, salary and outcome of the contact; 4) problems; 5) continued feasibility where the counselor can indicate his impressions of the employee and highlight any obstacles that may have arisen that may inhibit the employee from successfully securing a job; 6) plan for the following month; 7) justification for the services provided; 8) rehabilitation fees; 9) professional hours spent on the case; and 10) name and phone number of the counselor.

If an injured worker is involved in a plan to involve training or placement, the counselor must be aware of how the settlement of the case is progressing, for once a permanent disability settlement is reached, rehabilitation funds automatically end. Take for example, a worker who is going to be involved in a six-month training program. In requesting funds for tuition and counselor fees, the counselor must be able to reasonably estimate when the employee's case will be settled, in order that the cost of the plan is covered in advance. This again is different from a state system where an employee's rehabilitation plan may not be affected by the settling of the case.

Rehabilitation under the Longshore Act can involve limited or very extensive services. The services to be offered to an injured worker are designed to compensate him for the loss of **salary** associated with his injury. This is the main difference between the two systems, as the focus of the state system is to not only compensate his injuries but to provide him the means to become reemployed whether or not he has suffered a loss of earning capacity. While the definitions of disability may differ, the end goal of both programs is for industrially injured workers to be provided the means to return to meaningful and productive work.

**The Rehabilitation Process -- Referral by Attorney:**

In many instances the OWCP Rehabilitation Specialist may conclude that further vocational services are not feasible. Yet, as part of the litigation process in which an injured worker is claiming "total permanent disability," either the applicant or defense attorney may want a vocational evaluation and labor market study. Although the referral source is different and the party responsible to pay the counselor for the time involved is not the OWCP, the process is similar to that discussed above.

Referrals by an attorney usually carry with it the expectation that the counselor will be deposed and will testify at a formal trial before an Administrative Law judge. Occasionally, an applicant attorney may want to be present during the interview/evaluation with a defense-initiated referral. Although he has the right to be present, he does not have the right to interfere with the evaluation.

The applicant attorney is usually interested in an opinion by a vocational expert that corroborates the claim for total permanent disability, i.e. no wage earning capacity. Such a claim can have a large dollar value. If the injured worker was earning $600 per week, the disability payment is $400 per week for life if it is total permanent disability. Plus, if the worker dies, the benefit goes to his spouse as long as she does not remarry. Assuming a worker age 53 who lives to age 70, the value of the claim is approximately $353,600 (not adjusted). If he dies at age 70 and his spouse age 65 lives another 10 years, the value of the claim increases by approximately $208,000. Since the attorney gets paid anywhere from 10% to 30% of the final "verdict," the stakes are important for all parties.

The defense attorney is usually interested in an opinion by a vocational expert that confirms the qualifications and ability of the injured worker to earn wages at realistically available job(s). The higher the wage, the better. But any wage, even minimum wage, is better than nothing. If a minimal paying job is available then the judge may decide there is only partial permanent disability and order wage loss. Using the same scenario as above, but assuming there are jobs paying $5.00 per hour or $200 weekly that the worker could do, the wage loss partial disability to age 70 is $235,745. Plus, since it is partial permanent disability the spouse is not eligible for continuing benefits.

An analysis of the above scenarios shows that the total award in litigated cases before an Administrative Law judge is substantial, whether **total** permanent or **partial** permanent. The former is higher. The latter is usually greater than the disability awards under most state Workers' Compensation systems.

The preferred mental set of a vocational expert who receives a referral from an attorney, plaintiff or defense, within the Longshore system is the same as that needed as a vocational expert in personal injury liability cases. It is an adversary system. The stakes are high. The attorneys will use tactics to win with more intensity than is usually observed in state Workers' Compensation vocational benefits. Be prepared. Be thorough. Be professional.

And as President Truman remarked: "If you don't like the heat, stay out of the kitchen."

## NOTES

(1) Longshore and Harbor Workers' Act, Amendments of 1972, Excerpt from 92nd Congress, page 2

(2) Ibid

# CHAPTER 19

## Federal Employees Comp Act -- An Overview

### Program Goal

The Federal Employees Compensation Act is the Workers' Compensation Law that provides compensation benefits to civilian employees in the United States for disabilities due to injuries incurred while performing their job or due to employment-related diseases. When a determination has been made that an injured Federal employee is entitled to FECA benefits, the Workers' Compensation benefits are paid at the rate of two-thirds of the employee's pay rate if there are no dependents or three-fourths of the salary when there is more than one dependent. To be entitled to vocational rehabilitation benefits under the Federal Employees Compensation Act, the injured worker must:

(a) Have sustained a permanent and job-related injury.

(b) Be in receipt of or entitled to compensation benefits.

(c) Be prevented by the injury from performing his or her customary job duties.

There is a **definite** incentive under the Federal Employees Compensation Act to provide vocational rehabilitation services. This is due to the concept and benefit entitled **wage loss.** An employee can receive compensation as long as the medical evidence indicates total or partial disability and the employee is suffering lost wages due to the injury. Thus, this can be a lifelong benefit.

### Basic Benefits

The Federal Employees Compensation Act provides that employees who suffer job-related disabilities are entitled to:

(a) Continuation of regular pay for the period of the disability up to a maximum of 45 calendar days, for traumatic job-related injury.

(b) Compensation for wages lost as a result of job-related injury or illness.

(c) Medical care for disability due to:

1. Personal injury sustained while in the per-

formance of duty.

2. Diseases approximately caused, aggravated, or accelerated by employment.

(d) Vocational rehabilitation

(e) Scheduled awards

Compensation is provided for the permanent loss, or loss of use of each of certain members, organs, and functions of the body.

Vocational rehabilitation benefits include: vocational evaluation, vocational interest and aptitude testing, labor market research, and job placement services. Vocational plans may consist of:

(a) College training: This must be justified by vocational testing that includes administration of a battery that includes the Wechsler Adult Intelligence Scale, the Wide Range Achievement Test, aptitude test, interest inventory, and a personality evaluation.

(b) Vocational technical training: Testing must first be completed to justify the vocational technical training. This could be performed by a work evaluation center, colleges, qualified examiner, or a period of trial on-the-job training based on the individual's interests and work history.

(c) Job placement.

(d) Self-employment.

As mentioned above, the injured Federal employee receives compensation at the rate of two-thirds of his income if single or three-fourths with dependents. This is an untaxed dollar and therefore there is practically no financial incentive for the worker to return to the job. Also, medical and health benefits continue on simultaneous with the recovery process.

**Loss of Wage Earning Capacity**

When medically stationary, the Claims Examiner completes what is known as a Loss of Wage Earning Capacity (LWEC). The LWEC takes place when a determination is made that:

(a) The worker is not able to return to the usual and customary employment due to permanent disability.

(b) Their condition is medically stationary.

The LWEC is the factor in which the Federal Claims Administrator bases his rating of entitlement to future benefits for the Federal injured employee. In simplest terms, it is a transition step that moves the injured worker from Temporary Disability benefit structure to a Permanent Disability benefit structure.

The judgment factors that go into determining the LWEC is based upon three basic questions:

1. What are the permanent medical limitations?
2. What is the injured worker's work history?
3. Taking into consideration the above two factors, what job (or jobs) can the worker be reasonably expected to obtain within a fifty-mile range of his/her residence? (Taking into consideration only transferable skills - not potential training).

It is within this LWEC determination where there is an incentive for the Administrator of the Federal Compensation Act to provide vocational rehabilitation benefits to the injured worker. This financial incentive is that if the injured worker's skill can be raised through retraining, his overall LWEC benefits can be reduced significantly. For example, let's take a 35-year-old worker who was earning $2,000 per month when injured. While receiving his compensation benefits, he receives three-fourths of that salary or $1,500 per month in Workers' Compensation benefits under the Federal Employees Compensation Act. When he is considered permanent and stationary, the Claims Examiner can then proceed with a Loss of Wage Earning Capacity. If the injured worker does not have any transferable skills and is determined only to be able to acquire a job which pays a minimum wage, this pays $134 per week. The $134 per week times 4.3 weeks per month comes to $576 per month. The $576 is then reduced from the $2,000 making for $1,424 per month. The LWEC is then complete when the $1,424 is multiplied by the three-fourths making the amount of income that the injured worker could be entitled to for life $1,068 per month.

It is here where the vocational rehabilitation benefit comes into play. If this same individual can be retrained to become an electronics technician or printed circuit design technician, the starting wage could be in the neighborhood of $9 per hour plus pay increases over the years to come (since an injured worker is entitled to benefits for life, they are also re-evaluated for life). At $9 per hour, the monthly wage is $1,448 per month. This calculates to an LWEC of $552, or a savings of $414 per month over the minimum wage LWEC. Thus, when one calculates this over the working life of an employee, one can easily see the long-term savings of proceeding with a vocational rehabilitation program.

**Administration of the Benefit**

As mentioned previously, the responsibility for administrating the Federal Employees Compensation Act is the Office of Workers' Compensation Programs (OWCP), United States Department of Labor. The OWCP decides whether the employee, or the claimant acting on behalf of the employee, is entitled to benefits under the Federal Employees Compensation Act. A claimant refers to an individual whose claim for benefits and/or compensation has been filed in accordance with FECA. The claim may be filed for traumatic injury, an occupational illness or disease or death. There are approximately three million Federal employees covered by the Act. As of January, 1985, there were over 39,000 Federal employees who were receiving extended compensation benefits.

The various portions of the United States are divided into regions. For example, Region 9 covers California, Arizona and Nevada. For any given region, typically all claims are handled out of one central regional office. In Region 9 all claims are handled out of the San Francisco Regional Office.

Within this regional office, it is the Claims Examiner who is responsible for providing the benefits to which the claimant is entitled under the Federal Employees Compensation Act. A typical OWCP Claims Examiner has a much larger caseload than does his or her counterpart in the private sector. It is not unusual for a Claims Examiner to have as many as 1,000 open files that fall within his or her jurisdiction. This is compared to the counterpart in the private sector who typically will handle betwen 200-400 open files. The OWCP Claims Examiner's job is (as of this writing) further complicated by the fact that their cases are assigned according to alphabetical designation. In other words, one person may handle all claimants whose last name begins with a C or D.

The usual case in the private sector is for the Examiner to have account responsibility. For example, one Examiner may handle a large account such as Pepsi-Cola, Holiday Inns, United Parcel Service, etc. This gives the Examiner more of a sense of control because he is dealing with the same employer, same contact person with the employer and will have consistent expectations and communications regarding the setting from which the injured worker came. The OWCP Claims Examiners will be handling injured workers who come from separate environments as the United States Postal Service, Department of the Navy, Department of the Interior, the Air Force, etc. This leads to more confusion and less controllable case management than their counterparts in the private sector. It also means that the vocational rehabilitation counselor can be of tremendous assistance to the overworked FECA Claims Examiner in trying to facilitate a return to work with the employer of record.

Within each region, there is a Rehabilitation Specialist or Specialists that have the responsibility for seeing that the Federal injured worker receives the rehabilitation benefit. It is this Rehab Specialist who refers the claimant out for the vocational rehabilitation services. The Claims Examiner identifies the claimant who is entitled to and can benefit from vocational rehabilitation services. Once the case is identified, then it is referred to the vocational rehabilitation specialist. The Rehab Specialist is typically even more overworked and understaffed than is the Claims Examiner. It is not unusual for the Rehab Specialist to have responsibility for accepting referrals from as many as 15-20 or more individual Claims Examiners.

As stated in the OWCP/Dept. of Labor Rehabilitation Certification Handbook (January, 1985), it is "the mission of the Division of Vocational Rehabilitation, Office of Workers' Compensation Programs to assist injured workers covered by the Federal Employees Compensation Act and the Longshore and Harbor Workers' Act to return to gainful employment and providing vocational rehabilitation services." The Rehab Specialist starts the vocational rehabilitation process by conducting an initial interview with the injured worker. This is usually conducted through a telephone conversation with the claimant. They then make up a file and refer the claimant out either to a private rehabilitation firm or a State Rehabilitation agency.

It is the job of the Rehab Specialist to direct the vocational rehabilitation counselor, according to OWCP Policies and Procedures. Indeed, there are many procedures and forms that must be followed...

The OWCP Rehab Specialist has a 122-page document that is entitled "OWCP Guidelines." This is a resource book for both the Rehab Specialist and the private vocational rehabilitation counselor who is going to do work with the OWCP. It is not the intention of this chapter to quote from that resource. It is more to let the reader know that such a resource is available that covers the various details of performing work for the OWCP including:

(a) The vocational rehabilitation process
(b) Forms management
(c) Reports and reporting requirements for vocational rehabilitation counselors
(d) Bills and billing procedures by rehabilitation counselors.

If one is going to perform work under the Federal Employees Compensation Act, one should contact the Rehab Specialist in the nearest regional office. The Rehab Specialist has a specific process through which the counselor can make application for doing this type of work. The Rehabilitation Specialist will also require the qualified counselor to participate in an orientation and training program provided by OWCP.

# CHAPTER 20

## Vocational Rehabilitation Disability Insurance Income (Long-Term Disability)

### Your Success and Quantum Rehabilitation

Long-term disability vocational rehabilitation is a forensic application of vocational rehabilitation services. If you want to be successful in any endeavor, there are several principles to follow. **First,** you need to identify a goal. **Second,** you need to decide what you want to give up in order to reach your goal. **Third,** you need to develop a plan of action to reach the goal. Along with this plan is the behavior that you will do. You must work your plan. **Fourth,** you need to associate with people already successful in the endeavor you are pursuing. This is well illustrated by the training methods of the U.S. Olympic athletes. Napoleon Hill in his classic success book titled **Think and Grow Rich** refers to this as a Master Mind Group.

If you are not interested in the goal of providing vocational services to recipients of disability income insurance, then this chapter will be of no interest. If you are interested in this goal, read on.

In regard to your success, let us offer this analogy from physics and fitness. In the book **Quantum Fitness,** by Dr. Dennis Waitley and Dr. Dardick, the example of quantum fitness is adapted from physics. Dr. Waitley is a psychologist who works with astronauts and the Olympic training teams in mental rehearsals so people can achieve great feats. Dr. Dardick is a medical doctor who works with the Olympic team. "Quantum" can apply to the field of rehabilitation, in general, and to the delivery of vocational services to recipients of Disability Insurance Income.

Quantum, in the area of physics, is when a scientist by experimentation or participation actually changes the nature and the outcome of the performance of the universe. This language is that of physics. Quantum Physics is that branch of science that orders the universe and studies how that universe interacts and how all the components interact. Quantum vocational rehabilitation with any particular group of people or disability insurance system, is the study and application of how to interact with the components of the system to be more successful, to bring more order, and to accomplish a goal that **you** want to accomplish and that **other people** want to accomplish.

Quantum vocational rehabilitation is creating a "win-win" situation for all components of the disability insurance system.

Quantum endeavors in any field are not for the average person. Do you consider yourself an average consultant? The typical consultant will not like the work in the area of disability insurance. This does not mean you are unable to do it. If you see yourself as average, it means you will have to learn different behaviors and different skills in order to succeed. This chapter addresses some of these skills and behaviors.

**TEN TIPS and Extra Income for You**

At the end of this chapter are Ten Tips. If you follow those tips, and some of the other things discussed, you ought to generate over the next twelve months $600 to $1,000 of extra income for yourself. This is a typical total billings for one case of long-term disability. This amount is for an evaluation and labor market research, not the implementation of a plan or job placement services.

If you start developing a clientele or a referral base with that one case and if this leads to other cases, then you may be able to generate several thousand dollars, up to ten, twelve, or fifteen thousand dollars over the next twelve months. The information in this book and this chapter is not only informative, it also is practical. It relates to financial goals that you may have.

One frequently hears the words "accident and health insurance," "LTD" and "long-term disability insurance." All of these phrases will be referred to as "Disability Insurance Income." Generally, the principles apply the same way.

You need to approach the claims person and claimant in a Disability Insurance Income program differently than you do with straight Workers' Compensation.

You need to learn the language that is part of the disability insurance income system.

One of the key criteria of vocational consulting in a Disability Insurance Income business is that of "forensic environment." (The abbreviation **DII** will be used for Disability Insurance Income.)

One of the things that makes DII have a strong litigation undercurrent is bad faith legal action. This is the consensus as a result of a number of interviews with attorneys who are involved in these lawsuits. In many states, bad faith lawsuits are most prevalent and involved with DII benefits.

**Types of Policies/Tort Law**

There are individual noncancellable contract policies and group contract policies, such as offered through professional organizations.

Usually the individual contract policies are preferred in terms of the benefits one expects if disabled. Naturally they cost more.

The common denominator for group and individual policies is that they are contracts. They are not a benefit that you automatically get because you are an employee and somebody is paying for it through payroll premiums to a Workers' Compensation carrier. This is a contract **YOU** have. This means the issue of tort law and contract law easily comes into effect if there are disputes. If somebody in bad faith does not fulfill that contract they are likely to incur substantial damages through courts of law. Cumulative damages can occur if someone does not fulfill that contract.

It is this legal, tort law background that makes the delivery of rehabilitation services different. There is an obligation of a DII carrier to follow guidelines put forth in the insurance code. The insurance carrier for the DII program is required to "fairly" adjust the case. They need to show that they have the interest of the insured (for those of you who have your own policy you are the insured) above their own interest.

They have to maintain the delivery of the benefit at a fiduciary standard. The concept of fiduciary is important. It means that they have to work in a very trusting and caring way. They have to take the insured's interest at heart when an insured is disabled and receiving benefits. If for some reason an insurance carrier does not do this, they risk punitive damages frequently in amounts of 15 to 20 times the policy benefits.

**Disability Defined in the Policy**

One of the key definitions that pertains to DII is the concept of disability. This is important to keep in mind. It is not the same definition as Workers' Compensation disability. Furthermore, a distinction is made between **sickness**-caused disability and **accident**-caused disability.

Read your own policy, what is it for? Is it when you fall off the ladder? Or does it also cover you when you become ill because of a disease or illness of some sort? These are important definitions if you are the person receiving the benefit.

These are the kinds of questions that should be asked before a person purchases the policy. If a policy excludes sickness and that is the cause of disability, they would not qualify for the benefit. An example will illustrate this concept.

Assume the person disabled has benefits **only** when there is an accident and not when there is sickness or illness. In the process of your vocational counseling you discuss information that is vocationally relevant regarding the treatment, recovery time, and multiple diagnoses. You determine that some of the problems preventing the person from returning to work and effecting residual functional capacity have to do with an underlying disease or illness process.

You briefly discuss this information in your report under a caption titled "Medical Situation." In this instance, the claims person may take that information and try to justify a legal reason for stopping the benefits. If the disability is sickness-related, then for this particular example, there are no contractual benefits. In such a case, you have unwittingly become an "adversary" and have served more as an "investigator," albeit unwittingly, than a professional rehabilitation consultant.

One of the guidelines of the Ten Tips is "Don't do anything until you can get a copy of the policy." Otherwise, you may unwittingly be giving information that could hurt one side or the other and not fulfill your role of being a vocational consultant. If you are going to be "used" by a party, try to know how you are being used and what effects it may have. Then with candor and integrity, you are able to discuss it with the client who comes to the counseling session.

**Definition of Disability - Phase One**

A thorough vocational evaluation requires you to know the policy description for several reasons. Usually in the DII benefit policy there is a definition that discusses how being disabled from doing your own job is different from being disabled from doing any kind of work. This is an important distinction.

A policy that says money is paid if you are unable to do your job means that if you lose the job you were doing or you must change your occupation then you probably collect the benefits. Most Disability Insurance Income policies only do this for a certain period of time, such as the first two years. Then after two years, another definition of disability applies.

**Disability Defined - Phase Two**

Typically, in order to receive benefits after two years, a person must be unable to do any other occupation that he or she is reasonably qualified for by means of age, education, and training and work history.

Does this mean, using myself as an example, that after two years of not being able to do the occupation of a rehabilitation counselor the insurance company, according to the policy, could conclude that I am not disabled because I may be able to do the work of a cashier at a self-service station?

Certainly I have enough education to count and read and work the cash register. This is within my mental capabilities and let's assume within my physical capabilities. It may not be what I am interested in, but at least it is within my capabilities.

In most states, there is another standard for acceptable employment that has to be met. This is a standard that is not discussed in the contract. It comes from case law. It is the type of standard you only learn about by surveying and talking with attorneys. This is a standard that is set by the courts as a result of case litigation. The courts interpret the contract.

Most insurance companies try to shape their contract statements to the latest court decisions. However, the policy the client purchased five or ten years ago does not necessarily have that same contract wording based on a recent court decision. In most states, the court interpretation varies between being "liberal and liberal" (not a misprint).

In one major state, California, if you have an injury or a disability that prevents you from doing an occupation, the standard set by courts is any occupation that you are reasonably qualified to do based on age, education, and experience, **and** that would return you back to some type of "realistic comparable economic level," or income level. The comparable income level aspect of this standard is noteworthy. That means if I were disabled, I would not be forced to accept a cashier position even though I could physically and mentally do it, unless it paid me comparable to my rehabilitation counseling earnings.

This comparable income standard opens up another question. What is comparable? Are the Social Security disability benefits being counted?

It gets complicated. You need to know how DII is approached, otherwise you may unwittingly fall into situations that are embarrassing -- not necessarily illegal or unethical, but just embarrassing. You need to know how the claims person is thinking. This requires a reading of the policy. It requires a basic layman's knowledge of case law standards. Then you are able to be candid and forthright with the claimant. Otherwise you will be deceptive due to ignorance.

It is recommended that you secure the DII policy and read through the definitions. This enhances your objectivity and thoroughness.

**Earnings and Motivation**

In discussing a claimant's financial situation, the following suggestion is given.

"I want to talk to you about your economic situation and your finances. I want you to understand that I need to know this information because it may have a bearing on your interest and motivation to return to work. For example, if you are earning more money right now by not working than you could if you went back to your same job, then sometimes that creates a disincentive to return to work."

Most legal/claims departments that handled DII policies have an "earnings" standard. **IF** a person is earning by disability income two-thirds of their predisability wages then it is generally figured there are motivation problems.

You might ask yourself this question. "If I could earn two-thirds of what I earn as gross wages right now, how would that affect my lifestyle?"

Keep in mind the two-thirds of your gross income. For most people, there would be no lifestyle changes if they received two-thirds of gross wages. That is why the earnings standard exists. If a person is capable of maintaining their same lifestyle without working, they may have little incentive to return to work. Here is an interesting example that illustrates the earnings standard.

**The Case of Bill:**

Bill, age 40, was a disabled attorney. The long-term disability income benefit was the main issue effecting rehabilitation. The attorney qualified for the Disability Insurance Income benefits because he was unable to do his occupation as an attorney. Yet, he had set himself up in a solo practice as an attorney. Does this seem confusing? It was.

Being an attorney, he understood the subtleties of contracts. He had a private Disability Insurance Income policy. When he filed his claim for benefits for Disability Insurance Income he went to his employer (a major Workers' Compensation defense firm) and secured a very detailed description of his job duties. He submitted them to physicians. They wrote and said "you cannot do those duties."

This medical documentation established his eligibility. He is receiving Disability Insurance Income benefits for the extent of his contract. At the same time he is setting up another law practice on his own, **only** his duties are different.

He was able to show that he could not do his same occupation. Once the time period ends for this first definition of disability and the other definition that says "any occupation reasonably qualified to do" begins, then his benefits will stop.

He thought through very carefully the medical information he received from physicians and correlated it with typical duties. He had a stress and strain heart attack problem. He was relatively young, 40-years-old. The job duties he was doing at the time he had the heart attack were much more demanding than he is going to do in his solo practice. He was a trial lawyer. He is quitting trial law. He is pursuing another type of law practice. He will avoid trials and the associated stresses.

**Recurrent Disability Defined AND How Long to Wait**

Another definition in Disability Insurance Income policies that becomes important is the definition of **recurrent disability.** Associated with recurrent disability is the definition of the **elimination period.** These terms refer to aspects of policies that describe when your money begins being paid if you are disabled today. Sometimes you have a 7-day, 15-day, 60-day, or 90-day waiting period. The particular waiting period depends on the selection a person made.

The shorter the wait period, the more money a person pays for the contract. The longer the wait period, the less money is paid. No disability money needs to be paid until the elimination period ends. This is the "wait period." A person must wait until the benefit "kicks in." No money comes for this particular insurance benefit until the wait period has elapsed. This is pretty straightforward -- a person chooses it, the carrier fulfills their obligations.

The concept of **recurrent disability** becomes important in relation to the "wait period." Particularly when you as a "helper" are providing services to someone receiving Disability Insurance Income benefits. An example will illustrate the importance of this concept.

Assume you are a rehabilitation consultant. You are attempting to help a client who is receiving Workers' Compensation vocational benefits and Disability Insurance Income benefits. You have heard the terms "elimination period" and "recurrent disability." However, you never studied their definitions. You identify an OJT for machine operator for your client. It is a light job and medically appears appropriate. At least it appears appropriate enough to try it.

You want the employer offering the OJT to be properly motivated. You do not want the employer to view the OJT as "free labor and terminate the worker when it ends." There may be a labor code that requires an employer to pay a wage for work performed. In any event, you structure the OJT so that the employer pays a wage and the client becomes an employee. The employer/employee relationship exists.

What you have done in this OJT, albeit with good intentions, is to cause the Disability Insurance Income benefit to be eliminated, by most contracts. The person is no longer disabled, as defined by most disability income contracts. He is earning wages. Even though it is wages during a training period, they are nevertheless wages. What happens if after a month or **even after as short a time as a week**, the person cannot do the job? Wages have been paid.

You may have told your client "Look, it's okay, you can give it a try, and if it doesn't work, it's alright." You may continue to work with the person through Workers' Compensation. But what about the Disability Insurance Income? What if this amounts to a substantial amount? Did you tell the client prior to trying the OJT that once they earn wages and are "off disability" that a new elimination period starts? They may have to wait 90 days for their next payment. Would they have confidence in your genuine desire to help with such a scenario:

1. Work for wages one week.
2. Lose disability insurance income benefits 13 weeks.

The answer is self-evident. If you were the client, you would feel duped.

If you as the consultant had studied the policy you could have approached the OJT differently. You may have secured a signed statement from the claims person indicating that this one-week or one-month or two-month rehabilitation plan using an OJT would not be interpreted as a real work experience.

This above scenario happens too often. It causes attorneys, physicians, judges, and clients to view rehabilitation consultants as people with "good intentions but no common sense." Inquire during your initial interviews if a person has other sources of income, such as a private disability insurance policy. If they do, try to secure a copy. Explain why you need to review it. If they have an attorney, call him and explain your concerns.

**Residual Disability Defined - Money When Not Working**

Another concept that deserves understanding is the term "residual disability." As an analogy, think of the concept of residual **income.** Most people do not get money for **not** working. There are some businesses such as multilevel marketing businesses where if you built the business to a certain level, you would have income continuing even if you never showed up and worked in the business. I do not mean dividends necessarily, but other kinds of income that were merited because of the effort you put forth previously. For most people, this does not occur.

Purchasing disability insurance is an attempt to generate "residual income" if an individual is unable to work because of an injury or accident or disease. Residual disability attempts to deal with that money source.

The term residual disability is defined differently by various insurance companies and by different contracts. It implies a degree of disability less than 100%. Usually it is a percentage of the amount of money that you lose. A concept similar to wage loss as used in Workers' Compensation. An example will illustrate this important term.

Let us assume that you, a rehabilitation consultant, were disabled and went back to work. You could not be a rehabilitation consultant, however. You were a claims technician in the rehabilitation department of an insurance company, where you were able to use your professional knowledge but in a claims function.

You were monitoring and supervising cases. You did not talk with clients. Assume your disability caused you vocal problems. You could not speak. Speech is an important ability for most types of counseling.

The term residual disability requires the carrier to look at the income you are generating in your new occupation. They pay you a percentage of the difference between your current wage and that previously earned as a rehabilitation consultant. Understanding how this is calculated and what it equals may be the factor for motivation.

You would want to know what gross wages (before payroll taxes are subtracted) you need to earn so that this amount **after** taxes is subtracted **plus** the residual disability income that is received is at least equal to or greater than the amount of full disability income received. In short, why return to a job that in the "bottom line" analysis causes you to receive less money when all sources are taken into consideration? A thorough study of the contract is needed.

**Partial Disability Defined:**

Associated with the term of residual disability is the term "partial disability." Partial disability is different because it is a fixed payment. Assume you are able to work half-time as a rehabilitation consultant. You cannot perform all of your duties all of the time. Partial disability would pay you a fixed amount, let us say $1,000 a month, as spelled out in the contract since you are only working half-time. You would generate your wages for half-time plus you get the $1,000. In most instances, this gives a person an incentive to return to work because they correctly conclude that for at least a period of time, they will receive some money from Disability Insurance Income plus earn wages. Usually that "period of time" is pretty short, like six months.

Partial disability is one of the more recent and creative ideas that Disability Insurance Income policy writers have developed. They are trying to create contracts that give people a proper balance: giving enough money to help them maintain their standard of living but not so much to create a disincentive to recover and return to work.

**What to Expect from Claims Persons**

The provision of vocational rehabilitation is new to Disability Insurance Income policies. If you plan to do rehabilitation work with Disability Insurance Income claimants, be prepared to work with a relatively unsophisticated claims person when it comes to rehabilitation. They are not Workers' Compensation claims professionals who in many states have worked with rehabilitation professionals. Rarely will you interact with someone who has that sophistication.

What does this mean to your responsibilities if you want to develop this as a business? It means you need good communication skills. You must use words that create a mutual understanding. You will wear the hat of an educator. They are not going to understand what you mean when you say "OJT." You must explain what you mean by such terms as OJT, labor market research, transferable skills analysis, vocational testing, vocational evaluation, or work hardening. Without your help, they will not understand what you **really** mean when you use these words.

They will want to know how much it is going to cost. They will want specific estimates. Frequently they will give you dollar limits such as "I'll authorize $300. When you reach that, don't do any more until you call and tell me what the status is."

The claims person gives dollar limits because they are treading in unknown waters. They are attempting to responsibly control the case costs for an unfamiliar service. They are **not** trying to undermine your professionalism. They are **not** trying to provide low quality services. If you think a higher dollar limit is necessary, they expect you to say so **and** to give a logical rationale. An example will help illustrate this issue.

If you charge $60 per hour, then $300 represents five hours of service. This is not much time to spend initially. The "thick" medicals must not only be read but studied. You meet with a person one or two times. You may only be half done with your initial evaluation when the $300 is spent.

Now you must contact the claims person and discuss briefly your findings. He may wonder why you have not completed a labor market analysis. After all, you did spend $300. You will need to explain and "sell." You will need to teach that labor market research takes time.

What if the claims person says, "Okay, how about another two hours?" Then you must tactfully teach and say, "Well, let's discuss this. In an hour, I am able to call and speak with 14 to 16 employers. For each employer who has what sounds like an appropriate job opening, another 6 to 10 minutes is necessary to confirm the job as feasible or not. Usually I need to contact 60 to 75 employers to identify one feasible current job opening. If you can specify how many job openings you need in order to satisfy your requirements, I am able to tell you how long it will take. Minimally, I suggest four hours."

If you do not want to do this type of teaching with a positive attitude, then do not do this work. This teaching goes along with it.

If you want to do this work, it will be exciting because people are taught along the way. They develop confidence in you. You develop confidence in them. They teach you about the diversity of definitions and, right away, you will learn that not all carriers have the same definition. And, contracts and definitions of some carriers change over time. They change because of new case law decisions. The courts develop new definitions. This means that everybody you work with could literally have a different definition of terms in their policy. The exciting part is that it is new every time. There are new aspects. You learn something new. Yet you are still doing counseling, evaluation, labor market surveys, etc. You are delivering your professional services within a different structure.

**Claims Departments and Rehabilitation**

"Rehabilitation is not done a lot but it is recommended increasingly out of the Disability Insurance Income industry." I like this statement. It is taken from a book titled, **Disability Insurance Income**, written by Charles E. Soule. He has had many years of experience with the John Hancock Company in the area of Disability Insurance Income. He is not a rehabilitationist. He is a claims insurance professional.

Mr. Soule states that successful rehabilitation **must assume that almost all** claimants are candidates for rehabilitation **given the proper circumstances.** The circumstances he is referring to include the earnings level prior to disability, definitions of contract, motivation, and severity of the disability.

This powerful statement deserves repeating. From page 126 of his book, cited above: **It (rehabilitation) must assume that almost all claimants are candidates.**

If you, as a rehabilitation consultant, help claims persons solve their problems and help the disabled person, you will develop a substantial referral source.

The problem, Mr. Soule goes on to say, is that most claim departments do not know about rehabilitation professionals. If they heard of you, they do not know what you do. They probably over a luncheon with someone in the Workers' Compensation claims department heard those "horror stories." They have done no independent research on the more prevalent "success stories." You will need to show them what you can do.

**Interacting with Claims Person and Claimant: Personal Perspective**

Much of what is requested by the referral source is an evaluation and not necessarily the implementation of a Plan. If and when a Plan gets started, it comes later. This role of "evaluator" could cause conflict if not handled professionally with the client/claimant.

This section is written from a first person perspective. It is intended that this will enhance your learning and success.

I make my role and purpose clear. If I have been asked to do an evaluation, make recommendations, and not do anything else at this time, then I let the client know this.

Sometimes the person will ask, "Why are we doing this? What is the insurance company after?" I state what I think the carrier is interested in knowing. Usually, it is whether or not there are any other occupations that the person is able to do.

I go on and explain, "If you are able to do other jobs, I will tell you first, then I will tell the carrier second. I will also tell you and your carrier what it will take to accomplish your returning to work."

Here is an actual example with dialogue. **VRC** = Rehabilitation Consultant. **CLP** = Claims Professional.

I make a phone call to the claims person following my being contacted.

**VRC:** "Hi, this is Dr. Deneen, Larry Deneen, with Martin-Deneen Associates and I received your phone message regarding rehabilitation services."

(For some reason, a lot of the people I have talked with are long distance. They seem to work out of regional offices. You are frequently interacting with someone by long distance.)

**CLP:** "Well, we have this person, John Brown, and we'd like you to do some rehabilitation and find out the kind of wages he can make."

**VRC:** "Okay. Have you worked much with rehabilitation consultants?"

**CLP:** "No." Or, they say, "Yes, I have worked with a lot of people in New York but never anybody in California." Then I ask how they got my name. This enables me to follow up with a "thank you" to someone.

**VRC:** "I will need you to send all the medical records." (Usually this triggers the following reply.)

**CLP:** "Why do you need all the medical records? How about if we just send you the most recent doctor's reports?"

**VRC:** "Is that the treating doctor?"

**CLP:** "No, that is the doctor we sent him to for an exam."

**VRC:** "Then I think it would probably be helpful if I had all medical reports and all of the medical information."

I do not want to put myself into an adversary position unless it is definite that my role is such. Remember, they are not adversary people. Claims people are not "out to get that claimant." They have a fiduciary responsibility to keep his interest in mind. It is their obligation to **not** contact you with an attitude expressed by "Hey, we got this flakey policyholder and we want you to go wipe him out and find out what kind of job he can do." Does that sound as if the claims person has that insured's best interests at heart? These professionals are careful. They have been through the "wringers" the last few years in many states with bad faith suits. They are not going to talk to you that way.

**But,** you say, "What if they **do** talk to you that way?" My advice is simple: I would not work with that claims person on that file. I would not get involved. It is not worth it. There are too many professional claims people with integrity who are not going to approach it that way. You do not need this type of business. Just say that you do not work in this manner **but** you know somebody who does. Ha!

Back to the illustration.

**VRC:** "Let me tell you what I need and why. I need the medical information because I want to be sure I know what the treating doctor is saying. If all I have is the medical consultant's opinion and I start discussing that with the claimant, he is going to say, ,Well, I only saw that doctor once and it was one of those ten minute interviews. I didn't even take my clothes off or stand up on the table and jump up and down or anything. You know, he just sat there with his head down and checked off some things.'"

**VRC:** "Therefore, I would like to have information that allows me to say, ,Well, your treating doctor who's been seeing you for two years has said there ought to be some kind of work you could do as long as it was light. You are not able to do milk delivery work. You cannot handle the cartons or lift and bend. I realize this.'"

As you realize from this example, a teaching process is occurring. I may request the policy, the contract. This prompts a reaction of "Why?" Their real concern, interestingly, is that often the claims person has a difficult time securing a copy of the policy. They cannot give what they do not have.

In group policies, sometimes the injured insured does not actually get the contract. They receive a condensed employee benefit description package. They are not given the contract.

The courts in some states say the language used in the brochure is binding. Therefore, if it is a group policy ask if you can receive a copy of that brochure.

The claims professional is making a referral but they do not like paying the money. It does not say in their policy or the contract that they should pay $1,000 to a rehabilitation professional to do work. The problem is that they must pay the money **in order** to get your opinion **in order** to develop a program **in order** to get the person back to work, **in order** to get the person off disability, **in order** to reduce costs in the long run. This is a lot of "in order" connections.

They may not understand the connections. You will need to explain them. It is educational and time-consuming.

It is good to develop an ongoing relationship because it is difficult and not proper to charge your time for this educational process.

If you are going to charge for it, you ought to tell them, "Here's my cost. It's going to be $300 to $400 for the client to go through the initial rehabilitation process. Then, it's going to be an extra $100 because I have to talk to you for an hour and a half." It is recommended that you view educating the claims person as overhead.

**Social Security and Private Disability Income Policies**

Many group policies have an offset for Social Security disability income. If a person is covered by a Disability Insurance Income benefit and also eligible for Social Security disability, then that insurance disability benefit may get reduced and offset by some amount. For you as a practitioner, this has implications. You may want to develop proficiency in helping eligible people sign up and receive their Social Security disability benefits. The private carrier claims department may request this. You do not want to be an attorney and you are not practicing law by helping people complete forms and apply for benefits. You will need to study the Social Security disability program as administered in your state and secure the proper forms. Remember, you are not legally representing them in a court of law. Rather, you are coaching them on the administrative process of filing forms. If it is evident that legal advice is needed, refer them to an attorney.

## TEN TIPS TO ENHANCE YOUR EFFECTIVENESS FOR VOCATIONAL REHABILITATION WITH DISABILITY INSURANCE INCOME

1. Purchase and Read **Disability Insurance Income: The Unique Risk,** by Charles E. Soule, Dow Jones-Irwin, ISBN 0-87094-473-8, 1984. ($25.00) Chapters 1, 3, 6, 8, 14, 20, and 21 are particularly helpful. The information increases your knowledge of the factors and "hidden agendas" within a disability income contract.
2. Ask your contacts, current customers in Workers' Compensation, for the name, address, and phone number of a claims manager for the Long-Term Disability Insurance line.
3. Secure a copy of the policy whenever possible or **at least** a copy of the significant terms and definitions, such as disability, "any occupation," comparable earning capacity, recurrent disability, partial disability, residual disability, special offsets to benefits, cumulative elimination period.
4. At the time of referral, clarify with claims person the "real" goals of all parties and the criteria or rigor that must be met.
5. Learn how Social Security Disability benefits are provided and the definition of terms since many group or individual disability income policies have Social Security Disability offsets.
6. Explain your vocational evaluation and rehabilitation process to the claims person and be prepared to give specific time frames and cost estimates.
7. If claimant is represented, be sure to contact the attorney and discuss your vocational evaluation process.
8. Anticipate a lower level of vocational rehabilitation knowledge of disability insurance claims persons versus Workers' Compensation claims persons.
9. Approach **all** communications and interviews with objectivity and thoroughness regardless of the attitudes of other parties.
10. Demonstrate by words and actions your enthusiasm, candor, and commitment to excellence. Settle for only the best!!

# CHAPTER 21

## Forensic Implications: External Influences on the Consultant and The Need for Professional Objectivity

In this chapter we will clarify the very special working conditions of the vocational rehabilitation counselor who deals as a private consultant with industrially injured workers under the legally mandated provisions of the Workers' Compensation system. We have referred to this area of the rehabilitation counseling field as forensic rehabilitation because it is set against a legal background and implications of decisions made may have legal consequences. The vocational rehabilitation counselor dealing with cases in the Workers' Compensation system is a forensic counselor and works under basically different conditions than his peers in a nonlegal arena.

All the tools of the rehabilitation counselor -- work samples, vocational testing, labor market research, job-seeking skills, job development and motivational counseling -- are used and implemented. But it is the legal aspect, the differentiation of clients who qualify for the rehabilitation benefit from those who do not, and the determination of what constitutes a reasonable rehabilitation program, that gives vocational counseling in the Workers' Compensation system its forensic flavor in the use of these tools.

The word "forensic" itself can have positive or negative connotations. **Random House Dictionary of the English Language** defines it as "pertaining to, connected with, or used in courts of law or in public discussion and debate." In rehabilitation "forensic" can apply to an adversarial relationship between the injured worker and his attorneys and doctors on the one hand, and the employer/insurance representative team of legal and medical pros on the other. It can also be seen as an equitable and fair way of synthesizing the interests of the two sides of the case in a manner satisfactory to all concerned. This second perspective is the most productive way of looking at forensic rehabilitation counseling and is most often the goal of the vocational rehabilitation counselor in this setting.

**1. Advantages of the Forensic Rehab Climate**

Though the work of a rehabilitation counselor in the forensic climate may be more difficult and fraught with competing pressures, it can finally be a highly efficient and effective system for the delivery of rehabilitation benefits. Let's take a look at some of the advantages of this method of providing rehabilitation services to the injured worker.

1. In the Workers' Compensation system there is a formal appeals process involving attorneys, the state rehabilitation bureau and Workers' Compensation judges. The injured worker is protected against arbitrary decisions on the part of any people involved in the case.
2. In private rehabilitation services, there is a spirit of competition, helping helping to reduce paperwork inefficiencies and speeding up the development of a sound rehabilitation plan. Clients and customers get better, faster service.
3. In private rehabilitation service with its forensic implications, there is a need for professional consumer-and-client regulation of the quality of the vocational rehabilitation service provided. Whereas the less exacting and slower-paced bureaucracy finds more clients feasible, its eligibility lists frequently become overloaded, and deserving clients must wait longer for service. Professional regulation is needed to safeguard both the rights of clients and insurance representatives.
4. The forensic environment of private rehabilitation services creates a climate of careful scrutiny and documentation of all procedures. This promotes good business management and the maintenance of professional standards. Procedures and decisions are streamlined in this situation.
5. In private rehabilitation service, the third-party payment system alters the traditional counselor/client relationship. A new triad relationship is built up involving the payer of the bills as well as the external regulator of services, the state bureau of rehabilitation. Often more realistic vocational rehab plans evolve out of this larger team of involved pros.
6. The private rehab counselor is limited in the services he can perform to those functions legally defined by insurance contracts, state law, court rulings, or Work-

ers' Compensation rules and regulations. Other functions are beyond the scope of the benefit structure and may not be provided by the private rehab counselor. For example, all the client's medical services are provided and arranged by others involved in the medical aspects of the case. The rehabilitation counselor is free from extraneous concerns and may concentrate on his task of vocational rehabilitation. To authorize medical service for a client is outside the scope of the rehabilitation counselor's responsibilities.

7. The competitive, forensic climate of private rehab services promotes strong emphasis on returning the injured worker to a suitable job as quickly as possible. Reeducation or retraining plans are considered only after speedier and more effective rehab plans have been considered. The most feasible vocational rehabilitation plan is always to entice a former employer to bring his former worker back to the plant by means of a simple job modification. The solution, for the injured worker, is often also the most satisfactory plan. The next most feasible plan is to accurately explore and identify transferable job skills that a client already possesses to pursue direct job placement. This solution leads to greater completion rates, avoids tuition expenses and helps the client quickly regain a sense of self-worth and productivity. The last most feasible plan is to provide formal job skill training for clients lacking any transferable talents. This type of plan when properly developed and implemented gives the client new marketable skills.

**2. The Customer: Party-Crasher or Facilitator?**

Dentistry, medicine, psychology and some of the other professions have already felt the impact of a third-party payment source on their traditional professional/client relationships. Information gleaned from the workings of these new triad relationships will be of help to the practitioner in the emerging field of forensic rehabilitation.

In the first place, when a third-party payment source enters the scene, there is a revamping of established regulations. Self-regulation of professionals is no longer a visible method of regulation when an outside payment source appears. The new payers for the services are going to insist on having input into the pricing structure of the service provided by the professionals.

Ultimately, they will want to provide input into the general regulation of these professional services.

Secondly, third-party payment sources generally have access to specific and detailed information in which they can compare the competency and quality of the services of one professional with another. Like it or not, private professionals in any field, whether it be medicine or vocational rehabilitation, will have their skills critically appraised by others in the third-party payment system. Quality will be demanded by insurance representatives and client attorneys alike. This is an unheard of situation in areas where there has traditionally been direct payment by a client/customer for the professional services rendered or where clients are served by public agencies.

Lastly, when a third party arrives on the scene, there is an increased demand for detailed reports and legal forensic specificity on the part of professionals in order to determine the limits of liability and who should pay for that liability. This is most clearly seen in the aspect of medical benefits for industrially injured workers. The medical benefits must relate to that injury or disease which was caused by the person's work duties. A physician who diagnoses and treats some other ailment not caused by the job situation will not be reimbursed by the Workers' Compensation insurance representative. By law, the liability is only for those medical needs that have arisen out of the work-related injury or illness. This same concept will be refined and spelled out in more detail over the next few years as it begins to affect vocational rehabilitation.

For example, if an individual was an alcoholic before he was injured and then, as a result of his injury, is no longer physically capable of performing his former occupation, does the vocational rehabilitation benefit mean that he needs to be rehabilitated in terms of his alcoholism? Issues such as these will eventually be defined by courts of law. With such definitions the limits of responsibility for the vocational rehabilitation benefit will become clearer. It is the specific forensic and legal arena of Workers' Compensation cases that creates the need for clear determination of who is responsible for the payment of which services.

As a result, the counselor in this system is faced with a series of challenges unknown where there is no third-party accountability:

1. He faces a more rigorous accountability system.

2. He faces constant review of his counseling ability and case management skills by insurance representatives, attorneys, and regulatory agencies.
3. He must face the influence and weight of nonrehabilitation specialists.
4. He must be able to deal with the demand for extensive reporting, status summaries, thoroughly detailed rehabilitation plan development and full documentation of all services performed.

**3. Forensic Rehabilitation: A Triad Relationship**

The traditionally trained Master's rehabilitation counselor is probably in for several shocks when he looks into the field of private rehabilitation for profit. This growing field upsets many of the notions he was nurtured on through his days in graduate school.

The most important of these new ideas he will have to face in the area of forensic rehabilitation is the switch from the counselor/counselee dyad to the three-way partnership of customer/counselor/client. And his own position in the middle, often serving as mediator between contending interests, will perhaps be the most unsettling.

He can learn to live and work with this triad relationship when he learns that there are rules to play by. The client, the counselor and the customer all have their roles spelled out for them. Their relationship is regulated and influenced by the determination of attorneys, the state Workers' Compensation bureau, courts, and other certification bodies.

Let's take a closer look at each of the parties in this special rehab team.

**CLIENT,** according to **Webster's New World Dictionary,** is defined as "a person or company in relationship to a lawyer, accountant, etc. engaged to **act in his behalf.**" Webster's second definition includes "A dependent person under the patronage of another." The fourth definition includes, "loosely, a customer." In the relationship we are talking about, the client is the injured worker for whom a counselor "acts on his behalf."

**COUNSELOR,** also according to Webster is first "a person who counsels; an advisor." Counseling is defined as "the act or process of giving professionally competent advice" in the **Living Webster Encyclopedic Dictionary,** 1973. This clearly defines our vocational rehabilitation counselor in this triad relationship.

**CUSTOMER** is defined by **Webster's New World Dictionary** as "a person who buys, especially one who buys regularly." Thus, in our triad relationship, it is the insurance representative who most often pays the rehabilitation bill. He is the customer, the provider of the vocational rehabilitation benefits mandated by the state.

The needs, specific concerns, interests and biases of these three parties form the basic rehabilitation triangle in the forensic arena of the Workers' Compensation system. Fusing the vital interests of client and customer into a smoothly functioning and eventually successful rehabilitation is the hallmark of a skilled forensic rehabilitation counselor.

**4. Counselor Biases**

The traditionally trained counselor is taught to relate warmly and easily with his client, to understand the client's perception of his disability. This, in the traditional training scheme, is the way to motivate the client positively in accepting and dealing with his disability. These qualities are most often identified with compassion and sympathy. However, in a delivery system characterized by third-party payments, litigation and clients with "back disability," these very qualities can cause a counselor difficulty.

The counselor's empathy and concern for his client, his compassion and sympathy all heighten the counselor's identification with his client. They do not produce, however, the objectivity and detachment needed in the forensic arena of the Workers' Compensation system. The counselor in this system must also find ways of satisfying the needs of his customer, the insurance representative. The forensic vocational rehabilitation counselor must overcome, to some extent, his client biases. He is forced to assume the role of the professional expert whose objectivity is needed by both client and customer.

For example, the vocational expert is often asked in an appeal process to testify as to whether or not there is work a disabled person could do, and if such work exists in significant supply. This objective information is used by a judge to determine his ruling. The counselor's expert opinion might be the basis for not awarding benefits to a client. To be able to offer an opinion contrary to his client's imagined interests requires a high degree of objectivity on the part of the humanely trained counselor who has been taught the importance of client empathy.

Within the Workers' Compensation system a counselor must frequently confront a client with his lack of motivation and form an opinion of the client's feasibility for rehab which may run counter to the client's verbalized wishes. The forensic rehab counselor must also be prepared to recommend a vocational plan contrary to the client's expressed vocational goals. The client's expressed interests are but one factor to be considered in recommending a vocational plan. Labor market information, degree of residual disability, length of the plan, estimated wages at completion, tested interests, work adjustment and temperamental factors must all be evaluated and incorporated into a sound and objective rehabilitation plan. The net result may be significantly different than either the client or the customer was expecting. The forensic counselor needs to be tough enough to handle these situations in the litigious atmosphere in which he works.

As a professional, the counselor needs to be objective. And, in this field, he must be able to empathize with all significant parties in the rehab process while still forming his own objective judgment of the real needs of these parties.

**5. A Forensic Counselor's Needs**

More than any other type of counselor, the rehab counselor in the forensic arena needs specificity. Starting with the referral source, the counselor must know exactly what his customer is expecting to accomplish in the rehabilitation process. There must be well-defined behavioral objectives so that a client can effectively monitor the progress of his planning.

The counselor also needs all the specific medical and legal data he can get on this case. He needs an accurate and detailed vocational and educational history of the client, together with updated information based on some objective testing.

For every increase in the specificity of the information at the counselor's disposal, there will be a corresponding increase in his effectiveness as a forensic rehab counselor. His customers will feel more satisfied with the job he has done. The client will gain greater understanding and acceptance and the counselor, himself, is more likely to produce the successful rehabilitation he is aiming for.

The counselor also needs to fully understand the uniqueness of each client's case as that case interacts in the forensic environment molded by courts, attorneys, insurance representatives, physicians. The greater his understanding of the legal status of his client's case and options, the more effectively he can foster that client's feasible vocational interests.

**6. A Forensic Counselor's Responsibilities**

The counselor's responsibility to both client and customer is to make sure that his reports are clear, distinct and written well enough so that review in any court would not be embarrassing. If his report cannot bear the scrutiny of strict legal review, the counselor should probably go back to his evaluation to firm up his opinions. Decisiveness and clarity are vital to the forensic rehab process.

The counselor is also responsible for keeping abreast of all the current technical skills, including labor market research, employment development, rehab plan writing, counseling techniques for client motivation and commitment as well as the latest problem-solving approaches in aiding a client to select a vocational goal. He must also be able to anticipate problems in the implementation of his plan and meet such trouble areas before they are able to sabotage a rehabilitation. Constant vigilance over his report-writing clarity is also necessary to avoid the possibility of misunderstanding between client, customer, and the state rehabilitation bureau. Feasible plans can be delayed or prevented because of such misunderstandings. Neither the client's nor the customer's interest is served in such an event.

The forensic rehab counselor is not an expert in all fields. He has the responsibility of recognizing the limits of his expertise. He must let the other professionals, the lawyers and physicians, fulfill their roles and responsibilities as defined by law and regulations. If his client is represented by an attorney, the counselor must not seek to play the role of lawyer. He could be caught practicing law without a license. Nor must the counselor offer casual medical opinion. Misunderstanding and confusion almost always ensue when a rehab counselor offers "cheap medical advice." All medical questions from a client should be directed back to the consulting physician who has the responsibility of explaining his treatment and prognosis of residual disability. A counselor only gets involved in this aspect of the case after the medical opinions have been documented and have become part of the record.

It is the basic responsibility of the professional rehab counselor to use his expertise in determining the extent to which a disabling condition is a vocational handicap. He is not called upon to determine the nature of the impairment, the severity of the disability or what kind of a rating a particular client should receive. His task is to relate the disabling condition to specific work situations and make a determination of the kinds of employment the injured worker can seek.

Despite the fact that most rehab counselors are not medically trained, it is their responsibility to be able to understand and effectively review complex medical records. The counselor is responsible to clients, customers and the profession to glean from these records the relevant vocational information affecting a particular client's vocational assets and liabilities. A vocational expert who understands the requirements of the labor market, who is acquainted with the work performed in various industries and understands worker trait factors and job demands, can translate medical information into vocational data.

However, medical data in the forensic environment is sometimes complicated even further by conflicting opinions of physicians who represent the insurance representative and physicians representing the client. The best the rehab counselor can do in such a case is to use his vocational expertise and select from the varying opinions those which offer the best vocational opportunities for the client.

**7. Forensic Rehab as a Joint Effort**

We have seen that the vocational rehabilitation counselor brings all of his counseling and vocational skills and technology with him into the private rehabilitation setting under the Workers' Compensation system. He must, however, add to his skill repertoire the ability to function in the unique forensic environment of a third-party payment format. This third-party involvement has created what we have been describing as the forensic rehabilitation climate, where differences of opinion and aim are brought out in both formal and informal procedures. It requires new talents on the part of the counselor in working in this triad relationship of customer/counselor/client.

We have, in this chapter, identified and resolved some of the critical and serious differences the counselor will encounter in working with the industrially injured client. Most of these differences stem from the legal arena in which the counselor works and the strong regulations which control the delivery of all benefits under the Workers' Compensation system.

Whether it is the benefit of temporary or permanent disability, medical treatment, or rehabilitation, the issues of liability (who is responsible and who will pay) continue to arise. Like it or not, the counselor in this field is enmeshed in this system because he is concerned with the legal ramifications of eligibility for vocational rehabilitation benefits. Of the three persons involved in crucial decisions on this benefit, the counselor's role is the most difficult. What the customer wants in the way of rehabilitation benefits and what the client wants are not often the same thing. What the counselor recommends may satisfy neither party. These differences must be worked out by means of legal representation on both sides and by means of a review by Workers' Compensation judges or rehab consultants associated with the state rehabilitation bureau. In all cases, attention must be demanded of and required by the rehabilitation counselor for the weight of his professional judgments.

Counselors with an affinity for debate and who can tolerate criticism of their opinions by others will thrive in this environment. Such counselors who may work amicably with other professionals are badly needed in this field of forensic rehabilitation. Professional counselors who cannot work jointly with other professionals such as nurses, doctors, attorneys, rehab bureau consultants, claims examiners, will find it difficult to provide the quality of service needed in this area. Counselors who cannot tolerate the pressures of confronting clients, of legal debate and of peer review should avoid forensic rehabilitation. To quote President Truman again, "If you can't stand the heat, you'd better stay out of the kitchen."

# CHAPTER 22

## Attorney Viewpoint: Vocational Rehabilitation

Interview with Mr. Donald Gangemi
President, Northern California Chapter
of the Applicant Attorney's Association
by Lawrence J. Deneen, Ph.D., C.R.C.
Martin-Deneen Associates, Inc.

**Interviewer's Comments:** Research I conducted indicates that 79 to 86 percent of industrially injured rehabilitation clients are represented by an attorney. Their legal representative is a significant person in the provision of services. Good communication between applicant attorneys and rehabilitation professionals enhances the development, implementation and completion of Plans. This interview is an opportunity for rehabilitation consultants to learn more about our clients' legal framework and how their attorneys perceive rehabilitation consultants.

Mr. Gangemi was a Navy legal officer and is a graduate of Hastings Law School 1969. He was associated for 11 years with a San Francisco labor law firm. Currently he is associated with the firm of Norback, Durard, Colton, Gangemi & Schuler, a prominent law firm in San Mateo.

Mr. Gangemi is a certified specialist in Workers' Compensation.

Lawrence Deneen, Ph.D., C.R.C., is a vocational rehabilitation counselor, President of Martin-Deneen Associates, and a Commissioner on the Commission on Rehabilitation Counselor Certification. This interview was done in 1983.

**LD:** What do rehabilitation providers do that demonstrates objectivity in providing services?

**DG:** If rehabilitation professionals and CARP members (California Association of Rehabilitation Professionals) are interested in projecting an image of objectivity then they need to immediately endorse the concept of the injured worker's free choice of vocational counselor. Without that free choice there is a cloud over the selection of the counselor and an aura, at least as far as the injured worker is concerned, of mistrust.

**LD:** How would the injured worker freely choose rehabilitation consultants? Most clients that I work with have never been involved with rehabilitation or even heard of qualified rehabilitation representatives.

**DG:** It may be difficult for an unrepresented injured worker to select his own rehab consultant. Most of us who do Workers' Compensation know the rehabilitation consultant fairly well and their reputations are well established, at least among the applicants' bar.

**LD:** What would be a mechanism for implementing this suggestion?

**DG:** I would like to see it very similar to the free choice of physicians. Possibly an initial appointment by a carrier with input from the applicant attorney, and if the applicant is unhappy, within 30 days he would have an opportunity to change counselors.

**LD:** As a step in this direction, when a person becomes appropriate for referral to rehab services and is represented, would you like the employer or carrier to get your input at that point in time?

**DG:** Absolutely. Too frequently we merely get a letter indicating who the carrier has selected as the vocational rehab consultant with no input at all from us.

**LD:** What other aspects of objectivity are important?

**DG:** Counselors should have the strength of their convictions. They should make recommendations that they feel are appropriate and then do everything they can to carry them out. Too often I get remarks such as "It would be too costly to the carrier, and that's why we can't get that approved" even though a counselor might feel it is the best plan. They would not pursue it so as not to be in disfavor with the carrier. I feel that a rehabilitation provider employed by the carrier or in-house has even more difficulty. The financial considerations probably would be insurmountable to someone in-house who is working as an employee of the carrier.

**LD:** Assuming that you had input into the selection of a rehabilitation provider, what are the qualities that you would use in your selection so as to ensure that your client receives the best services?

**DG:** It gets back directly to objectivity. I have to be convinced that the counselor is objective in his or her evaluation of the applicant and proposal of the plan.

**LD:** At a recent seminar, two attorneys dealt with the issue of what they look for in a vocational expert as a defense attorney and as an applicant attorney. It was stated that they want someone who is objective who also agrees with their side. Can you comment on that concept of objectivity?

**DG:** This is the difficult plight of a vocational rehab consultant. He is being pulled two ways, first by the carrier who has the purse strings, and the applicant attorney who wants a plan that will restore the injured worker to suitable gainful employment. A consultant who will resist those influences and truly find the best plan for the injured worker is being objective.

**LD:** What are the criteria for suitable gainful employment that you feel are important? How do you evaluate the relative importance of those criteria since usually it is difficult to develop a plan where all of the criteria are met?

**DG:** All vocational counselors should, every morning before they go to work, read the rules and regulations dealing with due consideration being given to the employee's qualifications, interests and incentives, current injury earnings and future labor market. This is the critical portion of suitable gainful employment. You must motivate an injured worker. If you ignore interests, incentives and earning capacity, you have lost your motivation. All of us experience plans that go on forever and never achieve results. I think almost always those plan failures have to do with lack of motivation. Almost every time a plan is imposed on an injured worker that he or she is uncomfortable with or that he or she is resisting, it fails.

**LD:** What suggestions do you have where an individual wants to return and earn equal wages as before and yet given the severity of his limitations, this is not likely. What approach would you suggest when there is a conflict between "abilities" and the "incentive" to get back to suitable wages?

**DG:** That conflict appears very often. The injured worker needs expert vocational counseling and input from the applicant's attorney. Workers who have little or no skills, have limited education, and had high earnings are facing a crisis. I don't think enough is done to help them through that crisis with respect to restructuring their lifestyle, and with respect to convincing the injured employee that alternatives must be explored.

**LD:** You see it as important on such cases for the counselor to contact the attorney and get input at that point in time?

**DG:** It is a problem that has to be attacked from more than just one angle. More than just by the rehabilitation consultant who may or may not have gained the trust of the injured worker. The rehabilitation consultant needs input and the assistance of the injured worker's representative and possibly input from other professionals such as psychologists.

**LD:** Frequently it is heard from different attorneys, albeit a minority, that they do not want to be involved in vocational rehabilitation. They communicate a message that makes counselors reluctant to ask them to be involved.

**DG:** I can sympathize with some claimant/applicant attorneys who are reluctant to spend a great deal of time on vocational rehabilitation. Most of us have been forced to increase our caseloads to a degree that worries us. Vocational rehabilitation generates a lot of paperwork and time. We are often not compensated for informal meetings, conferences, review of correspondence and the like. While there is a procedure for compensation for applicant attorneys, it is not always pallatable to reduce the already low temporary disability benefits by 10% to create a fund. It is very difficult for an applicant attorney to spend a lot of time on uncompensated vocational rehabilitation when there are so many other time requirements in obtaining other benefits for which the attorney is compensated. As President of the Northern Chapter I am in contact with many attorneys. I believe that they fully represent all aspects of their clients' claims. They generally want to be involved in the crisis situations that we talked about and aggressively pursue on behalf of their clients any and all rehabilitation benefits.

**LD:** Rehab consultants gather lots of information. What do you think is necessary and relevant vocational information that should be gathered and evaluated by a vocational consultant?

**DG:** The injured worker's first face-to-face contact with the rehabilitation consultant is too often in the injured worker's home. I would like to see consultants interviewing injured workers in their office. I feel that they are intruding into the privacy of the person's home where, for example, an insurance investigator could not. Too often the reports indicate many factors about a person's private life that should not be brought up or disclosed to an insurance company or to the general public. I am much more comfortable with the counselor interviewing the injured worker in his office, in a professional setting, rather than in the injured's home.

**LD:** Would you make that one of your criteria for selection if you knew of a particular counselor who always interviewed in the home versus a counselor who used an office in a professional setting?

**DG:** I don't know of any particular counselor who interviews only in a person's home. I would like to see counselors, in general, changing their method of interviewing a client and calling them into their office.

**LD:** In the vocational rehabilitation process, before rehab even starts, it is determined whether an injured worker is eligible for rehabilitation. This usually requires a job analysis and having it reviewed by a physician. What would you like to see as an ideal approach to doing job analysis?

**DG:** It is indispensable that the applicant be present when the rehabilitation specialist visits the job site and formulates the job analysis. Too often a rehabilitation specialist will go to the job site without input from the injured worker and get a job description from a foreman or a manager. Then, the applicant and his attorney must review and correct a job analysis that is not accurate. If the injured worker were present at the time of the job analysis, much time could be saved.

**LD:** Do you think having the injured worker present at the time a job analysis is actually done and the people are interviewed would enhance the objectivity?

**DG:** Absolutely.

**LD:** In the rehabilitation publications of professional associations around the country, the ideal sequence of events described is that first you try to return the injured worker to the same employer in a modified job, secondly you try to return the injured worker to the same employer in an entirely different occupation, thirdly you would try to return the injured worker to a different employer using his transferable skills, fourthly you would try on-the-job training with a different employer, and finally you would consider formal training and returning a person to work using the new skills that he learned in the formal schooling. What are your comments on this typical sequence as an ideal approach?

**DG:** Your five-step procedure sounds very good. It is hard to disagree with it. I think in almost every case it is desirable to get someone back to his previous employer. That is what we normally strive for but with very limited success. The next step often attempted is direct job placement using transferable skills and it is a proper step **if there are transferable skills.** I think this is the area of most abuse. Most rehab plans that I see provide for direct job placement without any training and rarely state that the Plan will be reviewed in 60 days and reassessed as they should be. Sometimes there is an intimidation tactic going on with a threat of cutting off benefits and the like if the injured worker is not at a phone making telephone calls to prospective employers, or visiting prospective employers on a 40-hour basis. This gets back to motivation that we talked about previously. Without transferable skills, and a reasonable method of obtaining employment, most injured workers will not find suitable employment through direct job placement.

**LD:** Are you saying that the abuse lies in the misidentification of transferable skills?

**DG:** I think it is a high area of abuse. Those rehabilitation consultants who lack objectivity yield to a carrier's desire to limit the extent of the plan, and attempt to place someone who has very little chance of being placed, just to close a file quickly.

**LD:** Imagine for a moment that you are a rehabilitation consultant, a provider of services, and you want to work more closely with attorneys. You want referrals. You want to be the one who is selected by attorneys who specialize in Workers' Compensation. How would you proceed in the delivery of your services so as to enhance that relationship?

**DG:** That is a difficult question to answer. First of all, successful previous rehab plans are a key. A rehabilitation consultant who has repeatedly completed plans is invaluable, both to the injured worker and to the carrier. I think building up that type of a reputation is essential to success as a rehabilitation consultant.

**LD:** Well, assume somebody does that. They have a good reputation and have shown success. What else would you do to enhance your relationship with attorneys?

**DG:** As an attorney I appreciate very much getting a phone call from a vocational rehabilitation consultant informing me that something is going wrong with the Plan and we had better take some action to correct the Plan. By communicating early, we continue the flow of benefits and services and increase the chances of success. When I don't get those telephone conversations and the Plan "blows up," we need informal and formal conferences and a great deal of litigation. I appreciate the opportunity to anticipate problems and a chance to correct them before they become major problems.

**LD:** If you are still a rehab consultant and you want to enhance your business with insurance carriers, what would you do?

**DG:** Again, I am success-oriented and believe that the overworked claims adjuster or insurance person also does not want to see a lot of problems with vocational rehab plans. If there is something that the claims person can do such as provide necessary tools, get the transportation check sent or the like, I think they would rather hear about it from the vocational rehabilitation consultant than get a petition or get a formal letter from me demanding it.

**LD:** What do you see as some current issues that need to be faced by rehabilitation consultants, the medical community, the Rehabilitation Bureau, attorneys, claims people, and most importantly, injured workers?

**DG:** First of all, I think vocational rehabilitation is one of the most valuable benefits that an injured worker can receive. We now have an orderly system to return an injured worker back to the work force. A major problem is a determination that a worker is not feasible for rehabilitation services. The result is that the injured worker is not entitled to further training, permanent disability is inadequate to sustain him or her, the Social Security disability system has been sharply curtailed, and a large number of honest injured workers are forced onto county assistance. We must resolve the problem of nonfeasible injured workers who are not totally disabled.

**LD:** Based on your variety of cases and your position as President of the Northern California Chapter of Applicant Attorney's Association, do you think in the bottom line that rehabilitation as it is being delivered to injured workers is working more than it is not?

**DG:** Absolutely. Many injured workers are getting valuable benefits and getting back to work as a result of the vocational rehabilitation system. The abuses that I see are the atypical rather than the typical processing of a rehabilitation plan.

**LD:** That is a very good endorsement. Thank you.

## CHAPTER 23

## Self-Employment -- A Rehabilitation Alternative

by Lawrence I. Kramer, Jr.

### Introduction By Dr.'s Deneen and Hessellund

### Rehabilitation Plans for Entrepreneurs - The Doers of the World

A recent reading of the book titled **The State Of Small Business: A Report Of The President**, May, 1985 revealed some interesting statistics. In 1970 there were approximately six million self-employed people. Today, there are over 12 million and this excludes those involved in agriculture.

Over 700,000 new corporations are started annually and an estimated 2.4 million sole proprietorships and partnerships are begun each year. This country is currently experiencing an entrepreneurial boom.

The role of small business in the country is significant. For example, only one percent of job growth occurs in Fortune 500 companies. Yet 66 percent of new jobs are created in firms of 1 to 20 employees. Using the definition of the Small Business Administration, **68 percent of job growth occurs by small business.**

Small firms with fewer than 100 employees generated 52.6 percent of net employment growth from 1976 to 1982. It is noteworthy that in firms with 1 to 19 employees, representing 20.5 percent of the jobs, a total of 38.5 percent of new jobs were generated between 1976 and 1982. Across all industries with the exception of retail trade, firms with less than 20 employees have experienced the highest employment growth rates from 1976 through 1982.

For firms with less than 20 employees, during 1976 to 1982 the services industry experienced an employment growth rate of 52.6 percent; finance, insurance and real estate 46.6 percent; wholesale trade 28.9 percent; transportation, communications and utilities 33.9 percent; manufacturing 42.7 percent; construction 24.8 percent; mining 72.1 percent; and agriculture, forestry and fishing 21.8 percent.

**The point** of these statistics **is to reinforce** that there is tremendous **economic activity** and **job generation capability in small businesses.** Yet, Rehabilitation Plans with a vocational objective of "self-employment" are frequently the last to be considered for a disabled individual to pursue. The reasons are well known. There is a high failure rate of new businesses during the first five years of experience. Most disabled individuals have no prior business experience that transfers to a new industry area. Most disabled individuals have limited amounts of capital to invest in a new business venture.

These reasons are quite valid and represent the primary reasons why a vocational consultant considers self-employment as a last alternative, and even then plans a role as a friendly "devil's advocate" with the individual.

**Another reason** why self-employment plans are infrequently considered for Rehabilitation Plans **is not so evident.** Most rehabilitation consultants have no background or experience in the field of business plan preparation, finance generation, capital formation, tax planning, or business organization structuring. Consequently, most vocational consultants are somewhat anxious and uneasy when an individual client expresses interest in being self-employed.

The accredited Master's degree programs in the country that prepare individuals for the profession of vocational rehabilitation counseling and the accredited programs that prepare individuals as nurse consultants do **not** include in their curriculums business courses or consulting courses which teach an individual how to start, finance, and manage his own business or another person's business.

In our experience most disabled individuals pursuing vocational rehabilitation are not equipped either by prior qualifications and experience or by the necessary capital to pursue self-employment. However, there are enough of these situations that occur **and** enough gainful vocational objectives through self-employment ventures that warrant a discussion of this special type of plan in this book.

We have personally been involved in the development of successful Rehabilitation Plans for a wide range of endeavors, including: a hog farm in Texarkana, a street sweeping business, janitorial service, bowling alley, landscaping construction business, home remodeling business, restaurant business, liquor store and deli business, manufacturer representative business, hair styling and cosmetician business, manicurist consultant business, limousine driver/chauffeur business and many others.

Most self-employment Rehabilitation Plans are challenging and fun. They require careful screening. They require special knowledge and sensitivity on the part of the vocational consultant. It is usually recommended that a business consultant more experienced in the starting and managing of business enterprises work jointly with a vocational rehabilitation consultant.

Mr. Lawrence Kramer of Kramer, Blum and Associates is a business consultant with a practice in San Francisco, California. He has had over 20 years experience in providing consulting services for individuals setting up either profit or nonprofit enterprises. He has developed a special service in which he consults vocational rehabilitation consultants in the delivery of rehabilitation benefits to disabled workers. It is intended that the addition of his excellent chapter will provide a framework and knowledge so that rehabilitation practitioners are able to more effectively consider self-employment alternatives when feasible.

**Background of Mr. Kramer**

Mr. Kramer has been providing feasibility assessments of self-employment cases first for the California State Department of Rehabilitation and then for counselors and carriers in the Workers' Compensation system since 1964.

Mr. Kramer is a principal of Kramer, Blum and Associates, Inc., a prominent California management consulting firm. His professional experience includes consulting, managing a small manufacturing firm, managing nonprofit organizations and teaching.

His community activities have included 16 years as an elected school and college board trustee and membership on many agency boards of directors.

He received his education at Antioch College, Yellow Springs, Ohio and Harvard University.

**Self-Employment Plans**

"I want to go into business for myself."

These words, when spoken by an injured worker have the power to set the teeth of a rehabilitation professional or insurance carrier's representative on edge. The conventional wisdom is that self-employment plans are too risky.

The purpose of this chapter is to show how carefully screened self-employment can be a cost-effective, satisfying rehabilitation alternative for the well-prepared injured worker. In the first part I will describe a screening process designed to help the rehabilitation professional make a preliminary judgment as to whether a self-employment case should be considered further. In the second part I will present the characteristics I am looking for and the procedures I use to judge the feasibility of a proposed self-employment case that has passed preliminary screening by the rehabilitation consultant.

**Preliminary Screening**

The rehabilitation professional's responsibility in the preliminary assessment on a self-employment case is to find out whether or not the client is serious about pursuing self-employment or is merely indulging in a fantasy about being his own boss. Fantasies about self-employment are very common. They have very little chance of being converted into a successful business **unless** the person involved has the discipline and determination to convert the initial fantasy into a workable self-employment plan to which he is committed.

A screening tool that counselors of my acquaintance have found particularly useful is "The Questionnaire to Assess Your Readiness for Self-Employment" designed by Kramer, Blum and Associates, Inc. The questionnaire is designed to provide prospective entrepreneurs with an organized framework within which to consider the realities of being self-employed. A copy of the questionnaire is included in the Appendix.
Among the issues addressed are:

- the specific business they wish to enter
- their preparation for that business
- prior experience
- their expectations
- the demand for the product/service
- the existing competition
- how they plan to price their product/service
- their marketing plan
- initial prospects for business
- a time management plan
- working capital requirements
- a budget projection for the first 12 months

Consultants using the questionnaire state that out of 20 persons who request the questionnaire, only one completes it well enough to satisfy the consultant that he should have his plan further assessed by a specialist in self-employment plans. What has happened, of course, is that the fantasies about being one's own boss and controlling one's own hours tend to evaporate in the face of the reality constraints presented in the questionnaire.

This is just as well. Self-employment, particularly at the outset, is tremendously demanding and usually requires the willingness to put in long hours and cope with waves of frustration. Anyone who cannot discipline himself to complete the questionnaire is not likely to contend with those aphorisms of self-employment - **Murphy's Law:** "everything that can go wrong, will go wrong;" and **Kramer's Corollaries:** "everything will cost more and everything will take longer than you anticipate."

**Feasibility Assessment**

The prospective entrepreneurs who pass the initial screening by the rehabilitation professional are referred to a specialist in assessing self- employment cases. This has been my role in over 2,200 cases. Out of this experience I have identified some qualities that I am looking for in candidates for self-employment. These characteristics include:

- self-discipline
- the willingness to take responsibility for the proposed enterprise
- prior experience in the field they wish to enter or in a few cases, a partner with such experience
- tenacity
- the ability to plan
- access to at least minimally sufficient capital to initiate the enterprise.

**Attitudes and Ownership**

Injured workers considering self-employment come to me with diverse attitudes. Some are grasping at straws. They made good money before being injured. Now they can no longer perform that former work. They are looking for an alternative. Often they are desperate. Others see an opportunity to get help to do something they might not have been able to do otherwise, i.e., become self-employed.

In the most promising cases the injured worker has retained the decision making power over his prospective self-employment. He is not waiting for my blessing. He may (or may not) consider the validity of my assessment, particularly if it is negative. He reserves the "go/no go" decision for himself. That's appropriate because it is critical that the prospective entrepreneur be willing to take responsibility for his venture.

**Case Example**

A graphic example is provided by two similar cases. In both instances the injured workers wanted to enter the dump truck business. When I asked one how much the used truck he wanted would cost, he said $35,000 to $40,000. When I asked where the money was coming from, he responded it would have to come from the carrier. My next question was "...and if it doesn't?" He said then there was no business.

The second man wanted a more expensive truck costing upwards of $75,000. He, too, would have liked as much help as possible from the carrier. But when I asked him what he'd do if the carrier didn't provide the capital, he said "Oh, I've worked out financing with the seller, arranged for second mortgage on my home for a down payment and I'm ready to go."

The person who is waiting for the carrier, the rehabilitation professional, the rehabilitation regulator, the self-employment consultant or anyone else to make his self-employment begin and prosper is waiting for an event that will not occur. It is infinitely better for the prospect to have the attitude that "I'm going to do this regardless of what you say" rather than "I can't do this unless you (the carrier, counselor, consultant, etc.) do this or that." Phrased that way, the locus of decision making is clear. In the first instance it is with the injured worker, in the second it is not.

I stress the "ownership" of the responsibility for the proposed self-employment. In over 20 years of assessing proposed self-employments I have never seen a successful venture where the decision making was not in the hands of the entrepreneur.

**Self-Discipline**

One hallmark of successful self-employment is the ability of the entrepreneur to replace the discipline of the employer with self-discipline. The presence or absence of self-discipline often becomes obvious in the client's approach to completing the self-employment questionnaire. For many this is their first exposure to planning. They have been employed workers. The responsibility for finding work for them to do and managing and coordinating their activities has resided with someone else. Now they are responsible for everything.

They are responsible for completing the self-employment questionnaire, too. They can use whatever help they can find, but they have to work out a road map that they can live with.

The biggest stumbling block is often the one-year budget projection. People who have never been in business for themselves don't know how much even simple things cost -- like insurance or the operation of a vehicle. They tend to understate their projected expenses and overstate their anticipated income. Or they throw up their hands and say, "How am I supposed to know how much income I'm going to have next March when it's only November?"

The persons who can cope with these real and understandable frustrations, if not at the first pass, then on the second time around after some guidance, are showing the kind of self-discipline that self-employment demands.

**Hands On Experience -- Case Example**

Another important precondition for successful self-employment is intimate **inside** knowledge of the proposed business. No business looks the same from the outside as it does from the inside.

People who love to read flirt with owning a bookstore. They think that they will be able to read and discuss books with interesting people. I saw a bright young paraplegic with just such an idea. In reviewing his budget with him I noticed that he had made no provision for help. When I remarked on that he said he was going to work by himself. When I asked how he was going to move cartons of books and shelve them from his wheelchair he was shaken. Those activities were not part of his picture of owning a bookstore. You see, he had never worked in a bookstore.

The reality of any business, not just bookstores, is likely to be quite different from its appearance to an outsider. It is essential that a person entering into a self-employment venture have more than an outsider's knowledge of it. Ideally, this will be several years of broad experience in the business and/or having grown up in a family that ran a similar business.

The least desirable situation is that the injured worker have no direct exposure in the business he has selected. The prospect for success in such a case is very slight unless there is a knowledgeable partner and a very good written partnership agreement.

Sometimes, if the project is very well planned, an on-the-job training experience can be arranged as a prerequisite to further consideration of the proposal. Very often such a "real life" test will cool the ardor of the client for self-employment. In other cases, the on-the-job training may make the difference between disaster and success.

**Capitalization**

I've saved capitalization for last because it's an extremely touchy topic within disability compensation systems, such as Workers' Compensation system. The employer or carrier is usually not required to provide capital for a proposed self-employment venture. In some cases this is done voluntarily, but ordinarily it will be the responsibility of the prospective entrepreneur to find his own capital. Some of this may come from a permanent settlement of the disability claim, the balance may come from savings, an intrafamily loan or a second mortgage on real property owned by the injured worker. The source of the capital is much less important than the willingness of the injured worker to take responsibility for finding it. Very few small self-employments that I have seen are bankable and even fewer manage to get loans through the Small Business Administration. **The person who wishes to become self-employed must know that he won't have everything that he wants when he starts. He must be prepared to begin with what he has.**

Lack of capital is more likely to be a barrier to the person who wants everything to be perfect from the outset. Such a person can't start until he has this tool or that circumstance. This is often a means of postponing the taking of responsibility or of building in an a priori excuse for failure. "They didn't give me what I needed so I can't start (or I failed)."

**This attitude is fatal to self-employment. Success requires the willingness of the entrepreneur to take responsibility for implementing the venture.**

**A Caution to Rehabilitation Professionals**

One final point touches on the role of rehabilitation professionals in self-employment cases. Counselors or consultants are appropriately sympathetic to the difficulties their clients may have in preparing a plan for self-employment. The counselor should be an understanding listener, **not a partner.** He must not permit the client to transfer the responsibility for developing the self-employment plan to him.

If the counselor permits such a transfer he is likely to find himself developing a plan that he can implement, but that the client cannot. This type of involvement does not help the client. It misleads him. It wastes the counselor's time and the carrier's money. Self-employment is often lonely and demanding. The sooner a person considering self-employment learns this truth the more likely he is to adapt positively to it or abandon it. Either is a correct decision as long as it is the client's decision.

**Conclusion**

Self-employment is a hazardous pursuit. It is not for everyone. For the person prepared for its rigors it can be vocationally satisfying and financially rewarding. It is a disservice to the well-prepared injured worker not to consider his request for self-employment.

It is also a disservice to encourage an injured worker in a self-employment venture for which he is unprepared or ill-equipped attitudinally, experientially or financially. Misguided self-employment cases usually have unfortunate (and expensive) results. The worker who cannot meet the demands of self-employment will be better off looking at alternatives involving direct placement or retraining. One side benefit of the self-employment assessment process is noteworthy. Workers who are convinced that self-employment is not right for them are more willing to consider alternatives.

Clients desirous of pursuing self-employment are often the most imaginative and interesting clients a rehabilitation professional has the opportunity to work with. In addition, despite the Small Business Administration's extremely pessimistic statistics about the high mortality rate of small businesses it is our finding that **well-prepared** and **well-screened** entrepreneurs whom we have found to be feasible candidates for self-employment achieve at least modest success in the great majority of cases.

# SECTION III

## The Business of Private Vocational Rehabilitation

# CHAPTER 24

## Rehabilitation Benefit System As Predicator Of Ethical Standards
**by Jan Lewis, M.S., CIRS**
**Introduction by Dr.'s Deneen and Hessellund**

Ms. Lewis focuses her thorough knowledge of rehabilitation in a disability compensation system to that publicized topic of "ethics in for-profit" rehabilitation businesses. Her experience as a **purchaser and monitor** of private services, her counseling experience as a **provider** of private services, her **supervisory and quality control** experience as a manager of services provided, and her academic achievements enable her to "cut through fat" and put to rest the unfounded claims.

Her chapter should be required reading by all practicing rehabilitation consultants and those still in training. All faculty of rehabilitation counselor training programs and rehabilitation nurse curriculums should read her well-developed chapter.

In our opinion she lays to rest the concern that one's employment setting is a predicator of one's ethics. A person's ethics, that is, what he or she ought to do and does do in a particular situation is more influenced by factors such as view of the nature of man, religious values, professionalism, experience, and most importantly "common sense" of right and wrong.

### The Issues

Concern over the legal and/or ethical considerations related to private-for-profit vocational rehabilitation services has been expressed for a number of years. Private rehabilitation leapt into prominence in the early 1970's and, since that time, has grown at an extremely rapid rate. Debate over the "ethics" of being for-profit within the human services profession has been heated. There is a polarization of viewpoints, which have been predominantly published in a number of professional rehabilitation journals since 1981.

The faction feeling most strongly that for-profit rehabilitation represents a violation of the ethics of rehabilitation counseling and is a "crisis" for the profession has that viewpoint expressed by Juliam M. Nadolsky (1984) and by R. R. Cottone

(1982, 1983).

In his 1984 editorial in the Journal of Rehabilitation, editor Nadolsky comments:

"Although rehabilitation programs continue to operate within our society in 1984, in so doing, many of these principles have cast aside certain basic principles that have been historically associated with the rehabilitation movement. Perhaps the most basic principle, which seems to have been forgotten by a large and increasing number of personnel involved in the rehabilitation movement (i.e. those in the private-for-profit sector) is that an ongoing need exists for the government support of rehabilitation to meet the needs of citizens who are disabled and who lack the economic resources necessary to overcome the effects of their disability."

Nadolsky continues in this editorial to relate the decrease in federal spending and budgeting for funds for rehabilitation to a reduction in provision of individual services due to organizational pressures on the part of the Public Sector. Additionally, he states that the private-for-profit personnel accept the belief that rehabilitation should be an expedient process, in which the primary goal is to return the injured worker to their previous occupation or employer as soon as possible.

Nadolsky believes the private-for-profits do not embrace the basic principles of the rehabilitation process, and are contributing to the demise of a complex process and its underlying principles. He goes on to relate this to decrease in federal programs funding.

Cottone (1983) also reflects on the issue of confidentiality and counselor allegiance when the rehabilitation counselor is asked to serve the industrially injured worker at the request of the third party. When a rehabilitation counselor is asked to serve as an expert witness, there is concern that this violates confidentiality between the counselor and the client.

The other faction, represented by Sher (1979) and spokespersons for the National Association of Rehabilitation Professionals in the Private Sector, is of the belief that vocational rehabilitation is best provided within a free market environment. Welsh (1978) suggests that, with the degree of accountability built into the private profit system, if a counselor is not ethical, objective, responsive or efficient he or she will be unable to compete with the programs which are, and will soon go out of business.

The leading published author on the intricacies of for-profit rehabilitation, Dr. Ralph Matkin notes the increase in private-profit vocational rehabilitation companies is, and will continue to be, predicated on the assumption that Department of Rehabilitation agencies have been, and will continue to be, insufficiently funded to handle the needs of many disabled workers, particularly the industrially injured worker. (Matkin 1980, 1981, 1983, Rule and Wright, 1981, Brubaker 1981). The for-profit sector is just as vocal in support of their position as is the public agency sector in their respective position.

John Banks, former Executive Director of National Rehabilitation Counselor Association, responded to Mr. Nadolsky's editorial and he noted in his published response:

"Many have expressed anger over the fact that, in the official publication of the National Rehabilitation Association, profession is used in terms of employment setting rather than training, commitment and certification. The question is asked, Why does rehabilitation define a Rehabilitation Counselor as private-for-profit or state agency? We don't hear of doctors or psychologists referred to as private-for-profit physicians or state agency psychologist... NRCA has faced the crisis on "official language" (and closed minds) presenting the law that rehabilitation can only be accomplished in one way...Our profession transcends amoebic concepts that employment setting determines that you are the enemy or the "crisis"."

And so the polarization and the fractionalization within the profession continues.

**Workers' Compensation as a Vocational Rehabilitation System**

The provision of vocational rehabilitation services to the industrially injured must be examined in light of the evolution of the scope of rehabilitation services to both the industrially injured worker and to the handicapped individual over the past two decades.

Much of the structure of the present State Department of Rehabilitation (i.e. public agency) is derived from the 1973 Rehabilitation Act, with its attending definition of disability, emphasis on serving the severely disabled and the requirement that Individually Written Rehabilitation Plans (IWRP's) be provided. The socially disadvantaged were virtually eliminated from PL93-112 and the requirement that the severely disabled be served first, significantly narrowed the availability of rehabilitation services within the public agencies to those not meeting the definitions of disability and contained in the law. This continued defining of focus was again reaffirmed (and some feel possibly even more narrowed) by the 1978 Amendments. Again, the emphasis was on the severely disabled and particularly on the development of the independent living programs for those populations.

During this same time frame (1969 to 1977), studies were being undertaken with recommendations made regarding services to the industrially injured under Workers' Compensation. The National Commission on State Workers' Compensation Laws was established by the Congress in 1970. The task of this Commission was to study the State Workers' Compensation systems and to determine if their law provided an adequate, prompt and equitable system for compensation (Ross 1979).

That Commission's report, submitted in July of 1972, outlined major objectives of Workers' Compensation systems which has since been widely accepted in most states of the Union. Rehabilitation within the framework of Workers' Compensation was viewed by a number of experts including the preeminent Dr. Arthur Larson. According to the Model Medical Care and Rehabilitation Program report accepted by the IABC (1977), the goal of vocational rehabilitation for the industrially injured worker was restoration of an occupationally disabled worker to his or her optimum physical, mental, vocational and economic usefulness (Ross 1979).

In this report, the Commission concluded:

"In general, Workmans' (sic) Compensation is not doing an effective job of assuring that workers with work-related disabilities are helped to recover lost abilities and to return to their previous jobs, or, where this is impossible, to learn substitute skills. The major source of assistance in most states is the Department of Vocational Rehabilitation. These departments are largely funded by federal monies and are often associated with educational programs or other activities of state government with little formal connection with the Workmans' Compensation Agency ... despite the activities of the state DVR and the carrier's/-employer's, it appears that many workers who could benefit from vocational rehabilitation do not receive these services. Workman's Compensation should take a more active role in assuring vocational rehabilitation."

Ross (1979) notes the National Commission recognized the historic difficulty in attempting to bring Workers' Compensation cases into the existing state/federal structure. Therefore, the Commission urged the State Workmans' Compensation agencies to create specific agencies within the purview of their authority. The purpose was to provide timely supervision of the delivery of medical care and rehabilitation necessary to restore injured workers to gainful employment, and to keep the cost and management within the Workmans' Compensation system.

Following this recommended model, the State of California, in 1974, passed Assembly Bill 760, making vocational rehabilitation a mandatory benefit for the industrially injured worker. This law was one of the first, if not the first, mandatory vocational rehabilitation Workers' Compensation laws in the United States. It created within the Division of Industrial Accidents, a Rehabilitation Bureau to oversee the administration and provision of the Rehabilitation Benefits to the industrially injured worker. The California Labor Code gave the Rehabilitation Bureau and the Administrative Director the authority to promulgate rules for the administration of the benefit. The Administrative Directors Rules and Regulations define suitable gainful employment as "employment or self-employment which is reasonably attainable and which offers an opportunity to restore the employee as soon as practicable and as near as possible to maximum self-support, due consideration being given to the employee's qualification, interests, incentives, preinjury earnings and future earning capacity in the present and future labor market."

In 1976, a survey by the National Interdepartmental Task Force in conjunction with Syracuse University concluded that the median disability of 200 Workers' Compensation claimants studied from five states was 13%. In other words, they retained 87% of their income earning capacity. (Lynch 1978.)

In 1977, this same Interdepartmental Workers' Compensation Task Force recommended that compensation for wage loss be separated from any other benefits. The Task Force reemphasized the need for rehabilitating injured workers, stressed the need for reemployment and called for more private rehabilitation efforts. (Ross 1979.)

What emerges from a comparison of the Federal Rehabilitation Act of 1973 and the subsequent 1978 Amendments, to the recommendations of the above studies, is that two distinct systems of vocational rehabilitation service delivery were being defined by federal and state entities. There was the system envisioned by the Rehabilitation Act of 1973 for the severely disabled, and a

Third-Party Delivery System specifically for the industrially injured worker that began in 1972, and was implemented in at least one state by 1974.

**Eligibility Factors Based on Definition of Disability**

Given the results of the National Interdepartmental Task Force 1976 study, the general population of industrially injured workers are not eligible for services under the eligibility requirements of state/federal programs. The mandate of the public agency is to serve the severely disabled. The majority of the industrially injured workers do not possess the required level of disability to access this benefit structure, as noted by that study.

The Amendments of the 1978 Rehabilitation Law moved the State Agencies into the requirement to serve the severely handicapped with a major focus on independent living rehabilitation. This shift reduced the eligibility of the industrially injured worker to a lower priority in the state agency. This frequently rendered the industrially injured worker ineligible under those guidelines.

It is important to note the definition of disability varies depending on the system being applied. Vargo (1978) defined disability as the mal- or non-functioning of a body part, while handicapped is defined as a limitation in the psychosocial interaction of an individual in his or her environment.

The Social Security Administration, in determining eligibility criteria defines disability per Section 223 (D) (1) as "an inability to engage in substantial gainful employment by reason of any medically determinable physical or mental impairment which can be expected to result in death or which has lasted or can be expected to last for at least a continuous period of not less than 12 months. Section 223 (3) (2A) specifically notes that inability to do one's former work is insufficient to qualify for disability. An applicant must be incapable of engaging in any kind of substantial gainful work which exists in the national economy taking into account the applicant's age, education and prior work experience." (Grossman 1979.)

Most industrially injured workers who receive vocational services have a permanent or permanent partial disability which precludes him or her from performing their usual and customary occupation or the occupation performed at the time of injury. This is most frequently an orthopedic injury with back, knee and upper extremity soft tissue or traumatic injuries comprising the majority of the limitations (Deneen and Hessellund 1981). Most of these create a permanent partial disability. This does create a "decreased ability to compete in the open labor market." However, it does not render the individual either "severely disabled" under the definitions of the Rehabilitation Act of 1973, or disabled per the definitions of the Social Security Administration.

The California Workers' Compensation Institute, in 1982 and 1983, conducted a research study to determine the Economic Consequences of Industrial Injury. Based on a sample of 1,076 workers whose 1976 injuries produced permanent disability, the study was presented in "A Report to the Industry - Vocational Rehabilitation."

In this study, a number of significant factors are noted:

The study states:

"Injury: Every third rehabilitant has a back injury, about equal to the proportion of back injured employees in the disabled work force. However, injuries to the upper extremities, which account for 20% of all disabilities, produce nearly half again as many vocational rehabilitation claims. Few of the injuries requiring rehabilitation services are catastrophic. Severe burns, amputations and spinal cord and crushing injuries are relatively uncommon in industry and, consequently, relatively uncommon in the rehabilitant population. Instead, most of the rehabilitation activities centers on workers who suffer fractures or, in fully half the cases, soft tissue injuries (sprain, strain, torn muscle, etc.).

"Severity: Expectedly, the need for rehabilitation services increases with the severity of the worker's residual permanent disability. However, the worker's decision to participate in vocational rehabilitation correlates inversely to injury severity."

The table accompanying the above provides a comparison of the percentage of permanent disability rating to the percentage of rehabilitation eligible individuals.

| Percentage of Permanent Disability | Percentage of Rehabilitation Eligible |
|---|---|
| Under 10% | 13 |
| 11 to 24 | 25 |
| 25 to 49 | 36 |
| 50 to 69 | 52 |
| 70 and over | 71 |

The definition of disability, used by Public Rehabilitation Agencies, frequently eliminates the industrially injured worker from receiving services, particularly those workers with a disability of less than 70%.

Diamond and Petkas (1979) note the private sector seems to serve a narrow range of clients. Indications are that the large majority of referrals are the industrially injured (low back strains) with substantial work histories. In general, the handicapping conditions of these referrals seem less than those served by the State Department of Vocational Rehabilitation.

**Ethical Considerations**

The differences in the nature and extent of the disabilities of the clients served and the varying eligibility requirements of the Disability Service system providing the benefits make comparisons using the same Code of Ethics and standards somewhat akin to comparing apples to oranges. There are many basic similarities. However, the intent and the expectations of the respective systems vary in goal definition, eligibility to obtain access to these systems and the means of attaining the goal.

George N. Wright (1984) noted: Rehabilitationists suffer from fragmentation as no other profession -- particularly in specialization of function (i.e. counseling, assessment, adjustment, placement administration). Specialization and rehabilitation counseling may have several dimensions: By employment setting; by type of client or handicap; or by function. Still another specialization is by role where the goal of service may be other than traditional vocational and personal adjustment. His examples cited are Employee Assistance Programs, Health Maintenance Organizations and Forensic Rehabilitation. Wright suggests "perceiving ourselves as practitioners of various areas of psychology uniquely adapted to rehabilitation service can help to overcome a narrow and short-sighted professional self-image."

I would propose that the ethical requirements of each specialization within the broad profession of vocational rehabilitation consulting be viewed in the context of the disability system in which the services are being provided. By necessity, this includes the statutory requirements of the administration of the system whether it be State/Federal, Social Security or the Workers' Compensation Law. By examining the obligations of the client or worker and the consultant within each separate system, we can build a conceptual framework for the professional expectations and the ethical demands within the individual framework of the specific Third Party Benefit System in which the injured or handicapped individual is a participant.

**Philosophical Differences**

**Client Advocacy**

The National Rehabilitation Counseling Association's Rehabilitation Counselor Code of Ethics states:

"The primary obligation of the Rehabilitation Counselor is to his client. In all his relationships with the client, he will protect the client's welfare and will diligently seek to assist the client toward his goal."

The California Association of Rehabilitation Professionals' Code of Ethics states:

"The California Association of Rehabilitation Professionals members' primary obligation is to the injured worker or other recipient of services with whom the worker is working. While trying to facilitate vocational rehabilitation, the CARP member will resist any employment arrangements by business or other interests that exploit the injured worker or other recipient of services. The CARP member, in providing vocational rehabilitation services seeks to enhance not only the welfare of the injured worker or other recipient of services with whom a counselor is working, but the welfare of all others directly affected by the CARP member's professional role."

The National Association of Rehabilitation Professionals in the Private Sector has also addressed the issue of advocacy. Their Code of Ethics notes:

"Advocacy is a term used when referring to the act of pleading the cause or coming to the aid of another. NARPPS's members respect the integrity and interest of the people and groups with whom they work. With regard to disabled persons, advocacy takes into account such issues as the legal rights of handicapped people to achieve integration into the social, cultural and economic life of the general community. The role of the NARPPS member is an advocate, to protect and promote the welfare of disabled persons to maximize control over circumstances that interfere with their obtaining vocational independence."

All three codes stress commitment to the rights of the client or the worker. What comes into play in the dispute regarding the issue of client advocacy is the limitations and the entitlements of the client within the structure of the disability system providing the support or benefit.

In discussing the advocacy issue, another factor must be

included. That being the goal differences between the public and private programs. As discussed earlier, there are distinct differences in the eligibility standards for state/federal programs and the worker compensation systems. Additionally, the goal mandates of the respective programs are also different.

Ross (1979) summarized the issue well:

"An equally perplexing problem is the philosophical difference between programs. While the State Vocational Rehabilitation Programs seek to maximize a disabled person's potential, the objective of the Workers' Compensation system (Sawyer 1978) is to restore the individual to his/her preinjury employment, or, if that is not possible, to a state of employability as near as possible to that which he/she enjoyed prior to the occupational injury or disease."

In 1976, the Wisconsin Division of Vocational Rehabilitation formulated a Workers' Compensation Task Force, the mission being to study the problems that existed in the delivery of services to the industrially injured worker and to make recommendations for improvements. Lynch (1978) discusses the findings in detail. He notes that after examining the variables, the Commission concluded that the Vocational Rehabilitation Consultant must be specially trained in the complexities of vocational rehabilitation of the industrially injured worker.

"The Specialist should possess a thorough understanding of the factors associated with the industrially injured worker and have the ability to integrate these into the facilitative Rehabilitation Plan. The Specialist should also be able to communicate in an effective manner with the insurance carriers, physicians, attorneys and other parties involved in the rehabilitation process. Such communication will enhance the services coordination and decrease the possibility of confusion."

Lynch (1978) continued to address the findings of this committee and noted:

"Because the worker is in the enviable position of already having a job, efforts should be made towards returning him to that job. If this is not feasible, job modification should be considered. If this is not possible, then the employer should be approached regarding alternative employment in a new position. **Failing in this, attention should be focused towards obtaining suitable employment with a different employer or training to restore employability."** (Emphasis added.)

"If training or alternative employment is indicated, then the goal must be realistic and attainable. It should be based upon sound physical, social, psychological and vocational information."

This hierarchy for consideration of means to attain rehabilitation of the industrially injured worker is reiterated by Matkin (1983) and Deneen and Hessellund (1983) and generally is the accepted order for consideration of alternatives with the practice of industrial rehabilitation.

A view of advocacy often left untouched by private practitioners and public agencies is economic. A "real" advocacy program should enhance a person's purchasing power. It should demonstrably affect his earnings.

Evidence of this economic advocacy by private-for-profit service providers was noted by Dr.'s Deneen and Hessellund (1981). In two separate studies in 1977 and 1980, the average wages at closure of rehabilitation were $224 and $245 per week respectively. Clients, in these two studies, returned to work at 92% and 94% of their preinjury wages. This is a real advocacy. These results were collaborated by a more expansive study of the California Workers' Compensation Institute, (see Report to the Industry - Vocational Rehabilitation in Section IV).

Based on a review of the recommendations of the various State and Federal Task Forces and the above studies, there is a clear statement that the intent of vocational rehabilitation services for the industrially injured worker is to return the worker back to employment as soon as possible within the consideration of their status of time of injury.

## Confidentiality in Privileged Communication Relating to Testimony

As a consultant within a Third-Party System, specifically Workers' Compensation, the private consultant is often expected to enter into a potentially adversarial situation. When the testimony is requested by other than the industrially injured worker, the issues of confidentiality (ethically and legally) become a concern (Cottone et. al 1983).

Possibly, the issue of expert witnessing as it relates to privileged communications and client confidentiality is one of the most critical issues for licensure at this time.

The Third Institute of Rehabilitation Issues (TIRI) in 1977 issued a four part series dealing with the legal concerns of the Rehabilitation Counselor. While the ethical codes of the various rehabilitation counseling professional organizations frequently addressed the issue of Breech of Confidentiality, only a few states have licensure laws for Rehabilitation Consultants which directly address that responsibility. The six states which presently require licensure of rehabilitation counseling include four which have privileged communication provisions included in the law. It is notable that the State of California does not require licensing of Vocational Rehabilitation Consultants either in the Private or Public Sector.

It was noted by TIRI, there are some standard exceptions to the legal and confidentiality provisions. The exception germaine to this discussion is that an individual client can waive the privilege allowing the professional to testify in his or her case.

DeKraai and Sales (1982 page 372) note privileged communication prevents the compelling of a professional to testify unless the information which is to be presented falls under a statutory or judicial exception to that privilege.

Using a specific case example for one state will help illustrate the issues of confidentiality. In the California Workers' Compensation system, there is a requirement on the part of the employer to offer the legally mandated Rehabilitation Benefit to a Qualified Injured Worker within the guidelines of the Rules and Regulations. Once the worker accepts those benefits (as participation on the part of the worker is voluntary not mandatory), in effect, the worker also accepts the requirement of the California Workers' Compensation system for the issuance of reports which will be viewed by those parties with the statutory rights to access the information. The consultant has the obligation to advise the worker of the fact that the reports will be filed to the parties, including the worker's legal representative. The vast majority of the rehabilitation participants in the California industrial sector are represented by an attorney. Hence, the issue of confidentiality for the California industrially injured worker must be dealt with by the Rules of Practice and Procedure of the Workers' Compensation Appeals as well as the California Evidence Code.

Case reporting is a requirement of any insurance system. Written reports must be submitted in a timely manner to objectively reflect an up-to-date case status. Rehabilitation Consultants have a professional responsibility to inform the worker of the limitations of their confidentiality as early in the counseling process as possible. Ralph Matkin (1983) makes an important point: By providing disclosure to a client early in the relationship, the Rehabilitation Consultant can minimize the risk of a malpractice suit on grounds of Breech of Confidentiality or an invasion of privacy. The worker is also fully aware that issues discussed which are relevant to the ultimate employability of that individual will be presented in written documentation.

In August of 1983, the Rules and Regulations of the Administrative Director of the Division of Industrial Accidents pertaining to rehabilitation were amended to reflect the right of the worker (and the worker's attorney) to participate in the selection of the Rehabilitation Consultant who will provide services to the worker. The rule modification also gave an unrepresented worker the right to have access of all reports. This represents an additional safeguard to the rights of the worker.

The complexity of serving the worker and dealing with the issue of confidentiality is compounded by the fact that the Rehabilitation Consultant is serving other disciplines and not solely the worker. This is by virtue of the fact that the worker is a participant in a third-party system for disability services as opposed to a state or federally funded program (Diamond and Petkas 1979).

Lynch (1978) quoting again the Wisconsin study, summarized an important issue:

"As all industrial injuries are covered by the tenets of the State or Federal Workers' Compensation Laws affecting the injured worker, the Specialist should be prepared to make frequent court appearances to testify on his client's employability."

Expert testimony was, therefore, envisioned by the Wisconsin study, as an expected activity in a third-party disability system. Inherent in the involvement of those benefits is the fact that testimony of the consulting parties will be requested should there be a system dispute or breakdown and to determine wage earning capacity.

Testimony is addressed by the standards and ethics of NARPPS. NARPPS relates:

"NARPPS recognizes that a Rehabilitation Practitioner has the responsibility, when requested, to provide objective testimony. Rehabilitation Practitioners provide services within a legal system and, in addition to providing primary care rehabilitation services, are called upon to testify as to facts of which they have knowledge or to render a professional opinion on rehabilitation questions or disability factors affecting an individual. The testimony of a Rehabilitation Practitioner should be limited to the specific fields of expertise of that individual as demonstrated by training, education and experience. The extent of the Practitioner's training, education and experience needed to testify is determined by the legal jurisdiction in which the Practitioner is testifying. It is also permissable for a Rehabilitation Practitioner to render an expert opinion and answer questions about a disabled or handicapped individual who has been evaluated either in person or hypothetically."

In addressing the issue of confidentiality, the Code of Ethics of the California Association of Rehabilitation Professionals states:

"The CARP member regularly addresses the issue of confidentiality. If information which could be considered confidential in nature directly affects the development of a vocational rehabilitation program, this information may need to be made a matter of record. The key in confidentiality is to make certain that the injured worker or other recipient of services is aware, from the beginning, that the counseling process is being observed by others involved in the process."

The NARPPS Code of Ethics addresses confidentiality in much the same manner. In reviewing the National Rehabilitation Counseling Association's Counselor Code of Ethics, the implications to confidentiality when services are being provided by a third-party benefit system are not addressed.

**Role Differences and Similarities**

The research of Muthard and Salamone (1969) provided an accurate description of the role and function of the DVR Counselor in the mid 1960's. However, changes in work characteristics of that group over the past decade and a half suggest that job role modifications have taken place (Matkin 1983).

According to Matkin, numerous studies throughout 1977 through 1980 provide evidence of job role change, most notably that in the 1970's. The Rehabilitation Consultant is spending less time performing counseling and guidance and more time on case recordings and service coordinations. It is possible that many changes which have occurred in the State Department of Rehabilitation since 1960 are due to the legal mandates of the 1973 Rehabilitation Act which changed Rehabilitation Counselor case load composition.

The Fall 1983 issue of the **Journal of Applied Rehabilitation**

**Counseling** was a special issue regarding rehabilitation counseling: "State of the Art with Special Populations." Included in the "Special Populations" of Blind, Deaf, Epileptic, Older and Alcoholic clients (among others) were the Industrially Injured. Just as with the other designated special populations, counseling with the industrially injured requires consideration to the intricacies of the individual and the system providing the benefit. While the 1973 Rehabilitation Act required IWRP's, within the insurance rehabilitation system, the IWRP has its counterpart in the form of a Rehabilitation Plan which is approved under the criterion established by the Industrial Accident Commission within each state. This individually written Plan is scrutinized by all parties involved to insure the provision of the benefit as required by law. There must be a justification of the proposed vocational goal in relation to expeditiously returning the client back to work. (Matkin 1983).

There is no empirical data to support notion or myth that private practitioners are less client-oriented and more concerned with the financial rewards gained from their work than Public Agency practitioners. Kaplan (1984) comments: "These perceptions have cast the Private Rehabilitation Counselor in negative light and could have a deleterious effect on the type of relationships and information exchanged that exists." Kaplan then embarked on a study to compare attitudes towards clients. Research had previously shown that Rehabilitation Consultants have different attitudes towards different client types and that these attitudes may influence service delivery. Kaplan wished to determine if attitude difference was impacted by employment setting of the counselor or the disability benefit system in which the consultant works. Kaplan noted his study was inconclusive but did point out a possible inverse relationship between exposure to a disability group and a positive attitude toward that group on the part of professionals, with students having the most positive attitude. He notes, "It is unclear whether these findings illustrate that increasing exposure to clients worsens professionals' attitudes or merely provides a more realistic basis for appraisal of client abilities, which may be mistaken for a negative mind set."

## Summary

If procedures within the for-profit sector differ from an established professional code merely because of the for-profit or private nature, are services to clients affected and are professional ethics compromised?

Most Rehabilitation Consultants retain the belief that few medical conditions render a patient totally unable to work and that, with appropriate intervention, most injured workers can be returned to some form of gainful employment (Tuck 1979). Doctors Deneen and Hessellund describe private rehabilitation consulting as requiring total accountability. They imply this does not exist in other settings.

There are inept consultants in the Public Agency sector who only count "26's" rather than help clients. There are charlatans in Public Agencies that promise utopia and never deliver. Likewise inept consultants and charlatans exist in private-for-profit agencies too. This has nothing to do with Professional Codes and Ethics. It represents a lack of integrity within the individual. Let us not, therefore, generalize on employment setting as being the predicator of the ethics of an individual or of a professional. I propose a mutual respect within the specifications of the rehabilitation sector and an acknowledgement of the differing goals of a Rehabilitation Consultant providing services under a third-party Rehabilitation Benefit delivery system as opposed to the goals of the Rehabilitation Consultant providing services within the State/Federal program.

## References

1. Banks, J.R.; Letters to the Editor. JOURNAL OF REHABILITATION, 1984, p. 68.
2. Brubaker, D.R.; Identity and Organizational Problems in Professional Rehabilitation. JOURNAL OF APPLIED REHABILITATION COUNSELING, 1981, 47(1) p. 54-58.
3. Brubaker, D.R.; Budget, Administrative Battle Begins. Professional Report of the National Rehabilitation Counseling Association, 1982, 22(4) p. 1.
4. California Workers Compensation Institute; Report to Industry-Vocational Rehabilitation, Author, 1984.
5. California Association of Rehabilitation Professionals; Standards of Professional Behavior, Code of Ethics, Author, 1976.
6. Cottone, R.R.; Ethical Issues in Private for Profit Rehabilitation. JOURNAL OF APPLIED REHABILITATION COUNSELING, 1982 Vol. 13 p. 14-17.

7. Cottone, R.R., Wilson, W.C., Pullin, J.R.; Counselor Licensure Confidentiality and Privileged Communication. Implications for Private Practice in Rehabilitation. JOURNAL OF APPLIED REHABILITATION COUNSELING, 14(2) 1983.
8. Deneen, L.J., Hessellund, T.A.; Vocational Rehabilitation of the Injured Worker. San Francisco Rehabilitation Publications 1981.
9. DeKraai, M.D., Sales, B.D.; Privileged Communications of Psychologists. Professional Psychologist, 1982, 13, 372-88.
10. Diamond, Claude R., Petkas, Emmanuel J.; A State Agencies View of Private for Profit Rehabilitation, JOURNAL OF REHABILITATION, 3, 1979 p. 30-31.
11. Grossman, Howard; A New Concept of Disability. JOURNAL OF REHABILITATION 1979, 3, p. 41-49.
12. International Association of Industrial Accidents Boards and Commissions. Model Medical Care and Rehabilitation Program, Atlanta; Author, 1977.
13. Interdepartmental Workers' Compensation Task Force. Workers' Compensation, is there a Better Way? Washington D.C.; U.S. Government Printing Office, January 1977.
14. Kaplan, Steven P.; A Comparison of Public and Private Rehabilitation Counselors and Students Attitudes Toward Four Disability Groups. JOURNAL OF REHABILITATION, vol. 50, 3, 1984 p. 37-40.
15. Lynch, R.K.; Vocational Rehabilitation of the Workers' Compensation Client. JOURNAL OF APPLIED REHABILITATION COUNSELING, 1979, 9(4) p. 164- 167.
16. Lynch, Ross K. and Herbert, James T.; Employment Transfer Rehabilitation Counselors. JOURNAL OF APPLIED REHABILITATION COUNSELING, 1984, 3, p.43-46.
17. Matkin, R.E.; Insurance Rehabilitation - Counseling the Industrially Injured Worker. JOURNAL OF APPLIED REHABILITATION COUNSELING, Fall 1983, vol. 14(3) p. 54-57.
18. Matkin, R.E.; The Roles and Functions of Rehabilitation Specialists in the private Sector. JOURNAL OF APPLIED REHABILITATION COUNSELING, 1983, vol. 14 p. 14-27.
19. Matkin, R.E.; The Rehabilitation Counselor in Private Practice: Prospectives for Education and Preparation. JOURNAL OF REHABILITATION, 1980, p. 60-62.

20. Muthard, J.E., and Salomone, P.R.; Roles and Functions of the Rehabilitation Counselor. Rehabilitation Counseling Bulletin, 1969, 13, special issue.
21. Nadolsky, J.; The 1984 Crises in Rehabilitation. JOURNAL OF REHABILITATION, 50, 1983 (1).
22. National Commission on State Workmen's Compensation Law. The Report of the National Commission on State Workmen's Compensation Law. Washington, D.C., U.S. Government Printing Office, 1972.
23. National Rehabilitation Counseling Association Code of Ethics, Washington D.C.
24. National Association of rehabilitation Providers in the Private Sector, Standards and Ethics, Accepted 1981.
25. Ross, E.M.; Legislative Trends in Workmen's Compensation. JOURNAL OF REHABILITATION, vol. 45(3), 1979, p. 20-23.
26. Rule, W.R., and Wright, K.C.; Rehabilitations Unheralded Partner: Economics. JOURNAL OF APPLIED REHABILITATION COUNSELING, 1981, 12, p. 208-211.
27. Rules and Regulations of the Administrative Director, Article 12, State of California, Sacramento, 1983.
28. Cher, Paul L.; NARPPS, Key of the Survival of Rehabilitation in the 1980's. JOURNAL OF REHABILITATION, 1979, 3, p. 50-51, 74.
29. Third Institute of Rehabilitation Issues. Legal Concerns of the Rehabilitation Counsel, Part 1, 2, 3, and 4. JOURNAL OF APPLIED REHABILITATION COUNSELING, 1977, vol. 8, p. 5-14; 66-83; 130-149; 194-307.
30. Tuck, Marilyn; Psychological and Sociological Aspects of Industrial Injury. JOURNAL OF REHABILITATION, vol. 49, 3, 1983, p. 22-25.
31. U.S. Department of labor, Employment Standards Administration. Guidelines Rehabilitation Services for Private Rehabilitation Agencies, Washington, D.C., 1980.
32. Varjo, J.W.; Some Psychological Affects of Physical Disability. The American Journal of Occupational Therapy, 1978, 32(1), p. 31-34.
33. Wright, George N.; Professional Prospective and Planning. JOURNAL OF APPLIED REHABILITATION COUNSELING, vol. 15(3) 1984, p. 5-8.

# CHAPTER 25

## Private Versus Public Rehabilitation

Let us take a look at what distinguishes the private vocational rehabilitation counselor from his more familiar fellow workers in the public field of vocational rehabilitation.

The private rehabilitation counselor works for himself or with a group of his peers in a profit-making venture. Unlike his fellow counselors working for public or private nonprofit agencies, the rehab counselor in the Workers' Compensation system has customers whose needs he must directly serve if he is to continue in the **business** of rehabilitation. His customer's (generally the representatives of Workers' Compensation Insurance) needs are, at bottom, fiscal. The customer is looking for the cost-effective way of moving injured workers off his books. Whereas the public rehabilitation counselor seeks to find the most satisfying and "self-actualizing" type of work situation for his client, the customer of the private rehab counselor generally looks for the quickest and least expensive way of getting an injured worker back into the job market.

The conscientious private rehabilitation counselor finds himself in the middle. Experience has taught him that good rehabilitation often takes time and costs money. Experience has also taught him that there is not necessarily a correlation between expensive, long-term vocational exploration and training periods and **successful** rehabilitation. If he has been around long enough, he has seen cases where a small modification in an injured worker's former job has effectively, quickly and inexpensively rehabilitated a worker. He has also seen exhaustive vocational evaluations and two-year training programs fail with certain clients. There is no universal scale he can reckon with to determine how much and what kind of rehab is going to work for which clients. He recommends (and defends when necessary) the rehab plan most likely to get a worker quickly and satisfactorily back to work at a skill and salary level as nearly matching his former position as possible.

But in doing his job, the private vocational rehabilitation

counselor will discover that he has a lot more people to keep happy than does his fellow counselor in the public sector. The public rehabilitation counselor is primarily accountable to his client and indirectly to his supervisors and the general philosophy of the agency for which he works. The private rehabilitation counselor is accountable to his customer, the insurance representative, the various medical personnel who may be pushing for different vocational goals and lawyers on both sides of the case who are out to make the "best deal" for their clients. There is also the state rehabilitation bureau, anxious to guard the interests of the injured worker. The private rehabilitation counselor is caught in a vise of competing interests.

His only answer is to decide in each individual case what he considers to be necessary and effective rehabilitation and to objectively document this opinion as fully as possible. If he has all the facts, and has them straight, he may be able to "sell" his plan to the host of "experts" involved, not the least of whom is the injured worker himself. It's a tough job.

Let's take a look at some of the specific factors that make the job of private vocational counselor so unique and challenging, the factors that transform the helper into a businessperson and the businessperson into a helper.

**1. Total Accountability**

All actions and decisions of the private vocational rehabilitation counselor are open to challenge by the many parties concerned with a case in the Workers' Compensation system. While some of these parties are professionals and skilled in their own fields of expertise, they are not trained in vocational rehabilitation counseling. They are dependent on the professional judgments supplied to them in the form of reports from the private rehabilitation counselor. They will approve or disapprove rehabilitation plans, accept or reject feasibility determinations largely on the basis of information supplied to them in the ongoing reports of the professional counselor as he works with an injured worker toward reentry into the labor market.

To achieve truly effective rehabilitation in this area, therefore, the vocational counselor must be able to produce accurate, complete and easily accessible information on the continuing process of his rehabilitation work. The information contained in his reports must be well-substantiated and detailed enough to convince the most cost-conscious claims representatives, the most skeptical of attorneys, the most cautious of physicians, and even the sometimes unrealistic injured worker, himself. These reports need to survive the scrutiny of the state Workers' Compensation rehabilitation regulators. They will also be reviewed by compensation judges in deciding on the settlement of the claim. In selected appealed cases the reports may be reviewed by the State Supreme Court. On the basis of the private vocational counselor's reports, decisions and orders are issued by the state regulatory authority.

This is truly total accountability, making a convincing and complete case to a host of interested parties and simultaneously doing justice to your client.

**2. Referrals**

Unlike your counterpart in public rehabilitation establishments, you are totally dependent for your livelihood on referrals. These referrals come primarily from insurance representatives who, on behalf of employers, are responsible for providing rehabilitation benefits. Referrals also may be made directly from self-insured employers, attorneys, physicians or the rehabilitation bureau. These are some of the people whom we spoke of as being people to whom you are accountable. Now we see why accountability is an important fact of life for the private rehabilitation counselor. If his sources of referrals are not convinced of the quality of his rehabilitation work, our private rehabilitation counselor's source of referrals dries up. He soon finds himself with no more new cases, and eventually no rehabilitation business.

Those counselors and agencies that will remain successful over time are not the individuals who promise inexpensive plans to the referring agents. The successful professional will:

1. Provide timely services.
2. Develop plans that are reasonable and successful.
3. Conduct thorough, visible evaluations.
4. Maintain clear verbal and written communications with the referring agent and all concerned parties.
5. Provide services in a manner consistent with the procedures for a particular jurisdiction, whether it is state Workers' Compensation, Longshoreman, Social Security, Federal Workers' Compensation, etc.

**3. Extra Responsibilities**

The private rehabilitation counselor devotes a large part of his time and effort to many noncounseling activities.

It is part of his regular responsibility to attend hearings with the state rehabilitation bureau whenever there are disputes in a case. Here the counselor must be assertive in stating his position and the reasons for the actions taken in any particular case. Present at such hearings are rehabilitation bureau consultants, insurance representatives, insurance attorneys, the injured worker and his attorney.

In addition to his vocational counseling, rehabilitation plan development and ongoing monitoring of the client's progress, many private counselors must do their own vocational testing, labor market research, job analysis and job development. Every plan recommendation must be thoroughly researched and documented. Because of the thoroughness required, it is our opinion that the average counselor functioning in the private sector can effectively handle a caseload limited to twenty to thirty active cases.

Since the private rehabilitation counselor's livelihood is dependent upon his reputation "on the street," this reputation must be carefully guarded. Total professionalism is required at every step of the way. He must be in full and open communication with all referring sources. When a problem arises in a case, he must be prepared to deal with it immediately and convincingly. Negative feedback on any particular case has a way of filtering back through the industry. Reports of two or three cases which were not adequately managed will be noticed while the twenty or thirty successful rehabilitations may be quickly forgotten.

**4. Reasonable Vocational Plans**

Reasonableness is one of the key concepts in the private rehabilitation field. One must have reasonable expectations of the success of a rehabilitation plan. Vocational goals must be reasonable. The vocational rehabilitation benefit is set up in such a way that the reasonable plan, which can be agreed on by all concerned parties, is the plan that most often moves the injured worker back to suitable gainful employment at the earliest possible moment. This often means that the private rehabilitation counselor must weigh a quick return to work over maximizing his client's potential. His goal is to return the client to a suitable job quickly and with the long-run potential of matching his preinjury earnings. Thus reasonable rehabilitation plans in the private sector often involve a higher concentration of on-the-job training and placement planning than generally found in the public sector. The rehabilitation firm, therefore, establishes a delivery system which more readily produces on-the-job training and job placement plans. Research by one of the authors indicates that of closed 1977 cases the completion rate of direct placement and on-the-job training plans was 75% versus a 43% rate for formal training programs. A repeat study with a different sample in 1980 demonstrated a completion rate of 81% for direct placement, 77% for OJT, and 64% for formal training.

**5. Staff Turnover**

The operator of a private vocational rehabilitation service must accept the fact that he is going to experience staff mobility. Even though he may be well-paid, once a counselor learns this specialty field of counseling and gains confidence in his ability, the temptation becomes strong to strike out on his own if the temperament and capital exist for a private venture. Today's staff counselor becomes tomorrow's competitor.

A major factor accounting for this mobility is the newness and growth of private vocational rehabilitation counseling services. The authors, since January 1975, have hired and supervised over sixty-five professional staff members, twenty-three of whom eventually decided to start their own private rehabilitation services.

**6. A Litigious Environment**

The private vocational rehabilitation counselor finds himself at the center of many contending parties. That is the way vocational rehabilitation in the Workers' Compensation system is set up. It is believed that out of the contention of the various involved parties will come a fair and equitable rehabilitation plan. The private rehabilitation counselor must ready himself for this environment, do all his homework and be prepared to defend his professional opinion.

He must also play by the rules. If he recommends a client to a certain type of work from which he is medically precluded, and the worker is reinjured, the counselor may be liable for malpractice. Suitable gainful employment must be consistent with medically defined limitations. A counselor does not have to be a lawyer to work in private rehabilitation. However, he must do his job thoroughly, objectively and conscientiously. There is no room for careless or incomplete work in the private vocational rehabilitation field.

## A Case in the Life of a Private Rehab Counselor

Let's see just what the private rehabilitation counselor in the Workers' Compensation system does and does not do that matches the work of his counterpart in the public sector. So far we have looked at the theoretical issues of marketing, overall accountability, and the litigious climate of the private rehabilitation counselor. Now let's take a closer look at how these issues affect our private counselor's day-to-day activities, what particular skills he must use and how he copes with all the competing pressures involved in rehabilitating an injured worker.

We'll follow our counselor through an imaginary, typical case, from the worker's initial injury all the way through the labyrinth of the Workers' Compensation system and back to work.

It's a fine spring day and Mr. V, a structural iron worker, is about five or six floors up, working on the shell of a building downtown. He is tying some pieces of iron together when the bolted cement floor on which he is standing is somehow loosened and goes crashing down, with Mr. V aboard. When they get to Mr. V down there on the ground, they find both legs shattered, and quite likely Mr. V's career as a structural iron worker as well.

He is taken to the hospital and given the best medical treatment available. Six months later, after Mr. V's ankle has been fused and he is once more able to get around, it is obvious that he is not going to do structural iron work anymore. Medically, Mr. V is identified as a Qualified Injured Worker.

But, where is our rehabilitation counselor at this point? Chances are, he is working on about twenty-five or thirty other cases and doing the best he can. Word may have gotten out "on the street" that Mr. Josh Cullen, M.S., (that's what we'll call our sample private vocational rehabilitation counselor) is an effective man. To the insurance representatives, that means Josh has a knack for getting people back to work. The insurance person handling Mr. V's claim has all this information on Mr. Cullen via the grapevine (the world of private rehabilitation is still pretty small and closeknit). Maybe Josh has even dropped by this insurance representative's office once or twice just to let him know he is in the rehabilitation business. He may have left a resume.

Now the insurance representative has Mr. V on their books and the rehabilitation nurse is making suggestions about early referrals for rehabilitation being more likely to succeed. Mr. V is able to get around. He could get to see a rehabilitation counselor. The insurance representative thinks of Josh and gives him a call. Since Mr. V has an attorney, the insurance representative also calls the lawyer to insure agreement with the vocational rehabilitation referral.

Josh is informed briefly that they have a thirty-five-year-old structural iron worker who fell when a floor gave way and that he fractured his right leg and had a triple arthrodesis of the left ankle. The client is ambulatory, but can no longer work at heights and will have to change occupations. Would you please give us an evaluation?

Josh is agreeable. He only has about twenty-four active cases at the moment. He asks the carrier for medical records and whatever information they have on Mr. V's work history and educational background. He also asks whether or not the former employer is looking into any modified situation for which Mr. V might be suitable.

Soon, hopefully, Josh receives the case in paper form -- insurance referral, medical records, work and personal data. A file is set up for Mr. V in Josh's office. An appointment is made to see the new client in a week or ten days.

The time comes for the initial interview and Josh gets his case in human form. Perhaps for the first time Mr. V is able to ask someone, "What's going on? Can I get back to work? When? What kind?" He's not making phone calls to claims persons, never returned. He's not getting evasive answers from doctors. He's talking to Josh who is an effective counselor. Josh has a way of allowing Mr. V to feel that he is really interested in what's happening to him in this life crisis. (Here Josh is no different from any good counselor, public or private). But, Josh is also able to fill Mr. V in on exactly where vocational rehabilitation fits into the Workers' Compensation system and what to expect. He's able to spell out the nature of the vocational rehabilitation benefits Mr. V will receive and for what period. He can promise Mr. V that he will try and get through to the doctors and get some good solid medical opinions. Mr. V begins to feel that here is someone with whom he can start to make some plans.

Once Mr. V begins to feel at ease in the situation, Josh can start collecting the data he needs to form a clear vocational picture of his client, past and present, his vocational assets and liabilities, the family situation and financial pressures. Just about everything in his life will affect his eventual success or failure in vocational rehabilitation. What is Mr. V's social background, his current lifestyle? Does he have a supportive family situation which will help him through this crisis of readjustment? Aside from what the doctors say about Mr. V's injury, how does **he** perceive his medical situation? Is he facing the facts of his limitations or trying to pretend they do not exist?

Josh will want to go into Mr. V's educational and work history in detail. How did Mr. V get along in school? What subjects did he like and dislike? Which jobs did Mr. V like best, and why? What does Mr. V do in his spare time? Is he a reader, or does he go in for more active types of hobbies? Answers to these questions and others enable Josh to identify transferable skills, work attitudes, and work/educational achievements. Mr. V is probably amazed at what he has accomplished as he listens to himself discuss his work biography. This enhances his self-esteem. It builds rapport and trust with Josh.

Finally, perhaps Josh and Mr. V get around to a little daydreaming about what Mr. V would like to do with his future. Josh may hear some pretty wild ideas: "I want to be an airline pilot," or "I want to go to college for six years." Or Mr. V may tell Josh that he wants to go back to his old job as a structural iron worker and nothing else. He may want to be guaranteed the same income he enjoyed before his accident. It is at this point, after several ideas have been tossed out on the table, that Josh can help Mr. V start reality-testing. Which of these ideas are really practical in terms of Mr. V's present physical limitations, his family's need for a quick source of income, his past educational achievement, his work history and the current labor market? Some ideas are quickly weeded out. Some are left for Mr. V to mull over for a while.

Josh will plan a series of tests of Mr. V's achievement level, his special aptitudes and interests at future interviews. He will seek to match up the areas of interest and aptitude seen in the test results with Mr. V's expressed vocational interests and the current labor market. Is there a fairly high correlation? Or is Mr. V's self-assessment inconsistent with what the testing reports?

With all the data on hand, Josh will be able to make some tentative predictions of the most likely vocational goals for Mr. V to pursue. Though this is all work done by most rehabilitation counselors, Josh might find himself stressing the shorter-term rehabilitation plans over the long ones. His concern is to get Mr. V back to suitable gainful employment, an adequately paying job consistent with his skill and interest level. An opportunity for advancement consistent with his preinjury work adjustment is required. This is the kind of plan consistent with the interests of his customer, the insurance representative. Most importantly, it is the kind of plan that meets the needs of Mr. V.

During this initial phase, Josh will report to the insurance representative and Mr. V's attorney. His impressions of the client and the results of testing are tentative at this point. He follows up the initial interview with a comprehensive diagnostic report that summarizes initial impressions of the client. This report discusses services provided, medical status, expressed interests, motivators for vocational rehabilitation, transferable skills, and specific recommended steps to be pursued.

A report of testing results may be forwarded to all concerned parties after having discussed the results with Mr. V. If, because of the client's reading and academic level, paper and pencil testing is not appropriate, Josh may recommend a more performance-oriented evaluation involving hands-on testing in an actual work situation or work sample approach. It is this testing where Mr. V may be performing a variety of work tasks: assembly, electronics, mechanical, filing, typing, 10-key operating, etc. Mr. V's ability to learn through actual performance may be assessed.

Throughout the testing/evaluation phase and following it, Josh and Mr. V move into counseling. From the initial interview through work skills assessment and the testing sessions, everything is fairly straightforward. It is information gathering and information giving, with lots of critical listening. Now, however, the counselor gets into the rather specialized area of blending client information with his up-to-date occupational data. He may be asked to provide a number of highly specialized services: labor market information, detailed job analyses that clarify the physical requirements of the work, background information of the various training resources in the field under discussion, the possibilities of on-the-job training programs, job search skill training, coaching the client to call employers for interviews on his own, and scheduling interviews for appropriate job openings. All of these active procedures are discussed in reports sent to the insurance representative and other concerned parties.

Josh will let all parties know that Mr. V is "on the job," actively participating on a full-time basis, and that a plan for rehabilitation will soon be developed. Reports usually go to the insurance representative and other concerned parties every three or four weeks, summarizing case activity. This documents the provision of services by Josh and the involvement of Mr. V. After all, Mr. V is probably being paid $224 per week tax-free for his participation (the amount paid varies depending on the particular state). His vocational rehabilitation needs to proceed like a full-time job. Once a vocational objective and the necessary services to reach the objective are identified, Josh will work it up in the form of a documented rehabilitation plan. This plan clearly states the vocational objective, the amount of time expected to reach the goal and the expected earnings for the client on completion of the plan. Also spelled out are the specific vocational services that Josh expects to provide in implementing this plan, such as counseling, employer contacts, and structured job placement, together with projected costs of the rehabilitation plan.

This is where the real pressures are put on a private rehabilitation counselor that are not experienced by counselors in the public sector. Josh's carefully worked out plan for Mr. V's rehabilitation must be fully documented and justified on the basis of information from a wide variety of sources, medical reports, testing information, labor market data and local wage rate data. The strength of Mr. V's motivation and level of interest and education must be assessed and used as a basis for predicting successful completion of the plan. If direct placement is the most feasible plan because of transferable skills, then labor market information, the client's job-seeking skills and the details of the structured job placement services need documenting.

If formal training is necessary and feasible, the rationale for selecting the school, graduate job placement rates, post-training job placement services, and Mr. V's responsibilities regarding attendance and grade average need documentation. Josh must be able to stand behind this plan and defend it when necessary to the insurance representative, the medical team, the attorney, and the state rehabilitation bureau within the Workers' Compensation system.

If, on the other hand, a vocational plan is not identified in a timely fashion (say, ninety days from referral date), then Josh must be able to state why and address the feasibility issue. The following are questions which must be addressed:

**Is Mr. V** medically ready to enter a plan?
Has Mr. V been on-time and appeared for all scheduled counseling sessions?
Has Mr. V been cooperative and active in identifying vocational objectives?
**Has Josh** conducted a thorough evaluation including exploring modified work with the original employer, focusing on transferable

skills, conducting interest and aptitude testing, setting up a situational assessment, conducting labor market research, providing continual counseling centered on reviewing specific, realistic vocational objectives?

If the answer is yes to all of these questions, then Josh should staff this case with his peers (if he hasn't already) to obtain additional suggestions. He must then address the question, "Is the client likely to benefit from further services?" If yes, then state how and establish a time parameter. If not, then it is time for a meeting of all concerned parties or a nonfeasibility determination.

If Mr. V pursues formal training, Josh must be ready to provide the support needed (all good counselors provide this) and to carefully monitor Mr. V's progress reporting back to all parties concerned. Regular contacts with the school and with Josh are necessary. Josh will need to provide convincing answers to the many people involved in the Workers' Compensation rehabilitation benefit. He must have done his homework well and be prepared to defend his plan before arbitration panels if necessary.

If all goes smoothly, Mr. V will have completed his training on the date projected in the rehabilitation plan. Now, it is still up to Josh to see his client through all the preparations that go into job hunting: practice in interview techniques, resume writing, looking up sources for job market information, the process of answering ads and setting up interviews.

If Mr. V pursues direct placement toward a vocational objective or following the completion of his formal training, Josh must coach him, meet regularly with him to reinforce his job search efforts, monitor his keeping job interview appointments, observe his making a substantial number of employer contacts on his own and schedule him to call employers from the rehabilitation office.

In addition, Josh needs to call selected employers and schedule interviews for Mr. V. A job placement specialist working with ten clients should schedule one to two interviews per client each week. A client working for himself should be able to minimally call forty to sixty employers per day and schedule two to five interviews per week. This is pursuing job placement like the full-time job it is.

Once Mr. V gets that job, a job he can handle and feel contented with, satisfied with the prospects for growth and increased earning power, Josh is just about finished. However, he will keep an eye on how Mr. V is doing on the job for thirty to sixty days.

Mr. V was a clean case and proceeded through the system with relative ease. Yet the rehab consultant still had much more to do in the way of reporting and keeping all sides reasonably satisfied with the case progress than his counterpart in the public sector. These are the pressures the private rehab counselor works under, part of the challenge that makes the job so tough and so rewarding. The challenge is maintaining communication with all parties, responding to customer expectations and meeting client needs all at the same time.

# CHAPTER 26

## Accountability: An Old Ethical Problem Revisited

The problem of accountability discussed in the last chapter is certainly one of the most important concerns of the private rehab counselor. But it is more than just a concern of behavior, reacting and reporting to the various parties involved in most Workers' Compensation cases. It is also the ethical problem of doctor/patient or counselor/counselee relationships. This problem is as old as the helping professions; medicine has enshrined its ethical response in the Hippocratic oath.

There is not much discussion of ethical matters in most training programs for rehabilitation counselors. That, perhaps, is because for the counselor working in a public setting, there is little or no competition for his loyalty. He is generally accepted as **the** advocate of his client's interests. The matter is ended there. The confidentiality of patient/doctor communications is respected and transferred to the field of counselor/counselee interchange. Decisions are based solely on the best interests of the client and how well they serve his long-term vocational success.

In the field of private rehabilitation, however, a third party has entered the picture. The counselor is now faced with a "customer" who is paying the bills for his service to the client and who is paying for the benefit to the client through temporary disability. This new triad relationship of customer/counselor/-client puts the counselor in the middle. What happens to the question of the counselor's ethical responsibility to his client? If there is a conflict between the interests of a cost-conscious customer and the long-term, fully rewarding rehabilitation interests of the client, where do the counselor's loyalties lie? Are there ethical answers to these questions of accountability when a third party enters the case?

Earlier counselors in the field of private rehabilitation were forced to rely mainly on their own judgment or personal interpretations of the code of ethics set up by such allied professional organizations as the American Psychological Association, the American Personnel and Guidance Association or the National Rehabilitation Counseling Association. But these codes, helpful as they were, did not cover the unique problem areas of the private rehab counselor with third-party involvement in his case work. The customer/client dichotomy did not occur in these other counseling settings. Responsibility was still primarily to the client.

There is a new movement now, however, in the field of private rehabilitation. The Commission of Rehabilitation Counselors Certification has recently taken a special interest in clarifying these ethical issues. There is currently an Ethics Committee of this organization chaired by one of the authors, attempting to come to grips with some of the unique problems posed by third-party involvement in rehab cases. Future counselors in the field may have more specific guidelines to help them. For the present, private rehab counselors are pretty much on their own in resolving these ethical issues.

**1. Customer/Client Confusion**

Strictly speaking, a customer is a buyer of goods or services. But, by implication, the customer is also a user of those goods and services. Thus, in the fields of private psychotherapy and private counseling, the customer is both the buyer and the user of the psychotherapist's professional services. It is a two-sided relationship between buyer and seller. The rules of confidentiality and advocacy are fairly easy to follow in these cases. The therapist or counselor is accountable only to his "customer" in all ordinary situations. Complete confidentiality is expected.

A client is also defined, and commonly understood, as one who employs (uses) the services of professionals or businesspersons in any branch of business, or for whom the latter acts in his professional capacity.

Perhaps this terminology used in the field of private rehabilitation services is unfortunate, but the field seems to be stuck with it. This is of little help, however, to the private rehabilitation counselor caught, as he is so frequently, with issues dividing his loyalties between his customer, the insurance representative, and his client, the eventual "user" of his services.

Some counselors may find personal answers in considering as their "customer" the person or organization to whom they report, and their "client" as the individual to whose needs they respond. But this may be a rather naive solution to a complicated problem. Aren't the client's needs and the customer's needs often the same? Or is it perhaps the job of the counselor to discover some common ground where the interests of both parties are served?

These are the questions that will need answering as the field of private rehabilitation grows and more counselors are faced with the difficult problem: "Can I fully respond to my client's needs while reporting back to my customer what the customer needs to know, that a cost-effective rehabilitation has been accomplished?"

**2. Confidentiality and Open Communication**

The rehabilitation counselor in the public sector is not generally called upon to face an ethical problem regarding client/counselor communication. Unless there is an obvious danger to the client or another person, exchanges between counselor and client are privileged information. No one else need ever know what interchanges occurred. There can be a free exchange of feelings, attitudes and information.

In the field of private vocational rehabilitation counseling, however, confidentiality is crucial because anything that is said between the client and the counselor may eventually be heard or brought out with an attorney at a case conference, with the rehabilitation bureau or in court under oath. Both parties, counselor and counselee, should be aware of the fact that they are working in a legal system and that whatever is said may eventually be heard by a third party. It creates, for both counselor and counselee, a kind of "Anything you say may be used against you" feeling. This is not the ideal climate for effective counseling.

One ethical answer for the counselor is to make his client aware of the potential for third-party sharing of counselor/counselee communications. The client may be alerted to the fact that certain matters discussed, insofar as they are relevant to the probability of success or failure of the client's rehab plan, may eventually become part of the public record and be seen in reports the counselor submits to others involved in the case. Personal data, family information, financial status as they affect the client's rehabilitation, all become part of the official record. That is built into the Workers' Compensation system. A counselor, after informing the client of these conditions of the system, may offer to discuss, off the record, client problems which are really not directly involved in vocational decision making. This can sometimes enhance the client/counselor rapport and promote a more open counseling atmosphere.

The lack of the confidentiality of information in Workers' Compensation files and the availability of this information to insurance representatives, attorneys, and the state rehabilitation bureau, is a necessary contingency of third-party benefits. In the area of counseling, where feelings and attitudes are so difficult to capture and put down on paper, these feelings may be recorded and be open to gross misinterpretation. The counselor must strive for objectivity and accuracy in what he reports and only discuss what is vocationally relevant.

Suppose, for example, that a private rehabilitation counselor observed his client as appearing discouraged at a particular interview and described it in a report as "depressed." If this is noted in the public record, it can be magnified out of proportion. Perhaps a client's attorney seeing this in the file will conclude that his client is more in need of psychiatric treatment for depression than for starting a vocational rehabilitation program. A fleeting observation by a counselor can end up in costly psychiatric examinations and delay the implementation of rehabilitation plans. The insurance representative is unhappy, and the client loses confidence in the counselor.

In general, the private rehabilitation counselor must seek to be an ethical realist. In light of all he knows about confidentiality within the Workers' Compensation system, he must learn to steer a middle course. All factual, relevant data should be reported so that his rehabilitation decisions may be adequately supported. Personal and attitudinal statements are better left out. As long as the client appears motivated and is following his vocational plan, there is no need to introduce information that might be confusing and divert attention from the main goal of restoration to productive and satisfying work.

**3. The Ethics of Billing**

The private rehabilitation counselor is dependent on fees for his livelihood. These are fees that represent actual services he performs for his customer, usually the insurance representative. These fees must be realistic and represent adequate compensation for the amount of time the counselor spends working on a case. Ideally, this time basis should be a fair means of balancing the value of the service to the insurance representative and the output of effort on the part of a professionally trained counselor.

The conscientious counselor, in building his rehabilitation plan, realizes that every case is different. He may be able to come up with a simple job modification and return the worker to his original employer. In some cases elaborate, long-term and costly training programs are required to get a client back to work. He can only bill his customer for the amount of time he actually puts in on the case.

Clients, and sometimes customers, may equate the length and cost of a rehab plan with assurance of success for that plan. Should the rehab counselor go along with these prejudices, and perhaps unnecessarily inflate his billable hours by going through ritual testing, job analyses, etc.? The counselor is the professional in the case, and his judgment of what is required for effective rehabilitation should be the determining factor. An ethical counselor will provide and bill for the service needed. He won't provide extras to convince either the client or customer that he is giving better service.

Take, for instance, the client who is interested in becoming a dental technician. There happens to be a school for dental technicians right down the street from the counselor's office. They have a six-month training program with relatively low tuition. After the completion of selected interest, aptitude and dexterity tests, the counselor decides that this dental technician training program is right for the client. The client agrees and wants it. A plan is drawn up, authorized by the insurance representative and approved by the state bureau of rehabilitation within the Workers' Compensation system. The customer has gotten a bargain: a six-month training program with low tuition, a minimum of testing and a few counseling hours. But, ethically, the counselor may have reservations about this simple, inexpensive plan. Not enough research has gone into the study of either the client or the vocational potential in the field of dental technicians. Now, if a counselor is seriously interested in building a record of success and thus generating more business from this particular customer, and a better reputation "on the street," he wants to assure himself of the success of his plan. He should recommend labor market research on the employability of dental technicians in his particular locale. It may take another three to five hours of billing, but the counselor will have more confidence in his plan and be more certain that he has done his best for both client and customer. The ethical and practical areas meet here. The plan that insures success for the client the first time around is certainly more cost-effective than a gunshot approach that may involve several plans and a lot of billable hours for the counselor.

Other ethical questions in the area of billing involve outright fraud. Here a counselor may pad his bill to the insurance representative with hours and service never performed. But these behaviors go beyond the realm of ethics. They are matters of outright criminality. An emerging field, such as private vocational rehabilitation counseling, is particularly vulnerable to such incidents of fraud. So far there are no relative value schedules to determine how long a labor market search or a job analysis should take. It is not possible to predict with certainty how many hours of individual counseling any particular client may require. There are just too many variables for any absolute set of values to be placed on these services. In this area, a counselor's reputation is his most important asset. Meanwhile the professional organizations may begin struggling with some form of objective standardization of fee schedules and of the needed hours to accomplish specific tasks.

**4. The Ethics of Marketing Rehabilitation Services**

The marketing of vocational rehabilitation services depends on the type of rehabilitation firm you are talking about. The larger organizations may have full-time marketing people on their staffs. Partnerships and one-man operations rely on their day-to-day contacts in the field to promote new business.

Successful marketing of services depends to a large extent on what kind of a name the firm, partnership, or individual has made. "Street talk" in this industry is your strongest marketing tool. What produces new business in this field is word of the successes of the old business.

The most ethical kind of marketing you can do in this field is good, professional and competent work on a day-to-day basis -- setting up a reasonable time frame and reasonable expectations for a customer and then delivering as promised. Initially focus on transferable skills. Schedule testing to be completed by a certain date. Prepare reports in a reasonable time limit. Complete rehabilitation plans established within a definite time limit. The point is to let your customer know that he can expect a certain amount of completed work in a stated time frame. You do not promise that you will make his client into an engineer in six months. You promise that you will devote "x" number of hours to developing and implementing the best vocational plan possible for his client. And you follow through on that promise. That is ethical marketing in this field.

**5. How a Client Can Judge a Counselor**

The rehabilitation client is entitled to know more than whether or not he is getting the services of a trained professional rehabilitation counselor. He also should be able to determine, to some extent, the ethics of his counselor, and precisely where the counselor's loyalties lie. Private rehabilitation counselors, because they are generally retained by the insurance representative, are particularly vulnerable to client distrust. "How can he be interested in my rehabilitation when the insurance company is paying his bills? Isn't he just trying to get me off the disability lists as quickly and cheaply as possible?" These are natural questions for a client.

However, there are ways that a client can make some rough assessments of his counselor's ethics, his interest in quality rehabilitation over strictly dollar-saving rehabilitation and his honest and open interest in the client's total vocational situation. The conscientious counselor can coach a client in determining whether or not he is receiving the ethical and solid vocational services to which he is entitled. The client can be taught to ask and answer such questions as these:

1. Is the counselor working with me to achieve a goal that is mutually acceptable? In other words, are my interests being furthered?
2. How competent is my counselor technically? Has he explained to me just what my role is going to be? Has he made it clear what my role within the Workers' Compensation system is? Has he outlined the kind of steps I will be going through in the rehabilitation evaluation? Has he prepared me for what I am to expect during this process and how to get the most out of it?
3. After we got past the initial discussions of my vocational history and present limitations, did the counselor take a detailed work history and focus on my transferable skills? Did the counselor administer tests and make attempts to develop a series of vocational options? Were the test results explained and were specific job areas suggested to me to accept or reject? Were training programs and job development services explained to me? Was I given labor market information and ideas of the salary levels I might expect in various fields? Have specific vocational objectives been reviewed? In short, was my counselor acting like a professional and filling in my informational

gaps so that I could more effectively make a solid vocational decision?

The truly competent and ethical counselor realizes that the vocational decision is always the client's. This is not to imply that a client can select any alternative or occupation he desires out of the 12,000 or so listed in the **Dictionary of Occupational Titles.** Vocational rehabilitation is not the equivalent of the G.I. Bill. A skilled rehabilitation counselor guides clients into areas of suitable gainful employment and encourages a client's decision making throughout the process. A decision made **for** the client will not bear the weight of commitment that a client decision carries. Without this commitment, no vocational plan has much chance of success.

Once the counselor has worked with the client over a period of time, discussing at length the client's capabilities, limitations, interests, skills, and experience, he has helped that client form a more accurate vocational picture of himself. Next, the competent counselor communicates all available job market information -- salary levels, job availability, potential for growth -- to the client.

The counselor helps the client weigh the alternatives and consequences of each possible choice within the framework of the client's values. A number of feasible options are identified, all with a good probability of success. The client must now commit himself and choose. If he doesn't, then the counselor will select what appears to be the most feasible alternative and recommend it to the client, the insurance representative, and the Workers' Compensation Rehabilitation Bureau.

There may be several or hundreds of vocational alternatives that a person is capable of doing. In most Workers' Compensation jurisdictions a client will not be forced to choose a goal in which he has no interest. At the same time, if the only occupations the client is willing to pursue are not considered "reasonable" or "practical" by the regulatory authority then no services may be feasible.

# CHAPTER 27

## Rehabilitation Nurse Perspective: Accountability and Cost-Effectiveness in the Industrial Rehabilitation System

by

Cindy A. White, R.N., B.S., M.A.

### Introduction by Dr.'s Deneen and Hessellund

Ms. White delivered an excellent lecture at a 1983 seminar in Atlanta, Georgia. Due to a number of requests by seminar sponsors and participants, attorneys, counselors, and regulators she developed her talk into an inspiring paper. It is a near-verbatim reflection of her well-received talk.

Cindy A. White, R.N., B.S., M.A. is the 1982-83 President of the Georgia Association of Rehabilitation Nurses. She has taught nursing school courses in rehabilitation, orthopedics, neurology and other rehabilitation-related subjects, and she has been a Director of Nursing in a private rehabilitation center whose nursing service and in-service education programs she developed. At the time of this paper she was a Rehabilitation Nurse Consultant in the state of Georgia.

Her enthusiasm is evident from the script. Her goal of making rehabilitation a "Double Win" situation is evident.

### Presentation by Ms. White

I would like to begin by sharing these nine hints which recently appeared in a Georgia Nurses' Association Newsletter. They are entitled "The Habit Patterns of a Winner."

1. Don't condemn, criticize or complain ... The big rewards are paid for finding the solution, not the difficulty.
2. Show real, honest and hearty appreciation.
3. Think good thoughts about other people ... and yourself.
4. Give before you get.
5. Smile often ... it generates enthusiasm, friendliness and goodwill.

6. Be an effective communicator by listening. Encourage others to talk about themselves.
7. Think, act and look happy and successful ... and you will begin to think, feel and actually become happy and successful.
8. Never engage in worry conversations or participate in gossip sessions.
9. Always greet others with a positive, cheerful statement.

I felt it was appropro to the occasion, since when I received the brochure for today, the first thing which caught my eye was the title, "Everybody Can Win: Practical Techniques for Workers' Compensation Rehabilitation." And isn't that the bottom line for all of us -- we want to use our expertise in providing a particular service to our clients so that they can be successful in meeting the established goals, and thus through their winning we can win as do their families and significant others.

In order to be a winner there are techniques, guidelines, etcetera, which must be initiated and instituted. Here today, we have learned, and perhaps for some, relearned or reviewed, some of the techniques. As we carry out our responsibilities from day to day and apply the varied techniques learned, we are faced with many challenges. Some of which, due to our changing economy and legislation, threaten our very existence. Some of us, on almost a daily basis, are asked to justify our positions and the services which we provide. Thus, we hear more and more about accountability and the need for cost-effectiveness.

Nurses are not strangers to these terms. From the minute we enter the field of nursing we learn of our responsibilities and the accountability which accompanies the career which we have chosen.

We also learn very early that accountability begins with and ends with one's self. Regardless of the specialization chosen -- accountability to self doesn't change. I very strongly believe that if one doesn't have self-accountability -- one experiences difficulty in being accountable to others. Accountability is learned by the Code of Ethics studied and by the Standards of Care developed for the practice of nursing. As Rehabilitation Nurses our Standards of Practice are outlined by our licensing board and by our national organization, the Association of Rehabilitation Nurses. Both to whom we are accountable as

Registered Professional Nurses. This is a point of emphasis, which I would like to make -- we are, regardless of the specialty area in which we are employed -- Professional Registered Nurses **FIRST.** And the standards set to judge our accountability should be set by Registered Professional Nurses. Judgments made as to how well we meet the standards or if an implication is made that we have not practiced within these standards, should be made by our peers -- by other professional nurses. Development of a peer review board is a priority goal for the Georgia Chapter of the Association of Rehabilitation Nurses. The foundation has been laid through the development and publication of a **Core Curriculum for Nurses Practicing in the Field of Rehabilitation.** Building of the framework has begun in that a Task Force has been formed to work toward Certification of Rehabilitation Nurses. This Task Force has commenced to work on two major tasks which will allow for this process to become a reality -- one task is that of raising the needed finances; the other is that of updating and revising the present Standards of Care so that all facets of rehabilitation nursing are encompassed in the certification procedure.

This is a tremendous undertaking for an organization which was only conceptualized in the Spring of 1974 by a group of less than twenty registered nurses. Once this process is completed, everyone will again be a winner, in that nurses practicing in the field of rehabilitation will be certified to do so, and the criteria, which had to be met in order to be successfully certified, will signify expertise in the specialty area of rehabilitation, and the care and services provided to the injured worker will be of the highest quality. Completion of this process will also provide us with the tools needed to develop a peer review board which will also enhance our accountability.

As we work in the field of rehabilitation, in addition to self-accountability, and accountability to the State Board of Nurse Licensing, and the Association of Rehabilitation Nurses, we have accountability as well to the State Board of Workers' Compensation and to our employers. As a Rehabilitation Supplier, we must not only meet defined qualifications to become registered, but we must also adhere to the rules and regulations governing our practice as outlined in the Workers' Compensation rehabilitation laws. The quality of our work and the adherence to the rules and regulations are monitored by the State Board of Workers' Compensation.

Our accountability to the State Board of Nurse Licensing, the Association of Rehabilitation Nurses, and the State Board of Workers' Compensation, is clearly defined by written rules and regulations. The gray area, as I see it, lies within our accountability to employers, and this is the area where I see difficulties arise as I am working in the field. I hear a lot of discussion over loyalty; duty to the individual handing us a paycheck; need for job security; etcetera. Although I can understand these concerns, as a professional I cannot accept them. I believe that -- yes, we are accountable to our employers -- but our accountability comes into play, in that we accept a referral, we have a responsibility to strive to provide quality and objective rehabilitation services to the client, so that the individual is restored to the highest level of functioning -- physically, emotionally, socially, vocationally, spiritually, and financially. If we accomplish this, we have met with success and what more could any employer **ASK.** Thus, the ultimate accountability will be in the end result. By being objective, honest, and realistic with the employer regarding the client, his recovery, and his potential, one need not prostitute himself to justify his employability.

It is important also to realize and to educate the employer to understand that the only measure of success is not return to employment. Good medical management leading to medical stabilization and a decrease in monies spent on medical care is also a measure of success, and reflects a job well done. Thus, another measure of success is that of cost-control or cost-effectiveness.

Before discussing cost-effectiveness and how the nurse contributes to this, let me speak to one of the questions which I was asked to cover -- what techniques are utilized to enhance accountability? Participation in professional organizations; continuing education classes and seminars; self audits; and use of resources when needed and appropriate.

The following are questions I was asked to address on cost-effectiveness:

Why should a nurse be hired?
Why should a nurse be involved in the system?
Why should a nurse be used?
Why should her services be paid for?

Although I have only been involved in this facet of rehabilitation for eighteen months, I have found in meeting with nurses who have been in the field, even before 1975 when the mandatory rehabilitation laws came into existence in Georgia, that nurses' involvement with the injured worker has reflected a monetary advantage to the insurance companies. I also understand that this was substantiated by the pilot program conducted at Warm Springs in the early 1970's. Thus, early intervention and a team approach to rehabilitation is cost-effective. As to why a nurse should be hired and utilized in the system ... more importantly than the financial benefits, is the skills and the broad base of knowledge which she/he brings into the system. The educational process of a nurse is unique in that in addition to the physical skills, which are taught to administer on the care of the ill and injured, a nurse is also involved in course work -- psychology, sociology, preventative medicine, etcetera, which equips her to meet the needs of the **TOTAL PATIENT** and his family or significant others. As we all know, rehabilitation cannot be successful without meeting the needs of the entire family. This involves dealing with concrete issues such as teaching proper body mechanics, explaining the anatomy and physiology of the involved part, etcetera, as well as dealing with abstract concepts such as role reversals, altered body images, etcetera. Through the various affiliations and experiences with which we are faced throughout our educational programs, we are prepared to be accepting of and understanding of individuals from all walks of life. Thus, truly able to be a patient advocate.

As to why we should be reimbursed for our services ... this can best be answered by referring to the laws governing the practice of nursing in Georgia. Let me quote:

> "Practice of nursing as a registered professional nurse means the performance for compensation of any act in the observation, care, and counsel of the ill, injured, or infirm, or in the maintenance of health or prevention of illness of others, or in the administration of medications and medical treatments as prescribed by a physician practicing medicine in accordance with the provisions of Code Chapter 84-9, as now or hereafter amended, or a dentist practicing dentistry in accordance with the provisions of Code Chapter 84-7, as now or hereafter amended, or a podiatrist practicing podiatry in accordance with the provisions of Code chapter 84-6, as now or hereafter amended,

which requires substantial specialized judgment and skill based on knowledge and application of the principles of physical and psychosocial science, or the supervision and teaching of others to perform such acts."

I believe the key words are -- **specialized judgment, skills based on knowledge**, and **teaching of others.**

The teaching of others is a challenge. We have responsibility to teach the patient, the patient's family, the claim person, employer, and other team members, such as attorneys and physicians. Educationally, the biggest challenge I have faced and I believe it is true of most of the rehabilitation nurses which I am representing today, is in working with attorneys and physicians, to help them understand our involvement and the role we play in the system. Lack of this knowledge many times prevents the process of rehabilitation from working to the betterment of the client. I do not have any magical answers to convincing attorneys and physicians of our purpose and intentions, but I have found that objectivity, honesty, thoroughness of one's work and the timeliness of one's work can go a long way in gaining their cooperation and confidence.

I feel very strongly that if we practice what we have been taught and provide quality services within the boundaries of our role, rehabilitation nurses can only help enhance the rehabilitation system in the state of Georgia.

## References

1. "The Habit Patterns of a Winner," **Atlanta: Georgia Nurses' Association Newsletter,** 1982.
2. Georgia, **Law Governing the Practice of Nursing in Georgia,** 84-1001.(d). D.O.A.S. Printing Service, 1979.

# CHAPTER 28

## Getting Into the Business of Rehab

Helping others through the process of vocational rehabilitation is a challenging job in any work situation, public or private. It requires a very special kind of empathy with the client and a strong desire to help. It requires a real professional in the world of work and job requirements. The private rehabilitation counselor also needs the ability to work with a number of different professionals to fuse many different professional judgments into one comprehensive, sound and reasonable plan that meets the unique vocational needs of his client.

When an individual counselor decides he wants to go into the field of private rehabilitation, he is doubling the challenges he has set for himself. If he decides to go into the **business** of providing professional services on his own, he is further increasing the challenges, frustrations and rewards. He must deal not only with client/counselor interaction and the problems of multiple accountability that we have been discussing, with all their practical and ethical implications. He must also run his own business with all the challenges involved in that precarious situation. It all adds up to a long and fairly frightening list of challenges. Not all professionally trained rehabilitation counselors interested in the private practice setting have the inclination or stamina for such an undertaking.

However, the rewards in the form of earning potential are sufficient to tempt many young professionals into accepting the additional burdens and challenges of the private rehabilitation business.

### 1. Decisions, Decisions!

Deciding to open your own rehabilitation business is not an easy decision, and many factors must be considered. Opening any business involves a multitude of problems. Starting in the business of private rehabilitation is even more complicated since this is a "brand new" business field. First of all there are no universally accepted standards and no single best way of operating the business. A new rehabilitation counselor in this field has very little experience of others to fall back on.

Secondly, he must also count on some resistance from his peers in the field of vocational rehabilitation. To some extent, rehabilitation for profit is a brand new concept, and looked down upon in some professional circles. This attitude, however, has changed and is continuing to change as the industry grows. More and more student rehabilitation counselors are serving their internships with private rehabilitation firms. It is, however, a question which must be seriously faced by the counselor planning on striking out on his own.

The prospective rehabilitation businessperson must also look at the record of success among new business ventures. It is not an impressive one. According to Mr. Donald Dible, author of the best selling book, **Up Your Own Organization**, most new businesses fail within the first two years of operation. Therefore, the question of engaging in the private practice of rehabilitation must be seriously evaluated and approached. Examine the drawbacks: The long hours, the risk, the necessary family and financial support. "Is it worth the chance?" the counselor must ask himself.

According to Dun & Bradstreet, Inc., half of all business failures are caused by poor management. This includes lack of experience in the industry, lack of general managerial experience, unbalanced experience and simple incompetence. It is obvious that managerial experience is required to make a business successful. This fact becomes especially important when we consider that most private rehabilitation counselors come straight from a graduate program in rehabilitation counseling where business and managerial skills are not emphasized. Their training has been oriented toward the social and helping services with public employment as the career goal. In the past, state and federal rehabilitation programs have been the single largest employer of graduates of rehabilitation training programs. However, since 1975, the private rehabilitation industry has employed the largest number of vocational rehabilitation counselors in the state of California. As other states develop Workers' Compensation laws requiring vocational rehabilitation services, this trend will be felt nationally. It is hoped that the training institutions will recognize the need for some business/managerial skill development in their programs for rehabilitation counselors.

Meanwhile, before hanging his own shingle, the rehabilitation counselor should research the business of being in business for oneself. Three publications are recommended. The first is Donald Dible's **The Pure Joy of Making More Money,** a sequel to his best seller, **Up Your Own Organization.** A thorough reading of this book will help our would-be helper to feel more comfortable with issues surrounding the monetary incentive. "The profits of a company (private practice) will make or break it," Mr. Dible constantly emphasizes. The private businessperson needs to feel at ease with matters of money that go beyond simple calculation of his salary. Good management of expenses and income help him provide quality service at competitive prices. Ultimately he is able to provide his customers (the insurance representatives) and his clients with the best services at the most economical costs.

Mr. Dible stresses the need for a sound business plan for reaching projected levels of service and sales. This plan must give proper attention to the six critical business functions: marketing, innovation, production, sales, finance and management. This business plan is a declaration of the organization's goals and the procedures required to reach those goals. It is a written document, a realistic statement of company aims together with a list of the practical steps required to achieve those aims. Such a rational business plan can substantially reduce chances of failure.

Such a plan would discuss the details of financing, including profit and loss statements, accounts payable, accounts receivable and internal control of cash management. The key area of collections needs serious attention when setting up a business. However, for the private rehab counselor, whose customers are generally the more solvent insurance carriers, this area becomes less of a problem. Nevertheless, cash flow decisions require that accounts receivable be carefully managed. Accounts overdue thirty- to forty-five days should be promptly attended to. This is good business. It maintains cash flow and demonstrates to customers the firm's management capability.

The coordination of production and sales is critical or the new counselor/businessman may find his quality of service deteriorating as his sales curve rises. A good business plan will deal with these issues in advance so that an orderly process for delivering service can be developed and maintained. Mr. Dible discusses the development of a sales strategy for the new business. Understanding the role of salespeople and buyers, the importance of not knocking the competition and establishing a good working rapport with customers and clients alike is stressed.

Mr. Dible also discusses creative ways of financing a new business enterprise. He has some novel suggestions for raising capital that may not have occurred to you. For instance, if you have a Master Charge Card with a credit line of $1,600, a VISA Card with $1,600 credit and several retail store cards, you may already have $5,000 to $6,000 of financing readily available. To include with these cards several oil company cards, a Diner's Club and American Express Card, it's obvious that many people could establish a personal line of revolving credit in excess of $10,000 quite easily. If you are seriously thinking of going into business for yourself, Mr. Dible suggests that it's a good idea to get your personal credit cards in shape. Do not count on business bank loans.

The second book the new counselor should read is Gordon B. Baty's **Entrepreneurship, Playing to Win.** In his first two chapters he discusses the risk and rewards of private business fully and with great insight. His chapters on business planning, selling, accounting and working effectively with lawyers present a great deal of information in simple form. The would-be counselor will not be overwhelmed with a mass of unfamiliar jargon and terminology. In discussing the risk/reward conflict of being your own businessperson, Dr. Baty points out the need for a feeling of self-confidence in order to enjoy the full freedom of the risk-taking involved.

The third book to read is Bernard Kamoroff's **Small-Time Operator**. This easy to read book is loaded with practical information regarding licenses, insurance, bookkeeping, payroll taxes, and computers. Mr. Kamoroff's training as an accountant and his "C.P.A." designation comes forth, but it is palatable.

**2. Business Models**

Once you've considered all the problems and headaches of being your own businessperson and decided that the rewards, both personal and financial, justify this course, you are still faced with decisions that can determine the success or failure of your venture.

The business plan you develop will have a significant influence on the business model you want to set up to implement that plan. The exact structure you will use in your specific enterprise will require close consultation with an accountant and an attorney. But we can make a few general observations on the types of business models you will be considering.

Depending on many factors such as financing, availability of business and personal needs and temperament, you will be choosing from three major alternatives. You may want to set up your business strictly as a self-employment venture. You may want to set up a partnership with another rehabilitation counselor. Or, if your ambition and financing are greater, you may consider a corporation. Again, we go back to your business plan. The individual who has formulated a business plan emphasizing growth and long-term development will probably lean toward the corporate structure as his model. If you have one or two close associates in the field with whom you share some basic professional philosophy, you may find a partnership simpler to operate and easier to define responsibilities. If your financing is limited and you want to start small, working out of your home or a one-man office, then a simple self-employment plan will probably be the most suitable and least expensive to establish. This is the traditional practice that many attorneys, doctors and psychologists have used in getting started.

Each of these particular business models has its own tax ramifications, and these need close scrutiny by your accountant and lawyer. However, the primary consideration is to decide on the type of business you want to deliver based upon your business plan. With this plan identified, it is fairly simple to decide on the model best suited for the plan's implementation. Once you have decided on your business model, the actual mechanics of setting up that model is best left in the hands of the pros in the accounting and legal professions.

But, remember, you are in charge. It is your business. The accountants and lawyers work for you, using their expertise for the realization of your own personally identified goals and objectives. When you look for an accountant or lawyer, be selective. Cheapest is not best. You may have to shop around, seek advice from others before making your final selection. It's a matter of real importance. A good attorney and a good accountant can help you anticipate business problems you may encounter **before** you have to meet them head on. This gives you the opportunity to prepare for business difficulties and meet and resolve them in an orderly and stable manner. A good lawyer and a good accountant can free you to devote the major part of your time and effort to provide the quality rehabilitation counseling services you have set out to provide for your clients and customers. Whereas, if you are forced to spend 80% or more of your time on legal and accounting matters, your clients have lost and you are probably in the wrong field. You are the policy-setter for legal and accounting matters. It's up to your lawyer and accountant to implement that policy.

The particular topics of cash and accrual accounting methods are discussed in detail in the books already mentioned in this chapter. Your own accountant is in a better position to discuss the implications of these concepts for your particular business plan.

Remember, the importance of financial statements is to give you an ongoing record of your operating expenses and income received for a particular point in time. It enables you to constantly evaluate your business plan in relation to your daily business activity. It helps you anticipate problems before they happen.

**3. Employee Pay Models**

Learning theorists and students of human behavior have for years talked about changing behavior by means of different reinforcement models. As an employer in a private rehabilitation business, you are concerned with changing your employees' behavior through increasing their levels of productivity commensurate with reinforcement (pay). The learning theorists talk about two positive ways of bringing about the desired behavior -- a ratio reinforcement schedule or a time reinforcement schedule. These terms are directly applicable to your methods of paying employees and should be given careful consideration when hiring professional staff members.

If you decide on a **time reinforcement schedule,** you will pay your employees a wage based on hours or months of **time** they spend on the job. You are buying their time. This method of compensation gives your employees security and adequate support while they learn their new job. It helps you make accurate budget calculations in advance. This is the type of pay arrangement most rehabilitation consultants expect when they have completed their studies. It is also the normal method of payment in state and federal programs and for many jobs in private, nonprofit agencies. It frequently limits the horizons of the counselor and offers little stimulus for taking on extra work burdens. It produces mediocrity since all persons are paid the same depending on years of service, regardless of individual effort.

In a private setting, the upper limits of a counselor's earnings are as varied as the profit potential of the rehabilitation company for whom he or she works. The typical salary for a Master's level rehabilitation consultant with no experience either in a private rehab service setting or in working with the industrially injured varies from $1,500 to $2,000 per month. This salary is typically paid for the first six to twelve months of the counselor's employment. A principal drawback to paying the counselor a salary is that it does not give additional incentive for working longer hours or for working evenings when particular clients need to be reached after their OJT (on-the-job training). It also requires a management style that continually prompts and prods individuals to work more productively. If you are in a small partnership or a small corporation just starting in business, you are uncertain of the amount of referrals you will be getting and the amount of billing you will have. In this case, it is often difficult to determine whether or not you can afford a counselor on a fixed salary. All of this would depend on your particular financial backing, the number of referrals you receive, your skill in case management and your ability to control your overhead expenses.

The **ratio form of reinforcement** is less familiar to most rehabilitation counselors. This method of payment is similar to the commission frequently paid to sales personnel. However, in the professions of accounting and law, they do not describe this ratio system as commission, but rather as professional fees. In this method of payment, an individual counselor or evaluator is paid a particular percentage of each hour of service which is billed to the customer. For example, if a particular rehabilitation company charges $60 per hour for vocational evaluation services, then that counselor may be paid $20.00 for each billable hour he produces. This system of financial reinforcement allows the counselor to work longer hours if he wants to increase his earnings. It is a system particularly suited to "workaholics." It enables the counselor to work the number of hours that meet his personal needs as represented in his values and lifestyle, regardless of a prearranged salary or workweek. If a counselor, receiving one-third of the amount of his billable hours, wanted to work 60 hours a week, he would have the potential of earning $800 a week, or

$3,500 per month, assuming that out of the 60 hours worked he could bill 40 hours, a 66% efficiency.

This method has its drawback, however, when dealing with counselors at the apprentice level. Good time management skills are needed to make this system pay off for the novice counselor and these skills come only with experience. If the new counselor wastes time or does not carefully schedule and record his activities on a particular case, he is going to end up with a pretty small paycheck. It must also be remembered that beginning counselors in a private setting are not always fully efficient in working with employers, insurance representatives, attorneys, physicians, and are not skilled in dictating all the reports required. They are bound to have considerable hours categorized as lost hours. Lost time includes sessions with supervisors and excessive hours spent on reports, test interpretation, scoring, etc.

The ratio reinforcement method of payment is, in general, most suited to the entrepreneurial or business-for-profit system. It eliminates the need for tough management which may be required to push and prod workers in producing better service, qualitatively and quantitatively. The drive to produce more is generated from within. The counselor's need for producing an income to meet his lifestyle is a stronger motivator than a driving boss. It does **NOT** eliminate the need for peer review and internal auditing, which is desirable in any type of payment system.

In cases where the counselor has no strong roots in ethical conduct, this system can lead to fraud. Such a counselor may be too easily tempted to overcharge for a particular service, assuring himself a higher salary. Careful supervision is required so that the amount of time spent on a particular task is consistent with professional norms and not excessive. A counselor who has been found to be trustworthy and has gained good experience in providing private rehabilitation services is typically a good candidate for the ratio system of payment.

Clients and insurance representatives who utilize professional rehabilitation services ought to inquire of the providers of such services how the counselors are paid. There are implications regarding both the quantity and the quality of the work. Counselors on salaries, regardless of their level of productivity, are less likely to respond to crisis situations, to work weekend or evening hours. In many cases these are critical times for getting the job done. On the other hand, counselors paid on a ratio basis may be more apt to charge for activities not justly billable to an insurance carrier. This, too, is greatly dependent upon the internal management controls of the rehabilitation firm. There is also a greater tendency under a ratio system of payment to recommend services that may not be actually required in a particular case. This may require close scrutiny by rehabilitation specialists within an insurance company and certainly careful supervision by supervisors in a particular rehabilitation firm.

For the client working with a counselor paid on the ratio system, he is more apt to be given the counselor's home phone number and find the counselor available a greater number of hours on any particular day. For many clients, the opportunity to speak to their counselor and get questions answered as they come up is an important and helpful part of the rehabilitation process. It enables them to cope more effectively in day-to-day situations.

**4. Paying for Long-Term Employment**

Typically in most organizations, as employees work more years they expect and, in most cases, deserve pay increases. In its simplest terms, it is the longevity formula. Frequently your pay system is well worked out and firmly based on your business plan and overall philosophy. In that case, you can tell an employee when you hire him what he can expect to earn, provided he delivers quality services, after he has been with you two years, five years or ten years. Having such a goal frequently enables a new employee to tolerate the initial frustrations of working with industrially injured workers in the complicated Workers' Compensation system.

If your system of payment is for productivity regardless of the length of time a counselor has worked for you, then complicated longevity scales are not needed. You simply pay the individual according to the quantity and quality of work that he or she does -- taking into account the degree of supervision necessary. Generally, in an organization of three to ten employees, the maximum that could be paid would be 40% of the counselor's billable hours. This assumes that the individual has no marketing or administrative responsibilities and provides full-time counseling service. This would be the journeyman pay scale and implies that the counselor needs minimal supervision. Entry levels in the ratio system are generally in the range of 20% to 30%.

In terms of monthly salary, what does this mean? Assume a journeyman counselor who is paid for his productivity and, assuming he is not a partner and has no other interest in the corporation, is paid 35%. Carrying a full and regular caseload he should be capable of billing twenty-five to thirty-five hours of **necessary** case services per week. This assumes that he works forty to fifty hours a week. At this rate, his monthly earnings should range from $2,275 to $3,185, where the firm's hourly rate is $60. If the counselor puts in more hours, he is able to bill more time and increase his earning power.

Eventually, counselors working on this system and at this level of productivity are usually given an opportunity to join profit-sharing plans, become partners in the corporate structure, or receive special bonuses. This is traditionally the model that exists in many accounting and law firms. As the person reaches journeyman status, demonstrates continued competence and quality work, demonstrates loyalty and professional ethics, and develops his own reputation in the field, he becomes more valuable to the firm. It is at this point that the employer and individual feel upgrading and advancement is needed to maintain a healthy incentive.

**5. Billing Systems and Codes**

The private rehabilitation service depends, in general, on insurance representatives for payment. The customer, or insurance representative, requests service for an injured worker, the rehabilitation counselor's client. The client receives the service, but, in most cases, it is the customer who pays the bill.

Good consumerism requires that a private rehabilitation business inform the customers as to the specific services performed and specific charges made. Thus, the rehabilitation counselor's customer needs precise information regarding dates, types of service provided, length of time required and specific amounts charged. Insurance representatives must have this information for their own internal auditing control. They also use this information to more accurately set reserves and maintain their financial solvency. Most of the information regarding billing codes and services is not relevant to clients since they are not the ones who pay for the services. However, it is important that they realize they are receiving the services as part of their benefit. They, therefore, have certain responsibilities and obligations for those services. The counselor should expect clients to be just as involved in vocational rehabilitation services as if they were paying for these services out of their own pocket. Anything less fosters dependency and a sense of irresponsibility on the part of the client.

In most states in which private rehabilitation services are provided, there is no mandated code for charges or categories of service. Each individual company has been left to its own judgment regarding how it charges for services. However, some general guidelines have emerged that are important for the delivery of quality service in a third-party reimbursement system such as Workers' Compensation.

Specificity and precision are required in your billing. To send a bill to an insurance company with an invoice number and a category called "rehabilitation counseling services provided, 15 hours at $60 per hour" is not sufficient. The exact nature of those fifteen hours of service need delineation and specification. This allows the insurance representative, your customer, to monitor the charges and to control them if they seem excessively high or unwarranted. Good controls on the cost of services provided is necessary in order to prevent an unnecessary inflationary spiral in rehabilitation costs.

Table A is one model of a billing codes schedule that could be used for different services. Most of these activities are relatively discrete and self-explanatory. Most of the services would be charged at a constant fee with the exception that some "group" charges would be less. The particular hour rate would be dependent upon business goals, financing, management decisions, and the particular geographic region. Rates for these services usually range from $45 to $70 per hour.

The proper method of using this billable code is illustrated in the completed invoice shown in Table B. These billing codes and their use in invoices are suggestions only. Your exact needs may require other systems. Many providers of rehabilitation services delineate services chronologically in the order of the dates provided, rather than by particular category of service. Both alternatives appear to be acceptable to insurance customers. The value of subgrouping services under billing codes on an invoice is that it enables an insurance representative to evaluate the total number of hours spent for one particular area of service. For example, if a review of the invoice indicates that 12-1/2 hours has been spent on vocational testing, then the insurance representative may be justly concerned with the amount of time spent in that area and ask for an explanation. If the total amount of time spent for job-seeking skills training is one hour, then the insurance person may be concerned with the quality of such job-seeking skills training. Most such training is performed in groups and may last one to three days.

## TABLE A: Billing Codes

01 Carrier case status discussion
02 Attorney contact (applicant/plaintiff)
03 Attorney contact (defense)
04 Employer contact
05 Job analysis
06 Medical records review
07 Physician contact
08 Vocational consultation/counseling
09 Vocational diagnostic interview
10 Motivational counseling
11 Rehabilitation counseling
12 Vocational exploration and planning (individual)
13 Vocational exploration and planning (group)
14 Vocational testing (administering)
15 Vocational testing (scoring, interpreting, explaining)
16 Vocational research
17 Labor market analysis
18 On-the-job training contact
19 Formal training program contact
20 Job placement assistance (individual)
21 Job placement assistance (group)
22 Job search skills training (individual)
23 Job search skills training (group)
24 Community agency contacts
25 Professional staff travel time
26 Rehabilitation Plan conference-carrier
27 Rehabilitation Plan conference-client
28 Rehabilitation Bureau conference
29 Rehabilitation Bureau contact
30 Conference preparation
31 Testifying at hearings
32 Case file review
33 Follow-up Rehabilitation Plan counseling
34 Report preparation
35 Rehabilitation Plan preparation (RB-2)
36 Letters/correspondence
37 Vocational planning

**TABLE B**

**INVOICE NO. 000**

Mr. John Doe
D & D Insurance Co.
One North St.
Our Town, CA.

Re: John Everyman
Claim No.: 000 1 000M

|  |  |  |
|---|---|---|
| 10 Motivational counseling (9-5-86) | .5 hr @ $60 | $30.00 |
| 12 Vocational exploration and planning (individual) (8-28, 9-5, 13-86) | 2.4 hr @ $60 | 144.00 |
| 15 Vocational testing (scoring, interpreting, explaining, 9-11, 12, 13-86) | .9 hr @ $60 | 54.00 |
| 16 Vocational research (9-28-86) | .2 hr @ $60 | 12.00 |
| 17 Labor market analysis (9-28-86) | .2 hr @ $60 | 12.00 |
| 20 Job placement assistance (9-14, 20-86) | .6 hr @ $60 | 36.00 |
| 22 Job search skills training (9-8-86) | 1.1 hr @ $60 | 66.00 |
| 26 Rehabilitation Plan conference-carrier (9-12, 13-86) | .3 hr @ $60 | 18.00 |
| 33 Follow-up Rehabilitation Plan counseling (9-27-86) | .5 hr @ $60 | 30.00 |
| 35 Rehabilitation Plan preparation (RB-2) (9-28-86) | .5 hr @ $60 | 30.00 |
| 36 Letters/correspondence (9-28-86) | .1 hr @ $60 | 6.00 |
| 37 Vocational planning (9-25-86) | .2 hr @ $60 | 12.00 |
| 34 Report preparation (9-28-86) | 1.0 hr @ $60 | 60.00 |
| | **Amount Due** | **$510.00** |

## 6. Other Business Considerations

So far we have been talking about a fairly small scale rehabilitation business where the counselors are the only professional staff and may work with a minimum of clerical help. But, as the field grows, more and more larger firms are appearing and some jobs are becoming more specialized. Imagine an optimal rehabilitation business situation and what an ideal staffing situation might be. Some ideas might occur to the novice rehab businessperson which he might be able to simplify and adapt for his smaller scale situation.

### Setting Up an Office

A total delivery system for private rehabilitation services might look something like this. There would be a skilled receptionist who would be able to handle the phone, file and type. You would also have an in-house typist, and perhaps some back-up part-time typists available for emergency situations. You would have a staff of competent rehabilitation counselors who are experienced and doing a good job. You might at the same time be breaking in a novice counselor, splitting his supervision among the journeymen counselors. Ideally, you would have a job developer. A good person in this position needn't be a Master's degree counselor. He could be a competent technician with only a high school diploma who is skilled and professional in how employers are contacted and jobs developed. Or he could have a Bachelor's degree with some experience in job development, hiring policies and Affirmative Action. The job developer could also do labor market research and provide information to the rehab consultant to justify particular vocational goals. You might also want a vocational evaluator on the staff to aid the counselor in making his vocational diagnosis. If you really want to get fancy you can add a marketing person to the staff who would bring in referrals, freeing up the counselors to spend more time working with clients and less time looking for referrals. You might even want a manager to take over the office functioning and handle billing, account management, and financial planning.

In practice, however, the counselor who goes into his own business won't have all these problems to worry about. His will be the simpler problems: How much office space do I need? What kind of furniture, equipment, etc.? How much of a typist's time will I need? What kind of answering service? All these can become major issues for the beginner in this field.

After the cost of professional staff, the next biggest item in the budget of a private counselor is clerical support, including salary for personnel, lease or rental of office space and equipment. These are items that must be met on a monthly basis. Regardless of the amount of billing, there is a minimum amount of paper processing to be put through your system.

The relationship between moving this paper and providing quality professional services is high in a private rehabilitation counseling setting. The most effective counselor in terms of vocational evaluation, counseling and job placement will be of no value in a system requiring third-party reimbursement if he is not capable of writing reports that document the work he has done. And this same excellent counselor will put himself out of business if he does not have the necessary clerical support to type those reports, type up billing sheets and be sure that they are sent out and collected in a reasonable amount of time. The connection between clerical support and quality professional service is direct and vital.

Equipment and space requirements will finally be dictated by needs. There are no standards, no preferred amount of square footage per counselor. It's possible to work in an office with only room for a desk, desk chair and chair for the client. Some clients might feel cramped in such a situation, but if the office has a window with a fair view, it can be usable. Perhaps an area of eighty square feet and shaped in a square would be a good minimum to start from. This size space can provide room for meeting with one or two clients at the same time (a man and spouse, for example) without a feeling of being crowded. The larger size offices, though they may be useful for staff meetings, are not needed for ordinary counseling situations. If an office has no window, more space should be provided.

In order to have "phone call work stations" for clients to use during their job search, additional space, tables, and phones are necessary. It does little good to market yourself as scheduling clients to receive 15 to 20 hours per week of job search involvement if you do not provide a work area for them. Once an area is provided you can effectively monitor their involvement, give regular doses of encouragement, and assist in their success of securing interviews. This extra space adds to overhead, decreases profits, **but** it substantially enhances quality. It helps you help clients secure job offers more quickly.

Your preferences and values in office size, space, decor and reception area will be an influencing factor in the amount of overhead costs you will have to meet. They will also be factors to be taken into account when deciding on your basic legal model -- self-employment, partnership or corporation. A different image may be required depending on your particular legal status.

It is important to stress that your major interest is in providing rehabilitation services. You are not interested in spending too much of your time in managing paper flow. Therefore, it is important to find the right person who is skilled, temperamentally suited and adequately motivated to provide these administrative/management services. Then you are free to provide the billable professional services and engage in the professional practice that you started out to do in the first place.

# CHAPTER 29

## Hidden Agendas

One of the most important distinctions of rehabilitation consulting in the private sector is the matter of accountability, total accountability, as we have called it. So far we have looked very carefully at this demand on the consultant to account to a wide variety of different people involved in rehabilitation. We have considered this matter from a practical day-to-day working viewpoint and we have considered the wider philosophical and ethical implications of the third-party payment system, the customer/counselor/client triad.

We have not yet examined what each of the parties involved in a rehab case brings to this system in the form of attitudes, biases, expectations, hopes, fears, his whole psychological climate. We are calling these factors the "hidden agendas." As discussions on a case open, hidden agendas do not immediately appear. They may be conscious or unconscious, but they have an important bearing on how a case develops and the odds for successful rehabilitation. Some of these hidden agendas are positive and may be used by the counselor in facilitating his rehabilitation plan. Others are negative, and, unnoticed, can often sabotage a quality rehabilitation plan and send the counselor back to square one.

### 1. Hidden Client Agendas

When the client first walks into the counselor's office, he brings with him a score of different and often contradictory attitudes. He may be confused and angry. He is often discouraged, his self-esteem battered by a long period of not being able to work and earn a living. He may be bitter as he speaks of his $224 weekly benefit being called a reasonable compensation for his preinjury earnings of $800 weekly. If he already has an attorney, there has probably been some "secret" communication between them and that is a "secret" agenda he brings into the counseling session. In his anger at a system that awards him a "pittance" in the form of temporary compensation benefits, he may approach the whole system with the agenda, "I want to get as much as I can out of this thing." He is often not looking at the rehabilitation process in terms of getting back to work and making as much money as possible, consistent with his aptitudes, skills and interests. At this moment he is conscious only of the dollar value of his lost earning power -- $575 a week. He is angry as he remembers a friend who got a $125,000 settlement from a car accident in which he merely banged up a knee.

But this anger is probably only a cover-up for the fear the client is bringing into his rehab situation. He's probably scared at the idea of facing a new line of work and that the new work is not going to pay him enough to support his family properly. With the loss of his earning power he has lost a lot of self-esteem. Doubts of his ability as a provider begin to gnaw away inside him. But he has to deny all this, put up a good, tough macho image, "My attorney is going to take care of me." He is dreaming up a big settlement. In reality, however, the settlement he finally receives will be relatively small in comparison to what he could get if he cooperated fully with a vocational rehabilitation program, probably not even equal to a year's earning power.

That's the negative side of the hidden agenda many clients bring with them into the rehab system. In reality, it has been the authors' experience that most injured workers, along with their fear, anger and depression, bring a strong desire for getting back to work. They are mostly afraid to admit it. Afraid because how can they, as "disabled" workers hope to go back to productive work. They aren't willing to admit this desire to return to work out of fear that it may upset their status as "disabled" and affect the settlement of their claim (a misunderstanding which the counselor can easily straighten out).

Most workers find more in a job than just a paycheck. Faced with a life of just sitting around the house, they would much rather be out on a job. It gives meaning to their lives, self-esteem, pride in being able to take care of one's family. After a while, the idea of staying at home with their spouse every day becomes intolerable. Home is a nice place to come home to -- but all day may be too much.

The skillful counselor learns to recognize and work with the hidden agendas of the client, to use them to further the process of rehabilitation. The client's anger at the system can be converted into a drive to beat the system by getting back to a well-paying job. The incentive of restored self-esteem and renewed ability to support the family can be a strong motivator.

The important thing is for the counselor to understand his client's feelings and thoughts, to recognize the conflicting agendas and direct them constructively.

**2. The Attorney's Hidden Agenda**

The primary agenda for attorneys on both sides of a case is not hidden at all. It is to get the "best deal" for their clients, the injured worker or the insurance carrier. But that is not the whole story.

Most attorneys for injured workers are sincerely interested in maximizing their client's independence, getting them through the system quickly and painlessly, and getting them back to work at a well-paying job as quickly as possible. It must also be remembered that this attorney's agenda is not always as unselfish as it sounds. He is generally not being paid on a time basis and the typical allowable percentage (10%) of the client's settlement in workers' comp is not enough to drag out a case indefinitely. This is one of the reasons most attorneys practicing in the Workers' Compensation field carry caseloads of 500 or more injured workers. They just do not have the time for unnecessary litigation.

On the other hand, attorneys on both sides of the case, insurance person as well as injured worker, offer unqualified support to their respective client. This can be either a positive or a negative agenda. Without a doubt, attorneys will represent only their side of the picture. They may not know about "lies" and will not encourage it. But they will represent their respective clients fully and usually accept what their clients say. This is part of the system. If you are to represent a client, you are for him 100%. However, the concerned attorney, if he sees that his client's case is totally built on false information, will need to have a talk with that client and clarify the issues. Such a case built on lies is going to probably crumble anyway, and the attorney has no interest in being part of this failure. The attorney will therefore attempt to build the best case he can for his client based on all the facts and data available.

Normally, the attorney entering a rehabilitation case is anxious to win, and to do so, if possible, on his client's terms. This fact is important for the counselor to realize. An attorney is most likely to accept a vocational plan if it is what his client **wants.** The skilled rehabilitation counselor will develop a vocational plan the client **needs.** What a client wants is often **not** what a client needs. The effective rehabilitation counselor communicates to attorneys by emphasizing the objective data on which the plan is based. A skilled counselor approaching the issue objectively can work out suitable and acceptable plans. There is no **one** right job for any particular individual. (Recent literature on the subject points to the fact that most persons will make six or seven major career changes during the course of their work history). There is no scientific or technical means of proving that a client can succeed in only one vocational area. A client attorney's agenda frequently changes if objective information is provided which justifies a more realistic direction.

**3. Hidden Agendas of Insurance Representatives**

Generally, the insurance representative is out to achieve the least expensive rehabilitation possible. This fact, while obvious to any counselor who has worked in this setting, is not always known to the client. Injured workers can sometimes fantasize epic rehabilitation plans assuming that the insurance representative is going to pick up the tab.

The insurance representative is willing to provide the necessary rehabilitation services, but their main concern is to get this injured worker off their books and back to work as quickly as possible. You won't hear much talk about maximizing vocational potential around the insurance representative's office.

The counselor acquires a good idea of the agenda of the insurance representative when a case is referred to him. There are plenty of clues to tell the counselor whether the insurance person is interested in being supportive of the injured worker in serious vocational planning or whether they consider him a flake or a fake. This information is not always an accurate basis on which a counselor can judge a client's real motivation. Often the "uncooperative" client referred to a counselor does sincerely want to get back to work. He may have some serious personal problems at the time, preventing him from acting as positively as he might in promoting his rehabilitation. The issue with the insurance representative may be merely a screen to hide the representative's own personal distress with too many claim files, not enough clerical help, etc. The counselor must see beyond the insurance person's biased hidden agenda to get an accurate picture of his client's motivation.

**4. Counselors Have Hidden Agendas, Too**

In this rehab climate we are discussing, all parties seem to have multiple motives, often conflicting with each other. The trained rehabilitation counselor's theories of client advocacy must be somewhat tempered by the special needs of the Compensation system, its third-party payment, client legal representation and multiple accountability.

Perhaps the fundamental agenda of most vocational counselors stems from their philosophical bias toward work as a value in itself. The counselor believes in work. This belief may conflict with values of others. His main interest is in getting his client back to some kind of paying job and avoiding the pitfalls that clients sometimes fall into during long periods of recuperation (e.g., the "compensation neurosis" wherein the client has lost faith in his ability to work again). The quicker he can get his client actively participating in his own recovery, the greater his chances of successful rehabilitation.

The counselor is subject to the many competing pressures built into the Disability Compensation system. While he is anxious to work with the client and fully respond to his needs, he frequently finds himself biased by **his** needs to cover himself in his reporting to others involved in the case. Whatever decisions he makes in the interests of the client must be defended with attorneys and medical teams from both sides, with the claims representative for the insurance institutions, and with the state rehabilitation regulatory bureau. Though his interests and concern may lie with the client, he has to cover all his flanks and be sure that his decision making is justified before everyone else in the case. This is a hidden agenda that the private rehabilitation counselor in this system must live and work with.

# SECTION IV

## Facts and Figures: Fantasy or Reality?

## Introduction to Section on Facts and Figures

by L. Deneen and T. Hessellund

For the **first time** under one cover reliable data is available regarding rehabilitation statistics: employability and completion rates, reemployment and success rates, costs, types of plans, factors of successful plans. The data includes information from many different carriers and rehabilitation providers in various regions of the country. Data from 14 states is included. In our opinion it is the most reliable information available.

This information is more tedious to read and digest. It "reads differently" than the other chapters of the book. It represents our attempt to provide you a cross section of **hard data** that due to its scope is representative of what you may encounter.

We are appreciative of the willingness of California Workers' Compensation Institute, Mr. Alan Tebb, General Manager and the National Council on Compensation Insurance Data for giving us permission to reprint the studies in their entirety. Through our text these studies will receive a wider distribution and be studied by more people than may have otherwise occurred. No editing of the studies has been done by us.

L.D. and T.H.

# CHAPTER 30

## Vocational Rehabilitation: Report to the Industry 1983

In 1974 California became the first state to enact a mandatory vocational rehabilitation benefit as an integral part of the Workers' Compensation law, the first state to complete the range of benefits to which injured employees are entitled as a matter of law.

This report describes the California experience, documents the advantages and limitations of mandatory vocational rehabilitation, and discusses the impediments that obstruct the program's effectiveness in meeting the return-to-work objective of Workers' Compensation.

California Workers'
Compensation Institute
November 1983

**Summary**

The enactment of California's vocational rehabilitation provision gave statutory recognition to the system's rehabilitation objective. Unlike other social insurance programs, only Worker's Compensation has the goal of returning beneficiaries of the program to the world of work. In combination with other Workers' Compensation benefits -- unlimited medical care and physical restorative services, wage-replacement payments during recovery, additional compensation for the permanent effects of the injury -- vocational rehabilitation completes the circle of resources directed at putting injured workers back into productive employment.

By any standard, the results are impressive. During the past five years nearly 22,000 severely injured workers have had their employability restored through vocational rehabilitation services provided under the Workers' Compensation law. Of that number, 80 percent are working in modified, alternative or retrained occupations, a success rate that would be higher but for the recent economic recession.

In the vast majority of cases, vocational rehabilitation services are being furnished to those who will benefit, i.e., workers whose injury prevents them from returning to their usual occupation, or whose injury, in combination with other factors, may preclude any meaningful attachment to the work force.

Despite physical limitations, nearly half of all rehabilitated workers return to work at earnings greater than before their industrial injury. On the average, rehabilitated workers earn about 95 percent of their preinjury wages.

The progress has not been without costs, however. The arrival of vocational rehabilitation as a mandatory benefit brought confusion, expense redundancy and bureaucratic turmoil. Some of these shortcomings had their genesis in the novelty of the change and the enabling statute's lack of particulars, but there are other structural and operational deficits. Examples:

* Vocational rehabilitation is an add-on benefit that duplicates the purposes of permanent disability indemnity. Today California employers are responsible for restoring the employability of seriously injured workers and, at the same time, compensating them for the "diminished ability...to compete in the open labor market" -- as if the vocational rehabilitation benefit did not exist.
* Delays in identification and referral of potential rehabilitation candidates by employers and insurers have made the benefit less immediate and productive for some workers.
* The increasing involvement of attorneys, and through them the courts, have introduced an adversary aspect into what is -- or should be -- an agreed, cooperative process.
* The administration of the benefits is marked by delays, legalistic procedures and complex reporting requirements. The delivery of the vocational rehabilitation benefit too often is dominated by paper, not services.
* Costs have escalated rapidly. When vocational rehabilitation became mandatory, employers' insurance premiums were increased an average of 2.7 percent to pay for the new benefit. Within five years costs doubled. Today conservative estimates place the cost of the vocational rehabilitation benefit at 7 percent, with a predicted increase to 10 percent of total incurred losses in the near future.

The problems surrounding the California vocational rehabilitation benefit may arise in large part from a misunderstanding of its purpose. Under California law, the employer's responsibility is to restore employability, not employment. Vocational rehabilitation in Workers' Compensation is not a work guarantee program. Neither is it an education benefit, nor the Workers' Compensation counterpart of the GI Bill of Rights. Instead it is, first and always, a return-to-work benefit.

In contrast to permanent disability benefits, vocational rehabilitation concentrates on ability -- what the employee can do -- rather than disability. This shift in focus, if accepted and implemented affirmatively, presents the opportunity to restore Workers' Compensation to its underlying purpose: Recovery from, rather than recovery for.

Rehabilitation and Workers' Compensation have been closely linked throughout the history of America's premier social insurance program. In the early years the linkage was more perceived than real; for example, some of the original state laws did not contain provisions for adequate medical care, the foundation of all rehabilitation activity in a global sense. Yet, after these shortfalls were corrected, much of the emphasis in the past -- indeed, even the recent past -- was upon the medical aspects of rehabilitation.

Over the past 70 years, state Workers' Compensation systems have earned deservedly high marks for the physical rehabilitation of the catastrophically injured worker. Only recently, however, have state systems turned to address the far more common (and frequently more difficult) challenges: Restoring the employability of a carpenter who fractured his knee or, more typically, the 44-year-old laborer with a soft tissue back injury.

Interest in vocational rehabilitation (in contrast to medical rehabilitation) began after World War II, spurred by a public awakening to what had been done to help thousands of disabled veterans. Progress was slow. It wasn't until the early 60's that the Council of State Governments published a model act -- the "Workmen's Compensation **and** Rehabilitation Law" -- which contained detailed provisions governing vocational rehabilitation services to injured employees. Few states acted on the recommendations, but some -- a few by statute, others by administrative regulations -- recognized the importance of the return-to-work objective of Workers' Compensation and began to strengthen the vocational orientation of rehabilitation.

The breakthrough came in the 70's. Some observers credit the heightened activity to the 1971-72 study of the National Compensation Laws, although its report made only a passing reference to vocational rehabilitation. Nevertheless, the legislative interest generated by the National Commission's recommendations also directed attention to the need to offer injured workers something more than medical care and disability payments. In 1974 California became the first state to enact a mandatory vocational rehabilitation benefit as part of its Workers' Compensation law.

**Program Scope**

The California Workers' Compensation law and its vocational rehabilitation component apply to more than 550,000 employers who employ about 11 million workers. Compensable work injuries exceed 1 million annually, although most of these -- upwards of 75 percent -- are minor incidents requiring only medical treatment. Of the remaining "disabling" injuries, i.e., resulting in one or more days lost time, few are potential vocational rehabilitation cases (although the percentage is increasing because of improvements in reporting procedures).

| Year | Disabling Work Injuries | Rehabilitation Files Opened | As % Disabling Work Injuries |
|---|---|---|---|
| 1978 | 360,453 | 16,845 | 4.7 |
| 1979 | 382,227 | 16,078 | 4.2 |
| 1980 | 373,959 | 24,624 | 6.6 |
| 1981 | 361,983 | 24,460 | 6.8 |
| 1982 | 331,314 | 30,717 | 9.3 |

**Source:** California Division of Labor Statistics & Research Rehabilitation Bureau, California Division of Industrial Accidents

The creation of a file by the state administrative agency only identifies cases to be monitored; it does not establish the need for vocational rehabilitation services. In fact, more than half of the files ultimately will be closed because the employee returns to work without rehabilitation intervention, or because the state agency determines the employee is not eligible for the benefit. About 18 percent of the files will be retired because the employee does not want rehabilitation services. The remainder, about 30 percent of the identified potential candidates, will be provided rehabilitation services under a specific return-to-work plan.

Some of the workers actively engaged in rehabilitation, about one in seven, will not complete the program because of disinterest, lack of cooperation, or inability to participate in the rehabilitation regimen because of medical limitations. However, the vast majority of injured employees complete the vocational rehabilitation program and return to the labor market.

**REHABILITATION PLANS COMPLETED**

| Year | Employee Working | Employee Not Working | Total |
|---|---|---|---|
| 1978 | 1,874 | 309 | 2,183 |
| 1979 | 3,278 | 482 | 3,760 |
| 1980 | 3,869 | 773 | 4,642 |
| 1981 | 4,421 | 1,062 | 5,483 |
| 1982 | 4,131 | 1,627 | 5,758 |

**Source:** Rehabilitation Bureau, California Division of Industrial Accidents

(The completion statistics do not recognize the considerable time-lag between injury, recovery and return-to-work. The figures report only the number of plans completed in the indicated year, not the number of cases in process. For example, more than two-thirds of the rehabilitation plans completed in 1982 were by employees injured in 1980. The result of the build-up in the pipeline shows in the 123 percent increase in rehabilitation plans completed during the 1978-82 period. The most encouraging sign, given the recent economic recession, is that 80 percent of the rehabilitated workers return to productive employment.)

Considering the scope of the California Workers' Compensation system, the rehabilitation segment is a small one. Potential cases identified for monitoring represent perhaps 10 percent of all lost-time claims. If the comparison base is limited to injured employees who qualify for and accept the benefit, the rehabilitation market in California Workers' Compensation is reduced to 2 percent of all disabling injuries. And if the measurement includes only successful return-to-work cases, then vocational rehabilitation affects only 1 percent of workers disabled by work injuries annually.

## A Two-Part Test

The enabling statute, while hardly a paragon of legislative clarity, is straightforward. In pertinent part it requires:

> When a qualified injured worker chooses to enroll in a rehabilitation program, he or she shall continue to receive temporary disability indemnity payments, plus additional living expenses necessitated by the rehabilitation program, together with all reasonable and necessary vocational training, at the expense of the employer....

Thus the mandatory aspect of vocational rehabilitation is binding only upon the employer -- at the option of the employee. If the employee chooses not to participate, the right to other compensation benefits are not affected. This feature of the California law is consistent with the agreed nature of the process -- rehabilitation services cannot be force-fed to an unwilling claimant -- but it creates potential motivational problems if the employee's only incentive is the continuation of compensation payments. Moreover, because entitlement to rehabilitation services cannot be settled, the employer continues to have a liability if a worker who originally declined the benefit changes his mind and requests rehabilitation several years later, usually after the proceeds of the permanent disability award have been exhausted.

The administrative regulations that implement the statute limit the vocational rehabilitation benefit to disabled workers who pass a two-part test. The first criterion is medical: Whether the injury prevents the employee from returning to his or her usual occupation, a determination usually made by the treating physician. If medical eligibility is met, the second step is vocational feasibility, a more subjective standard that attempts to evaluate, before the fact, if rehabilitation services will be beneficial given the individual employee's injury, interests and motivation. One-third of the potential candidates for rehabilitation services fail to meet one or the other tests, with medical eligibility the predominant disqualifier.

The statute vests authority to monitor and supervise the rehabilitation of injured workers in the Rehabilitation Bureau of the Division of Industrial Accidents, the state administrative agency. Current staffing is 28 consultants located in 14 offices throughout the state. (In a pattern subsequently adopted by a number of other jurisdictions, Bureau consultants do not provide rehabilitation services directly; rather, their function is to foster, review and coordinate the rehabilitation activities undertaken by insurers and employers.)

### A Three-fold Benefit

For qualified injured workers the vocational rehabilitation benefit is three-dimensional:

- A maintenance allowance, paid at the same rate as temporary disability indemnity, while the employee is receiving rehabilitation services;
- The cost of evaluation, testing, development and implementation of a specific return-to-work plan, job placement assistance and other professional services provided by private and public rehabilitation counselors; and
- The out-of-pocket expense of the rehabilitation plan itself, including tuition, books, transportation, tools, uniforms, additional living expense occasioned by the plan, even babysitting fees in appropriate instances.

The maintenance allowance accounts for the largest share of vocational rehabilitation dollars, typically about half the cost of the plan. Payments to professional counselors average about one-third of plan costs, with the remaining 15-18 percent allocated for the direct expense of training or retraining.

The percentage distribution of vocational rehabilitation costs is a function of the labor market. During the late 70's, when unemployment was down, the major emphasis was on shorter, less expensive (and usually more successful) rehabilitation programs -- for example, modification of the worker's preinjury job or direct placement of employees with transferable skills -- because job openings existed. Recently, however, as the job market tightened, more employees are being placed in formal schooling plans, whose longer duration impact the maintenance and training cost elements.

Not all rehabilitation candidates receive the three-fold benefit. If the employee is medically eligible, he or she will be paid the maintenance allowance during evaluation and testing to determine vocational feasibility, a relatively short period in most instances. If feasibility is not established, further entitlement to the vocational rehabilitation benefit terminates without participation in a return-to-work plan. In 1980, the latest measurement available, 28 percent of all vocational rehabilitation expenditures were made in so-called "nonplan" cases, down from 34 percent two years earlier. These results, while not optimal, suggest insurers and self-insured employers have begun to exercise more controls in the management of rehabilitation cases.

### The Rehabilitant Population

With rare exceptions, vocational rehabilitation under the Workers' Compensation law applies only to employees whose injuries result in permanent residual disability. Within that population, rehabilitants most frequently are younger, less educated and lower wage-earners than other permanently disabled workers. More than half are non-white. Most are blue-collar workers employed in manufacturing. Males predominate, although women are proportionately represented in the rehabilitated work force. Back injuries most commonly require rehabilitation services, but upper extremity impairments are nearly as prevalent.

**Age:** Half of the rehabilitated workers are under 40 years, an expected finding given the age distribution of the severely injured. Age alone may not be a significant determinant; nevertheless, there are fewer older workers in the rehabilitated population.

| | **Permanently Disabled Workers** | |
|---|---|---|
| **Age at Injury** | **% Rehabilitated** | **% Other** |
| Under 30 years | 25 | 27 |
| 30-39 | 25 | 24 |
| 40-49 | 31 | 18 |
| 50-59 | 19 | 22 |
| 60 years and over | -- | 9 |

**Source:** CWCI global study, 1983

Formal rehabilitation intervention may not be necessary for an experienced worker with readily transferable skills, or for one whose loyalty and abilities are recognized by a long-term employer. On the other hand, some older workers are more unwilling to accept a different role in a new work environment, e.g., eight of 10 qualified workers under 30 years accept the vocational rehabilitation benefit, versus only half of those 50 years or older.

**Education:** The need for vocational rehabilitation services decreases with educational achievement. Workers without a high school education are half again as likely to require vocational rehabilitation as a result of a job injury than other disabled employees.

| **Education Completed** | **Permanently Disabled Workers % Rehabilitated** | **% Other** |
|---|---|---|
| Grade school only | 24 | 15 |
| Some high school | 20 | 15 |
| High school graduate | 27 | 26 |
| Post high school | 29 | 44 |

**Source:** CWCI global study, 1983

The relative lack of educational achievement among rehabilitants seems an anomaly in light of California's mandatory education requirement. However, the high incidence of English language handicap among rehabilitated workers -- 24 percent -- suggests immigration may be a factor.

**Earnings:** Nearly 70 percent of the rehabilitated workers earn less than the statewide average wage at the time of injury, compared to the expected 50 percent for other permanently disabled workers. On the average, rehabilitants' earnings were only 90 percent of the statewide average weekly wage, a finding traceable to differences in experience and education.

**Ethnicity:** More than half -- 55 percent -- of all rehabilitated workers are non-white. Three of every 10 rehabilitants are of Hispanic heritage, while Blacks, Asians and Indians are twice as likely to be represented than in the injured work force generally.

| **Ethnicity** | **Permanently Disabled Workers % Rehabilitated** | **% Other** |
|---|---|---|
| White | 45 | 69 |
| Hispanic | 31 | 19 |
| Black | 18 | 9 |
| Asian/Indian/Other | 6 | 3 |

**Source:** CWCI global study, 1983

**Occupation:** Nine of every 10 rehabilitated workers are in a blue-collar occupation at the time of injury. Operatives account for only one-sixth of the permanently disabled workers but more than half of all rehabilitants. On the other hand, construction workers are underrepresented in the rehabilitant population which may be due to a combination of seniority rights, availability of alternative work and the worker's unwillingness to leave a high-paid occupation.

| | Permanently Disabled Workers | |
|---|---|---|
| **Occupation** | **% Rehabilitated** | **% Other** |
| White Collar | 10 | 21 |
| Blue Collar | 90 | 79 |
| Craftsmen | 9 | 26 |
| Operatives (non-transport) | 57 | 16 |
| Service | 11 | 11 |
| Laborers | 7 | 17 |
| Transport | 6 | 9 |

**Source:** CWCI global study, 1983

**Injury:** Every third rehabilitant has a back injury, about equal to the proportion of back injured employees in the disabled work force. However, injuries to the upper extremities, which account for 20 percent of all disabilities, produce nearly half again as many vocational rehabilitation claims.

Few of the injuries requiring rehabilitation services are catastrophic. Severe burns, amputations, and spinal cord and crushing injuries are relatively uncommon in industry and, consequently, relatively uncommon in the rehabilitant population. Instead, most of the rehabilitation activity centers on workers who suffer fractures or, in fully half the cases, soft tissue injuries (sprain, strain, torn muscle, etc.).

**Severity:** Expectedly, the need for rehabilitation services increases with the severity of the worker's residual permanent disability. However, the worker's decision to participate in vocational rehabilitation correlates inversely to injury severity. In other words, the percentage of eligible workers accepting the benefit **diminishes** as severity increases, with the highest acceptance among workers with comparatively minor permanent disabilities, i.e., those rated 10 percent or less.

| **% of Permanent Disability** | **% Rehab Eligible** | **% Accepting Rehab** |
|---|---|---|
| Under 10 | 13 | 86 |
| 11-24 | 25 | 63 |
| 25-49 | 36 | 72 |
| 50-69 | 52 | 61 |
| 70 and over | 71 | 50 |

**Source:** CWCI global study, 1983

Part of the explanation for the apparent incongruity lies in the fact that machine operatives dominate the lower permanent disability categories -- and a "minor" injury to the hand or arm is more disabling to an operative on a manufacturing line than to other workers. Still, the data suggest there may be other factors, operating independently of the injury's severity, that contribute to the worker's decision to undertake a vocational rehabilitation program.

**Perceptions:** One of those contributing factors may be attitudinal. Workers who viewed their injury as "very serious" -- a population that includes most of those whose permanent disability rated 10 percent or less -- were 60 percent more likely to be eligible for vocational rehabilitation services and even more willing to accept the benefit. The issue is not the objective measurement of the injury's severity, which presumes some disabilities are minor (except, of course, to the individual worker). Rather, it is the individual's perception of the injury's severity that may be controlling.

Workers who are "very dissatisfied" with their preinjury earnings and employment are more than twice as likely to be represented in the rehabilitant population. Similarly, workers who rated the postinjury relationship with their employer as "excellent" are three times less likely to undertake vocational rehabilitation, possibly because formal intervention is unnecessary with an enlightened employer.

**Significant Characteristics:** Determination of an injured employee's entitlement to vocational rehabilitation is not an exact process. The fundamental test is medical: Whether the employee will be able to perform his or her usual job. But beyond this consideration are other factors -- age, education, ethnicity, occupation, unconscious or volitional responses of the employee -- that influence both the identification of the need for and the acceptance of the rehabilitation benefit. In summary, significant variables include:

| **Characteristic** | **Permanently Disabled Workers** **% Rehabilitated** | **% Other** |
|---|---|---|
| Less than high school education | 44 | 29 |
| Earnings less than state average wage | 68 | 50 |
| Non-white | 55 | 30 |
| Machine operative | 57 | 16 |
| Employed in manufacturing | 58 | 30 |
| Upper extremity injury | 29 | 20 |
| Perceived "serious" injury | 56 | 35 |
| "Very dissatisfied" with wages at time of injury | 9 | 4 |
| "Very dissatisfied" with job at time of injury | 12 | 5 |
| "Excellent" relationship with employer after injury | 9 | 30 |

**Source:** CWCI global study, 1983

These characteristics are not absolute and, accordingly, cannot be used as predictors of potential rehabilitation activity with any degree of accuracy. Nevertheless, these factors provide insight to rehabilitation counselors in designing and providing services and to claims technicians in managing the delivery of vocational rehabilitation benefits.

## Costs and Results

Probably the most controversial aspect of vocational rehabilitation in California is its cost, an ever-increasing expense that has shown no abatement in the nine-year history of the benefit. Between 1978-80 the average rehabilitation expenditure on claim files closed during that period increased 42 percent ($2,327 vs. $3,303). If the cost comparison is confined to claims where the injured employee participated in a specific return-to-work plan, i.e., excluding expenditures for workers who did not qualify, lost interest or refused the benefit, the increase is even more striking.

| **Rehab Component** | **1978** | **1980** | **% Change** |
|---|---|---|---|
| Maintenance allowance | $2,168 | $3,545 | +64 |
| Evaluation, testing, etc. | 1,190 | 2,280 | +92 |
| Training, retraining | 860 | 1,102 | +28 |
| Total | $4,218 | $6,927 | +64 |

**Source:** CWCI cost studies, 1978 and 1980

More recent cost figures are not available, but educated estimates based on sampling project the average expense of rehabilitation plans completed in 1982 at the $11,000 level, and rising to more than $13,000 in 1983.

The same pattern also shows in the experience of the Workers' Compensation Insurance Rating Bureau, the insurance industry's statistical agency in California. With the introduction of mandatory vocational rehabilitation in 1975, the rating bureau calculated the new benefit would increase employer's costs an average of 2.7 percent. The actual costs, even in the start-up years, turned out to be somewhat more -- 2.8 percent of total incurred losses in 1975, 3.7 percent in 1976 -- and signalled the start of an escalation that continues to the present. The number of claims requiring rehabilitation involvement and resulting expenses increased consistently in subsequent years and though final figures are not complete, projections place costs at 7 percent of total incurred losses in 1982 -- upwards of $130 million -- with an expected rise to 10 percent in the near future.

Rehabilitation costs are a function of two interrelated factors: The duration of services and the type of return-to-work plan. A detailed study in 1980 found rehabilitation programs averaged 24 weeks in length, ranging from under 100 days for modified or alternate work plans to 226 days for formal schooling. Thus modified or alternate work programs were the least expensive -- less than half the average cost of all rehabilitation plans -- while formal schooling regimens were the most expensive, nearly half again the overall average.

Costs and success rates generally are inversely proportional, with the least expensive plans offering the greatest opportunity to return the worker to gainful employment. For example, 85 percent of the workers who complete modified or alternative work programs, which capitalize on the employee's transferable skills, in fact return to work. By comparison, only 52 percent of workers who participate in formal schooling programs find suitable work after completion.

The message in these findings seems apparent: Make as few changes as possible in the disabled employee's life. Modified or alternative work -- a substantially similar job in a substantially similar workplace, frequently with substantially similar co-workers -- provides the best chance for successful rehabilitation. Other, more complex training cannot match the cost-effectiveness of short-term rehabilitation programs that minimize the upheaval in the worker's environment. In contrast, formal schooling programs are the longest, most expensive and least successful.

Promptness (or the lack thereof) in the delivery of vocational rehabilitation benefits also impacts costs. The rehabilitation community consistently has advocated early identification of potential candidates, early referral, timely intervention and prompt implementation of return-to-work activities. These concepts are generally accepted verities, and the results of Institute research quantify their effect.

| **Time-lapse from commencement of services to program implementation** | **Avg. Plan Cost** |
|---|---|
| 90 days or less | $5,186 |
| 91-180 days | 6,092 |
| 6-12 months | 8,723 |
| 12-18 months | 9,178 |
| Over 18 months | 9,735 |

**Source:** CWCI cost study, 1980

Even more significantly, the prompt provision of services also enhances program completion and postrehabilitation employment.

More than half of all rehabilitated workers return to work at earnings equal to or greater than their preinjury wages.

| **Post-rehab Earnings** | **% Rehabilitated Workers** |
|---|---|
| Lower than at injury | 46 |
| Same as at injury | 9 |
| Higher than at injury | 45 |

**Source:** CWCI cost study, 1980

During 1980 the average preinjury weekly wage of rehabilitated workers was $259. Upon return to the work force these workers earned an average of $247 per week, or 95 percent of average preinjury wages. The real wage loss is understated, because it does not take into account wage increases that might have occurred had the employee not been injured. Moreover, other data indicates rehabilitated workers will not benefit from future wage escalation to the same degree as noninjured workers. Still, the record provides a tangible measurement of the results of vocational rehabilitation in the Worker's Compensation mode.

## Current and Future Issues

The results of mandatory vocational rehabilitation in California are both positive and promising, although considerable problems remain. The obstacles -- some inherent, others external -- run counter to the return-to-work objectives of Workers' Compensation and hinder the efficient, economic delivery of rehabilitation services to disabled workers.

**Benefit Duplication:** One of the major issues is the conflict between vocational rehabilitation and permanent disability benefits. On the one hand, California law requires an employer to restore the employability of a disabled worker. But other provisions require the employer to compensate the employee's reduced ability to compete in the open labor market -- the very condition the employer is obliged to correct in the first instance.

The California permanent disability benefit is structured on the theory that an injured worker with a given disability, age and occupation will need a specific number of weeks to adjust to the disability. Accordingly, the percentage of permanent disability translates into a period of weeks during which indemnity payments will be made, ostensibly to assist the employee's adjustment.

The concept -- euphemistically labeled the "rehabilitation theory" by the founding architects of the California system -- may have had some practical meaning when workers used the weekly payments for support while undertaking a formal or informal program of adjustment to their disability. Today, however, the vast majority of permanent disability claims, upwards of 80 percent, are paid in a lump sum -- much like damages. The prevalence of this practice raises grave questions about the efficacy of a system that permits cashing what was intended to be a rehabilitation benefit and, at the same time, imposing a redundant collateral responsibility on the employer.

**Delays:** The research literature and Institute studies establish the cost-effectiveness of early rehabilitation intervention, a goal frequently unmet in California. Some of the delays result from the permanent disability benefit structure and the rules of the litigation game that encourage the worker to preserve and maximize disability. Although the injured employee's entitlement to other compensation benefits are not affected by acceptance or rejection of vocational rehabilitation, many qualified workers elect to postpone rehabilitation activity until the dollar value of their claim is determined, a variation, perhaps, of the bird-in-the-hand metaphor.

Other delays occur in the process itself. Vocational rehabilitation is not an exact science, and trial-and-error is necessary in evaluating, testing, motivating and counseling severely injured workers; it is, in short, an intensely personal service that does not lend itself to a singular approach. Moreover, because successful rehabilitation is a cooperative venture, the injured worker's misunderstanding and misapprehensions must be allayed, processes which require additional investments of time. Conferences and documentation requirements of the state agency also slow the process.

Prompt initiation of rehabilitation services is dependent upon prompt identification of potential candidates. Nothing can happen until the need is known, and the record suggests the recognition of need by employers and insurers requires improvement. According to a 1983 Institue study, half of the potential rehabilitation cases reported to the state agency for monitoring are submitted late, on the average nearly 10 months after the disabling injury. While there may be justifiable reasons for delayed identification in individual cases -- the employee's fracture may still be casted, for example, or the compensability of the underlying injury is disputed -- the overall picture is distressing. The direct expense of late reporting can be quantified, as employers and insurers must pay the rehabilitation maintenance allowance retroactive to the time the report should have been submitted. The effect of late identification on the potential rehabilitant and the ultimate success of the rehabilitation program is clear -- and even more troubling.

**Attorney Involvement:** Most rehabilitation candidates -- 9 of 10 -- are represented by attorneys. The representation usually involves the permanent disability aspects of the claim, principally the amount of indemnity, and few attorneys were active in rehabilitation matters in the early years after the benefit was enacted. However, a recent decision of the Workers' Compensation Appeals Board, the state adjudicatory body, permits the workers' attorney a separate, additional fee for services in connection with vocational rehabilitation. Today attorney involvement in rehabilitation is commonplace.

This development may be the legacy of the legalistic orientation of the state Workers' Compensation agency, an orientation carried over to the procedures and administrative regulations of the Rehabilitation Bureau. Many proceedings are quasi-judicial in nature. Bureau consultants issue "Notices of Intent" and "Decisions & Orders" with "service upon all parties." Notices advising injured workers of their possible right to rehabilitation benefits encourage the employee to "contact your attorney." Other requirements are complex and convoluted -- and with confusion and uncertainty, the need for legal interpretation increases.

The residuals of this focus are now apparent. The incidence of appeals of Rehabilitation Bureau decisions has increased three-fold in the past three years. The body of decisional law on vocational rehabilitation in Workers' Compensation today exceeds 100 cases, up from 58 cases two years ago. Many of the decisions are necessary and welcome, given the vagueness of the enabling statute, but the trend is obvious. Increasingly, the vocational rehabilitation benefit is being administered by lawyers -- a far cry from the precepts underlying both rehabilitation and Workers' Compensation.

## Outlook

After nine years of development, vocational rehabilitation in the Workers' Compensation mode in California is still in its childhood. Some of the growing pains are subsiding, but adolescent problems emerge with each new court decision, each legislative session, each budgeting cycle. Few will argue that the program's ultimate dimensions and direction will be shaped in the next ten years.

The issue is not whether vocational rehabilitation is working. It is. Rather, the challenge is to undertake a series of design changes to make the program more effective and efficient. The improvements -- simple in concept but no less difficult because they require legislative action -- should include:

* A more explicit enabling statute. Lack of specificity in the existing law has led to confusion, uncertainty, misunderstanding and, inevitably, controversy that affect both program operation and outcome. The courts in adjudicating the controversies have shown a consistent ignorance of the return-to-work objectives of vocational rehabilitation and Workers' Compensation and, instead, substituted a doctrine of entitlement that encourages additional litigation. Statutory provisions that clearly define the rights, benefits and responsibilities of the employee and employer will narrow the opportunities for disputes and minimize judicial interpretation -- or misinterpretation.
* An active, adequately funded state agency. As originally conceived, benefit delivery in Workers' Compensation was expected to be self-administering, i.e., the elimination of fault and statutorily prescribed benefits would protect the injured employee without external assistance. If that hope proved naive and illusory for Workers' Compensation, it is doubly true for vocational rehabilitation. The scope of the benefit, its personal nature and the complex interaction with other benefits requires the state agency to take the initiative in providing meaningful assistance and creating an ambience of protection and mediation. Anything less exacts an immeasurable cost in interference with or delay in the vocational rehabilitation of injured workers. Affirmative management of the program will take financial support, professionalism, commitment and the willingness of the participants to accept a higher degree of supervision. Today these elements are largely lacking.
* Introduction of incentives. The employer's vocational rehabilitation responsibility is dictated by statute which, commbined with the concurrent and concomitant liability for permanent disability indemnity, sometimes

> produces a grudging response. On the other hand, the employee's participation is self-determined, and the acceptance or rejection of rehabilitation services may be motivated by short-term consequences. The solution lies in devising a program that encourages the willing participation of both employee and employer.

There are no quick and easy answers in this area. The predecessor statute authorized "voluntary" vocational rehabilitation, i.e., only upon agreement of the employee and employer, in which case the amount of the employee's permanent disability indemnity was calculated after rehabilitation, invariably a lower amount. What was intended to be an employer incentive became a disincentive for the employee, and little activity resulted during the 10-year life of the voluntary vocational rehabilitation provision. The mandatory statute is a step forward, but its optimal effectiveness suffers from a design flaw that fails to recognize and reward the self-interest of the principals.

All of these deficits have a common heritage: The enactment of an adjunct to an existing body of law without regard to the interrelationship of the parts to the whole. The laws of physics apply to other than mass and matter; changes in one component of a system produce consequences in other components, usually with unintended results. Systems analysts term the effect "suboptimization," a phenomenon in which the functional elements operate at cross-purposes to the overall objectives of the structure. It is an analogy that fits the vocational rehabilitation component of Workers' Compensation in California.

Real improvement will be realized only after acknowledgment of the interdependence of vocational rehabilitation to other parts of the benefit structure, to state administration, and to the benefit delivery process itself. Clearly, the need is for integrated, comprehensive change. Any other solution is palliative, not progress.

### Technical Notes

Information contained in this **Report to the Industry** in part is drawn from records of the Rehabilitation Bureau, Division of Industrial Accidents, and from reports of job injuries or illnesses filed with the Division of Labor Statistics & Research pursuant to California law. Both agencies are divisions of the California Department of Industrial Relations.

Other data are based on results of research studies conducted by the Institute. These sources include:

* Two cost studies of 25 percent of case files closed by the Rehabilitation Bureau during March-April 1978 and June-July 1980.
* A 1982-83 research study to determine the economic consequences of industrial injury. The data for this study are based on file review and structured interviews with a sample of 1076 workers whose 1976 injuries produced permanent disability.
* A survey to measure and evaluate timeliness in the reporting of identified candidates for vocational rehabilitation services; based upon an analysis of every fourth "Report of Disability Status" (Form RB-1) filed by insurers and self-insured employers during January-February 1983.

Further information may be obtained from the California Workers' Compensation Institute, 120 Montgomery, Suite 715, San Francisco, CA 94104

# CHAPTER 31

## Economic Consequences of Job Injury
## A Report to the Industry

Effective management of Workers' Compensation claims includes a continuous monitoring of the injured worker's progress -- from injury through medical treatment, rehabilitation and return to employment. However, little is known about the ultimate effects of job injury, much less the long-range economic impact of disability.

This report summarizes results of research to determine and measure the economic consequences of job injury and offers a basis to evaluate the adequacy and equity of the California program's response to the financial hardships that result from residual permanent disability.

California Workers'
Compensation Institute
December 1984

### Summary

Workers' Compensation is the oldest form of social insurance in the United States, the first to provide economic security to working men and women. In the event of a job injury, an employee is entitled to all necessary medical care, without deductible, coinsurance or other contribution. If the injury results in disability, the employee receives partial but tax-free replacement of lost wages at the employer's expense. Other employer-paid benefits -- vocational rehabilitation and reemployment services, payments to surviving dependents in the event of death -- complete the income protection objective.

By any measure California's Workers' Compensation program is the largest in the United States and exceeds the scope of parallel programs in most foreign countries. As a mechanism for delivering medical benefits, it has few challengers for effectiveness and efficiency. California's leadership in the rehabilitation of injured workers is established and accepted. But the record in income protection, particularly for permanently disabled employees, is less glowing and raises serious questions about the adequacy and equity of the California Workers' Compensation system. Consider:

* Income benefits replace less than 50 percent of earnings lost because of a job injury, substantially beneath the two-thirds wage replacement promised by the statute.
* On average, a permanently disabled worker's uncompensated earnings loss will total $18,000 over the working lifetime.
* Some workers fare better, others fare worse. Income benefits paid to younger workers who are permanently disabled replace 135 percent of lost earnings, more than double the two-thirds goal established by law and three times the replacement rate of workers in the 25-50 age group.
* Similarly, income benefits for very minor disabilities restore 88 percent of postinjury earnings loss, compared to only 32 percent replacement for the severely disabled.

The income protection imbalance in California's Workers' Compensation program affects all injured employees to a greater or lesser degree, but the heaviest impact falls upon those with residual impairments, particularly the seriously disabled worker. The Institute's research examines this population in detail and provides baseline information about their characteristics, the nature of their disabilities, and their postinjury participation in the labor force.

The study confirms the conclusions of many observers: That income benefits provided by the California law are both inadequate and inequitable.

## Framing the Issues

Workers' Compensation laws originated as a modern society's response to the accidents that were a natural outgrowth of the Industrial Revolution. Occupational injuries in the early 1900's were a fertile source of litigation, resulting in delays, uncertainty and red tape. An employee injured on the job had to prove the employer was at fault to collect medical expenses and lost wages. The employee's reluctance to jeopardize his job by bringing suit against the employer, in combination with the employer's formidable legal defenses, imposed a near-impossible burden upon the injured worker and his family.

The enactment of Workers' Compensation laws came after reciprocal concessions by employees and employers. In exchange for prompt, certain benefits, paid automatically regardless of fault, workers relinquished their right to sue in tort. Employers agreed to accept the financial responsibility for all workplace injuries, thereby permitting them to limit and budget their liability for workplace accidents. The legislative compromises were aimed at correcting an economic condition, not to curing a legal wrong.

Today Workers' Compensation is an integral part of a social insurance package that seeks to assure economic security to workers. Social Security and pension programs, both private and public, assume the task of handling old age retirement and survivorship. The state/federal unemployment compensation system addresses economy-related earnings loss. And Workers' Compensation affords protection against hardships that result from earnings loss caused by job injury.

The original Workers' Compensation laws explicitly recognized the income protection principle. All of the pioneering European systems -- and 10 of the first 11 U.S. acts, including California's -- emphasized earnings loss as the sole basis for indemnity. In the event of a job-related disability, the worker would receive a specified percentage of his preinjury wage.

The shift away from replacement of actual lost earnings began with the enactment of the 1911 New Jersey law which introduced a "schedule" of benefits for permanently (as opposed to temporarily) disabled workers. Under this schedule approach, the loss, or loss of use, of a bodily member became a proxy for future lost earnings; compensation then is paid for a certain period of weeks (or up to a maximum dollar amount), regardless of actual economic consequences.

The introduction of schedules in compensation acts originated largely as an administrative convenience. The economic aftermath of a residual permanent impairment often extends over an employee's working life, but Workers' Compensation administrators were unwilling to wait a lifetime to determine and compensate actual earnings loss as it occurred. Early resolution and prompt benefit payments, even for long-term disabilities, required a different approach. This perceived administrative need led to the development of schedules that allowed a specific dollar amount for equally specific residual impairments of an injury. To preserve the income protection theory, however, the drafters rationalized that the scheduled amount was not payment for physical loss but, instead, an estimate of future earnings loss that might result from the physical injury. Today, scheduled benefits are the predominant method for compensating permanent disability in the United States.

In concept, scheduled benefits for permanent disability work some rough justice. In practice, however, the conceptual purpose frequently is unmet. Disability schedules presume a direct link between physical impairment and future earnings in every instance, an assumption that ignores reality. For example, the adverse economic consequences of some injuries may continue long after the scheduled payments have been paid and spent. On the other hand, scheduled amounts may be paid even when there is no earnings loss, in which case the award resembles installment payment of damages, a concept alien to America's premier no-fault insurance program. Between these extremes are varying examples of over- and under-compensation for job-incurred disability.

As a mechanism for compensating the long-term impact of a job injury, a disability schedule inevitably creates equity problems. A schedule emphasizes certainty of result at the expense of individual differences. The historical California response to this conflict was adoption of a less rigid schedule that, at least in theory, attempts to predict the economic consequences of a physical impairment by permitting variations in the individual case. Some of the variables are objective, taking into account the age and occupation of the injured worker. But modifications also are permitted for purely subjective factors, e.g., pain and estimates of the worker's ability to bend, stoop, lift and perform the other physical requirements of working for a living. Most usually, the determination of these subjective factors are based on the worker's own description.

If the variables are objective, results can be predictable. But recognition of and allowance for subjective factors, which cannot be substantiated much less quantified, introduces uncertainty -- and where uncertainty exists, litigation follows. Today in California three of every four permanent disability claims are litigated. The predominant issue in the vast majority of these claims is not the existence but, instead, the

**extent** of permanent disability, a determination that encourages the involvement of attorneys and forensic medical testimony so that the "right words" will be used.

Dissatisfaction with the use of a schedule for predicting and compensating the long-term economic effects of job injury has increased in recent years. Moreover, both the adequacy and equity of benefits allowed by the schedule have been criticized repeatedly by employees, employers, administrators and legislators.

While the discontent is real, its roots are based on conjecture since hard data did not exist. Three years ago the California Workers' Compensation Institute authorized a research study to fill the vacuum. This report summarizes the findings and conclusions of that research and provides an objective basis for evaluating the performance of the California Workers' Compensation system in alleviating the economic hardships of industrial injuries.

## Job Injury and Earnings Loss

Despite seven decades of experience, relatively little is known about the economic consequences of job injury, much less how well Workers' Compensation responds to these consequences. State administrative agencies and the insurance industry are repositories of abundant statistics, although most of the figures -- nature and type of injuries, incidence rates, claim costs, etc. -- are only pertinent to operational aspects of the program. With few exceptions, little is known about what happens to the injured worker after the claim file is closed.

Three years ago, after nearly a year in development and design, the Institute commissioned a research project to determine the scope of postinjury earnings loss and to test the effectiveness of the California Permanent Disability Schedule in providing income protection after a job injury.

(While measurement of earnings loss attributable to job injury was the primary purpose of the study, these were other complementary objectives. These goals included determining the extent to which other public and private programs duplicate or supplement Workers' Compensation as an economic remedy, the causes and results of litigation, and the effectiveness of vocational rehabilitation in restoring disabled workers to productive employment -- issues which are or will be the subject of other CWCI reports. Because of the multiple objectives, the research project was labeled the "global study.")

The study relied upon two related data bases: (1) Responses to structured, personal interviews with a representative sample of California workers whose job injuries produced residual permanent impairments; and (2) Individual earnings records of the disabled worker sample as reported to the State Employment Development Department.

The latter data alone quantifies the extent and duration of gross earnings loss which occurs after injury. However, some portion of the loss may be due to factors unrelated to the injury -- retirement, voluntary withdrawal from the labor market, subsequent nonindustrial injury or illness, economic unemployment -- as related by the workers themselves during interviews. Only by melding the two data bases is it possible to respond to the study's two central questions:

* How much of the subsequent earnings loss is attributable to the injury?
* How well does the California system compensate injury-related earnings loss?

The research answers these questions in detail. Additionally, the data provide baseline information about the economic consequences to those who suffer job injury, while defining policy issues that must be addressed if the California Workers' Compensation law is to achieve the adequacy and equity promised by its enactment 70 years ago.

## Postinjury Earnings

In the four years following injury, a period during which earnings patterns stabilized for those who returned to the work force, permanently disabled workers sustain an average $17,800 earnings loss. Assuming the same degree of earnings loss continues to age 65, as it will for the severely disabled, then the average earnings loss over a working lifetime increases to $115,000.

Aside from the limitations of averages, these estimates of gross postinjury earnings loss suffer other inadequacies:

* In the first instance, the figures are overstated to an unknown degree because they are derived from wages reported to the State Employment Development Department. Not included are earnings from the so-called

"underground economy," i.e., cash payments made to some workers -- most frequently in the construction, transportation and service industries -- and which may not be reported for payroll and tax purposes.

* On the other hand, the figures are understated because they do not reflect wage increases that might have occurred but for the injury. While it is possible to estimate the potential effect of wage escalation, income benefits of the California law are based on earnings and benefit levels in effect at the time of the injury and, accordingly, no adjustment was made.
* More pertinently, the figures do not take into account the reasons for changes in earnings. The estimates are only measurements of gross postinjury earnings loss, **not** earnings loss attributable to the injury.

**"Peeling the Onion":** Nearly 60 percent of the gross postinjury earnings loss is experienced by workers whose permanent disabilities generally are not considered handicaps to employment or wage-earning ability. In some instances the earnings loss is attributable to the job injury, but much of it can be traced to other causes, according to the workers themselves. Thus, the gross postinjury earnings losses were offset by the amount of wage reductions due to noninjury factors, a process the analysts labeled "peeling the onion" -- stripping away the outer layers to arrive at estimates of net injury-related earnings loss.

Some of the reductions are based on the employee's own statements during structured interviews (e.g., "reached retirement age," "only wanted part-time work," "quit to be with family" and other examples of voluntary withdrawal from the labor market). Excluded also were earnings losses incurred after normal retirement at age 65; during periods of self-reported major illnesses that were unrelated to the job injury; and while receiving unemployment insurance benefits, when the employee was available and able to work -- earnings losses that would have occurred even if the worker had not been injured.

Other reductions, most usually made when the postinjury earnings pattern was inconsistent with the nature of the injury, were arrived at more subjectively. For example, the analysts concluded that an 18-year-old service station attendant's total absence of earnings except during the summer months probably was due to enrollment in college, not the minor injury he suffered four years earlier. Similarly, the earnings loss experienced by a 24-year-old female office worker after returning to work for two years at wages above her preinjury wages was ascribed to marriage or pregnancy.

Two other adjustments were made. Earnings loss that occurred after the employee's treating physician provided an unrestricted medical release to return to regular employment was eliminated as unrelated to the injury. Finally, if the employee returned to work and the earnings equalled or exceeded preinjury wages for three consecutive months, recovery was presumed to be complete and any subsequent earnings loss due to factors other than the injury.

The adjusting criteria assume that, after controlling for noninjury factors, earnings loss is a function of injury severity. In other words, the more severe the resulting disability, the greater the potential for earnings loss. If the criteria were valid, seriously disabled workers would be least affected by the application of the adjustments. For example, the most severely disabled workers would not have retired voluntarily, would not be eligible for unemployment compensation and would not be able medically to return to their former jobs; therefore, the difference between gross and net earnings loss would be least for these workers and greatest for those with minor disabilities. A series of comparisons validated this hypothesis and established the appropriateness of the criteria.

## Gross vs. Net Earnings Loss, by PDR

After adjustment for reasons unrelated to the injury, the net earnings loss in the four years after injury is reduced by 55 percent, to an average of $8,080 per worker. The projected earnings loss over the working life of these employees drops even more, 85 percent, to $17,700. With few exceptions, the gross vs. net differences are because of noninjury-related earnings losses of younger workers with minor disabilities.

## Adequacy & Equity

A comparison of net earning loss to disability payments shows the California program is neither adequate nor equitable. On the average, Workers' Compensation income benefits (for both temporary and permanent disability) replace only 49 percent of the net earnings lost by permanently disabled workers over their working life.

### Replacement Rate, by PDR

Moreover, replacement rates vary widely according to injury severity and the age of the worker. Workers with very minor disabilities, those rated under 10 percent on the California schedule, fare best, exceeding the two-thirds wage replacement intended by the Workers' Compensation law by a wide margin. Other disabled employees are less fortunate, however, and the degree of their economic misfortune progresses with the severity of their injuries. The exception is the permanently and totally disabled worker whose compensation approaches the program's wage replacement goal -- but then such workers are compensated, not according to the schedule, but by two-thirds of their average preinjury wages for life.

Compensation for younger workers exceeds their actual earnings loss due to work injury and, on the average, more than double the intended two-thirds replacement rate. Workers between 25 and 50 years, the majority of disabled workers, fare worse than their younger and older counterparts. With fewer years to retirement, workers in the oldest category suffer less earnings loss than the mid-group, but they recover proportionately more because the California schedule contains an upward adjustment for age.

### Replacement Rate, by Age

The limitations of the California permanent disability schedule, and the dimensions of the resulting inadequacy and inequity, are demonstrated in a matrix that combines severity and age in calculating the percentage of earnings loss replaced by income benefits.

### Replacement Rate, by PDR & Age

If two-thirds wage-replacement is the goal, younger workers are over-compensated. Older permanently injured employees, most notably those 25 to 50 years who dominate the work force, are severely undercompensated. Regardless of age, workers with the least disability are compensated best and, with the exception of permanently and totally disabled workers whose compensation is not predicated on the schedule, the percentage of earnings loss replaced declines with severity -- the wrong movement in the wrong direction affecting the wrong population.

The deficiencies of the California schedule as a mechanism for compensating permanent disability are manifest. The system may have been adequate and equitable when adopted 70 years ago; clearly, it is no longer. Today Workers' Compensation indemnity benefits in California bear no relationship to economic loss, and replacement of earnings loss due to the injury is not accomplished in any rational manner.

## Righting the Balance

Over the past 70 years the California Workers' Compensation program has earned deservedly high marks for its progressive features: scope and extent of coverage, expeditious delivery of virtually unlimited medical services, and the provision of vocational rehabilitation services. On the other hand, California's position in income protection for injured workers lags badly. For many years benefit levels have ranked well below the national median -- and usually at the bottom of a listing of comparable industrial states. Additionally, the Institute's research shows the distribution of income benefits lacks consistency and certainty in alleviating the financial consequences of industrial injury.

Correcting the deficiencies of income benefits could take a number of paths. The first and most obvious choice would be an increase in indemnity benefits. This approach has the virtue of simplicity, but its effectiveness is questionable if past performance is instructive. For example, during 1983-84 the state legislature doubled partial disability indemnity and increased benefit levels for total disability by 28 percent. Yet, even after the infusion of nearly $1 billion in additional benefits, the overall replacement rate -- the proportion of earnings loss replaced by income benefits -- dropped to 47 percent from the previous 49 percent.

### Replacement Rates
### Effect of 1983-84 Benefit Increase

Greater equity could be achieved through reallocation of benefit dollars and balancing over- and under-compensation among the various categories of permanently disabled workers. However, this approach would require reducing benefits for some, primarily the younger, less seriously injured employee, an alternative legislators have found unattractive in the past. Additionally, unless the reallocation were accompanied by another substantial benefit increase, the overall replacement rate would still remain at 47 percent, well below the two-thirds objective.

Another option, a variation on the reallocation theme, involves changing the California Permanent Disability Schedule. Adjusting the factors used to modify the percentage of disability according to the individual worker's age and occupation could moderate the peaks and valleys present in the current distribution of income benefits, although the effect would be muted by the schedule's continued dependence upon subjective factors.

The answer, then, might be to eliminate all subjective elements from the schedule and rely solely upon objective, measurable impairments as the basis for compensating permanently disabled workers. This approach offers certainty and uniformity -- but at the loss of the ability to recognize individual circumstances. Disability is not a constant. Different workers, even those with the same impairment, will suffer differing degrees of disability, a fact the Workers' Compensation program acknowledges by individualizing income benefits. More to the point, tinkering with the California schedule leaves unanswered the question of whether any schedule, flexible or static, can ever be an accurate and reliable predictor of the economic consequences of job injury.

Selection of the precise remedy to cure the California program's inadequacies and inequities requires addressing a more fundamental policy issue: the **purpose** of income benefits in Workers' Compensation. Is it indemnity for impairment of the worker's natural capacities? A substitute for common law damages? An approximation, however inexact, of potential loss of earning capacity? Or is it, as the original architects intended, compensation for actual loss of earnings because of job injury?

The resolution of this issue is the first step to righting the balance and reconciling the objectives of a modern Workers' Compensation program with the realities of contemporary California.

## The Permanently Disabled Worker

The prototypical worker whose injury results in permanent disability is a 39-year-old, white male, blue-collar union member. At the time he strained his back, he had more than five years' experience in his occupation, more than five years' tenure with the same employer, and earned $12,300 annually, about 8 percent more than others in the general work force because of experience and seniority. He was unable to work for 24 weeks because of his injury but returned full-time at the same or higher wages for the same employer. Compared to noninjured members of the labor force, the permanently disabled worker is older by nearly 10 years and, in part because of the age difference, is more experienced, less educated, and more likely to be married.

Averages, however, obscure the numerous variables within the permanently disabled population. Sex is a significant factor in differentiating earnings. For example, more than one-quarter of the workers are females, a group whose median annual earnings are substantially below males ($8,062 vs. $12,333). Only 2 percent of the male employees were working part-time when the injury occurred, compared to 14 percent of the women, findings which together with somewhat less job experience for women accounts for some -- though not all -- of the disparity in earnings.

## Annual Income at Injury

Occupation also is a factor in earnings. About half of the women are in white-collar jobs, particularly business services and retail trade. In contrast, nine of 10 males are blue-collar workers, for the most part in the manufacturing, construction and transportation industries.

Age patterns are similar for workers of both sexes (although females on the average are two years older), but women have higher education levels.

## Education Completed

More than one-third of the male workers did not complete high school, a finding that appears to conflict with California's mandatory education requirement. However, the fact that one in eight of the male workers do not speak English and the likelihood that they are twice as likely as females to be of Hispanic or Asian origin suggests that immigration may be a contributing factor to the comparatively low educational attainment of permanently disabled men.

### Ethnicity

**Nature of Injury:** Back injuries, either alone or in combination with other injuries, account for nearly half of all permanent disabilities. Impairments to upper and lower extremities each affect about a third of the disabled population. One in five disabled workers suffered an injury to the head or neck.

### Nature of Injury (multiple responses)

Soft tissue injuries -- strains, sprains, and muscle, ligament or tendon tears -- are the principal cause of disability in more than half of the cases. Fractures and crushing injuries are next in importance, accounting for every third permanent impairment, followed by cuts and lacerations (8 percent) and amputations (6 percent). No other injury type accounted for as much as 1 percent of the total.

Only 1 percent of the injuries are catastrophic. The vast majority, seven of every 10, are so-called "minor" disabilities, i.e., those rated less than 25 percent under the California schedule.

### Disability Severity

**Postinjury Employment:** A substantial majority of permanently disabled workers return to work after their injuries, and most are currently employed. However, 16 percent of those who are permanently injured -- every sixth worker -- never returns to employment after the job injury.

**Severity of Injury and Postinjury Status**

The severity of the injury -- measured either as the percentage of permanent disability or the length of convalescence (i.e., the duration of temporary disability) -- is the primary reason for leaving the work force. However, half of those who never return to work have "minor" disabilities, an indication that factors other than the injury -- or, more correctly perhaps, factors in addition to the injury -- may have contributed to their withdrawal from the labor market.

Workers who never return to the work force after the job injury are, on the average, 12 years older than their working counterparts and are more likely to be female, working part-time, and in white-collar occupations.

Of those workers who return to work after the injury, 85 percent go back to full-time employment. Another 7 percent start on a part-time basis but subsequently return to full-time employment. The remaining 8 percent continue in part-time work, either because of limitations imposed by the injury or by choice.

Most permanently disabled workers who return to work go back to the same job with the same employer, but a significant minority experience some displacement. Nearly three in ten return to work for a different employer, and 19 percent return to both a different employer and a different type of work. The injury and resulting disability are major factors in many of the job changes, but almost as important are dissatisfaction with the prior job or employer, lack of job openings because of the general economy, and "changing employers is common in my line of work."

Upon returning to full-time work, 86 percent of the disabled workers earn the same or more than before their injury. For the most part, the adverse impact falls upon workers who change employers, type of work, or both. However, for every worker in these circumstances who earns less, another earns more than before the injury.

Six years after the injury another 18 percent of the permanently disabled population leave the work force (compared to a 12 percent withdrawal rate among a matched sample of noninjured workers). Thus, 34 percent of workers permanently injured in a job accident -- 16 percent who never returned to work after the injury, plus 18 percent who went back to work for a time but now describe themselves as "unemployed and not looking for work" -- are out of the labor market six years after the job injury.

## Employment Status (Six Years Postinjury)

Severity of the disability is not a major factor among those who return to work for a time but later retire or withdraw from the job market. Various measures of severity -- permanent disability rating, duration of temporary disability, incidence of hospitalization, and mean amount of indemnity -- show no appreciable differences. Instead, the critical variables are age and sex. Workers in this group are significantly older than permanently injured employees who are working (a median age of 54 years versus 40 years). One in three are 60 years or older. In addition, women, regardless of age, are more than half again as likely to stop working at some time in the six years following their injury.

## Technical Notes

This report summarizes the results of Institute research into the experience of workers who suffered serious on-the-job injuries, which resulted either in permanent disability or, in fewer than 5 percent of the cases, a period of temporary disability lasting more than 12 weeks.

**Sample Design:** The study employed a two-stage sampling procedure. In the first stage, the Workers' Compensation Insurance Rating Bureau selected a stratified sample of 8,364 cases from a universe of 55,926 serious claims incurred under Workers' Compensation insurance policies issued in the 12-month period ending June 30, 1976. At the request of the legislature, the State Employment Development Department furnished earnings records for each of the selected workers under confidentiality requirements that protected their identity. Depending upon the date of injury, the individual earnings records ranged from one to nine calendar quarters preceding the disabling injury and 16 to 21 calendar quarters after the quarter of injury.

The original sample also included cases involving employees of self-insured employers, selected from the records of the Office of Self-Insurance Plans within the California Department of Industrial Relations. Approximately 800 claims were identified based on disabling work injuries that occurred in May and June of 1976 and which were still in "open" status on December

31, 1976. Although the proportion of self-insurer claims were under-represented -- about 10 percent, compared to a targeted 14 percent -- the analysts believe the resulting data are representative of the disabled workers' population during the study period.

In each case a survey form was sent to the insurer or self-insured employer with a request to provide the employee's last known address and other information from the claim file necessary to the study. A total of 7,081 survey forms (77 percent) were returned with sufficient qualifying information.

**Questionnaire Design:** The Institute contracted with Field Research Corporation (FRC), a San Francisco-based consulting firm with broad experience in opinion research, to conduct structured personal interviews with workers disabled during the study period. The questionnaire was developed by FRC under guidance of a research task force appointed by the Institute. The development phase spanned several months, during which research objectives were identified and refined, interview protocols established, interviewers trained and a pretest conducted. After approval of the final version of the questionnaire, a translation was produced for use with workers who preferred to be interviewed in Spanish.

A random sample was drawn from the 7,081 completed claims data forms and FRC then was provided the names and addresses of 3,374 disabled workers. To maximize the efficiency of the field effort, interviewing was restricted to workers living in the 10 Standard Metropolitan Statistical Areas of California, which collectively account for 85 percent of the state's population. After completion of prescribed tracing procedures to secure current addresses, 1,076 interviews were completed, or 32 percent of the **a priori** sample and well above the 15-20 percent completion ratio considered acceptable for opinion research.

| | | |
|---|---|---|
| Total Sample | (3374) | 100% |
| **Not Interviewed** | **432** | **13** |
| Out of state/country | 291 | 9 |
| Out of statistical area | 60 | 2 |
| Deceased | 73 | 2 |
| Language barrier, deaf | 8 | * |
| **Not Located** | 1257 | 37 |
| **Respondent Not Available** | **257** | **8** |
| Health reasons | 50 | 1 |
| Other reasons | 235 | 7 |
| **Refused** | 324 | 10 |
| **Interviewed** | 1076 | 32 |

Interviews were conducted in the homes of the workers between December 8, 1981 and March 24, 1982, and averaged approximately one hour in duration. To assure candor, all interviews were "blind", i.e., respondents were unaware the research was being conducted on behalf of the Workers' Compensation community. Instead, with the cooperation of the State Department of Rehabilitation, workers were informed the interviews were under the aegis of that agency.

Certain characteristics -- age, sex, extent of disability, attorney representation, etc. -- of the interviewed and noninterviewed workers were compared to test the representative quality of the interviewed sample. Women and workers who received vocational rehabilitation services were slightly more prevalent in the interviewed sample than were represented in the original universe. For all other variables, the distributions are consistently close and, accordingly, the differences do not require any qualification of the sample.

**Estimating Earning Loss:** An average preinjury quarterly wage for interviewed workers was calculated from data supplied by the State Employment Development Department (EDD). In each instance the amount was an arithmetic average unless earnings in the calendar quarter immediately preceding the injury quarter was greater, in which case the higher figure was used.

The average was multiplied by 16 to estimate the worker's expected earnings in the four years after injury, a period selected to reflect maximum rehabilitation of earnings potential. Gross postinjury earnings loss was arrived at by reducing the product by the amount of actual earnings reported to EDD.

The calculation of gross earnings loss did not take into account wage increases that might have occurred in the four postinjury years, nor take credit for quarterly earnings in excess of the individual worker's preinjury average -- adjustments that are estimated to approach parity.

The gross amount was reduced further by earnings losses caused by reasons other than the injury, according to the worker's own account related during interview or by other factors discussed in this chapter. Finally, the four-year net amount was projected to age 65 to produce an estimate of injury-related earnings loss occurring over the working lifetime of the permanently disabled employee.

**Acknowledgments:** The Institute gratefully acknowledges the cooperation of the Department of Industrial Relations, the Department of Rehabilitation and the Employment Development Department of the State of California, and the Workers' Compensation Insurance Rating Bureau of California.

Assistance in the preliminary analysis of the data was provided by Peter Barth, Department of Economics, University of Connecticut; and John F. Burton Jr., New York State School of Industrial & Labor Relations, Cornell University.

Special mention also is due members of the Institute's Research Task Force whose ungrudging cooperation, attention to detail and unwavering patience made the study's completion a reality. They are: Laurenfe C. Peabody, Liberty Mutual Insurance Co., chairman; Robert J. Benjamin, State Compensation Insurance Fund; George P. Janich, Fremont Indemnity Co.; Will B. Murphey, Industrial Indemnity Co.; James Smith, Fireman's Fund Insurance Cos.; Bert Zahner, Hartford Insurance Group; and James J. Holland, Travelers Insurance Co.

# CHAPTER 32

## Vocational Rehabilitation: 1985 Costs & Results
## California Workers' Compensation Institute

### Summary

With the introduction of vocational rehabilitation as a mandatory benefit under the California Workers' Compensation Act in 1975, premium rate levels were increased 2.7 percent to pay for what was then a new benefit.

Over the years actual costs have exceeded this projection -- 3.7 percent of total incurred losses in the 1976 policy year, 4.8 percent in 1978, 6.9 percent in 1980 -- with the upward spiral continuing into the present. Next year vocational rehabilitation expenditures are expected to reach 15 percent of incurred claims costs.

In the face of this cost explosion, the Institute board of directors last year authorized another vocational rehabilitation research study, the latest in a series designed to monitor the provision of rehabilitation services to injured workers, identify emerging issues and assist practitioners in the prompt and effective delivery of the benefit. (For a summary of findings from the 1978, 1980 and 1982 studies, see **A Report to the Industry: Vocational Rehabilitation**, December 1984.) The results of the 1985 research show:

**Escalating costs.** Overall, average vocational rehabilitation expense increased 284 percent since 1978, the first year CWCI measured rehabilitation costs. During the same period, the average cost of specific return-to-work programs rose 251 percent. In both instances, growth rates surpassed increases in inflation, benefit levels and total claims costs.

**Increased utilization.** Forty-five percent of claims with rehabilitation involvement result in development of a return-to-work plan, a substantial improvement from the 19 percent penetration rate in 1978.

**Successful rehabilitation inversely related to plan duration and plan cost.** Vocational rehabilitation regimens involving modified or alternative work with the same employer are the but the most successful in returning injured workers to preinjury earnings. By the same standards, formal schooling programs are the least successful and the most costly of all rehabilitation plans.

**Yet formal schooling programs continue to be the most common approach to the vocational rehabilitation of injured workers.** Nearly half (48 percent) of all rehabilitation plans involve formal schooling. Programs of modified or alternative work with the same employer, the least expensive but most successful, account for only 5 percent of all rehabilitation plans.

**Importance of timely intervention.** Delays, either in initiating or completing rehabilitation services, increase costs on an average from $76 to $726 for each month of delay.

**Benefit Cost**

The Institute cost study series measures the expense of vocational rehabilitation benefits in two ways: (1) Average rehabilitation expenditures in all claims with rehabilitation involvement, regardless of outcome; and (2) The average cost of developing and implementing specific return-to-work programs.

In both instances, costs are the sum of the maintenance allowance (paid at the same rate as temporary disability indemnity); the cost of evaluation, testing, development and implementation of a specific return-to-work plan, job placement assistance and other professional services; and the out-of-pocket expense of the rehabilitation plan, including tuition, books, transportation, tools, uniforms, additional living expense necessitated by the plan, etc.

Injured workers who may have a possible vocational impairment, i.e., unable to return to their usual occupation, are identified by the Rehabilitation Bureau of the California Division of Industrial Accidents through reports filed by insurers, self-insured employers and, in some instances, employees themselves. The creation of a file by the bureau only identifies cases to be monitored; it does not establish the need for vocational rehabilitation services.

The study shows 10 percent of the bureau files are closed without any vocational rehabilitation expenditure, most frequently because the employee is able to return to work without intervention. The current incidence of non-cost cases contrasts markedly with the 47 percent rate in 1978 and suggests the identification and monitoring mechanism is more precise and effective today.

In the remaining cases, vocational rehabilitation expenditures ranged widely, from a low of $13 to a high of $61,188. The average in all cases with rehabilitation expense was nearly $9,000, up 284 percent from the corresponding figure in 1978.

**AVERAGE COST—COST CASES ONLY**
**1978–85**

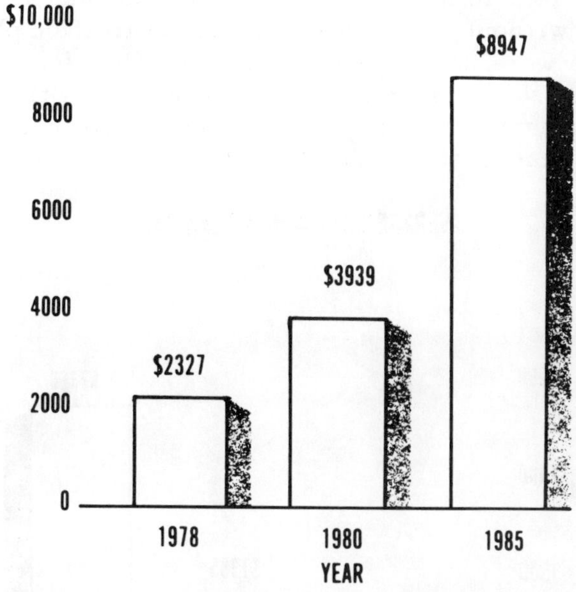


There is no single explanation for the rapid escalation. It cannot be attributed to inflationary pressures alone since the Consumer Price Index rose only 60 percent during the 1978-85 period. Nor are benefit increases solely responsible: The maximum weekly payment for temporary disability indemnity, which accounts for about half of all rehabilitation costs, increased only 45 percent during the same period. Longer duration of services and a slumping economy in the early 1980s also were contributing factors. But regardless of the reasons, over the past eight years vocational rehabilitation expense has increased nearly four times faster than the rise in total Workers' Compensation incurred losses.

**Plan vs. Non-Plan Cases:** The objective of vocational

rehabilitation is to provide the injured worker with the means to return to suitable gainful employment, usually through development of a specific return-to-work plan appropriate to the individual's abilities and interests. In the 1985 study so-called "plan cases" constitute 45 percent of the total -- a steady improvement from 19 percent in 1978 and 34 percent in 1980, a finding that indicates insurers are increasingly effective in getting qualified injured workers into the rehabilitation process. The remaining 55 percent were "nonplan cases," i.e., files closed without development of a rehabilitation plan because the workers were determined to be ineligible for the benefit, declined the services or failed to cooperate in the evaluation and developmental phase. Nonplan costs average $2,366 per case, 376 percent above the 1978 level.

**AVERAGE COST—NON-PLAN CASES**

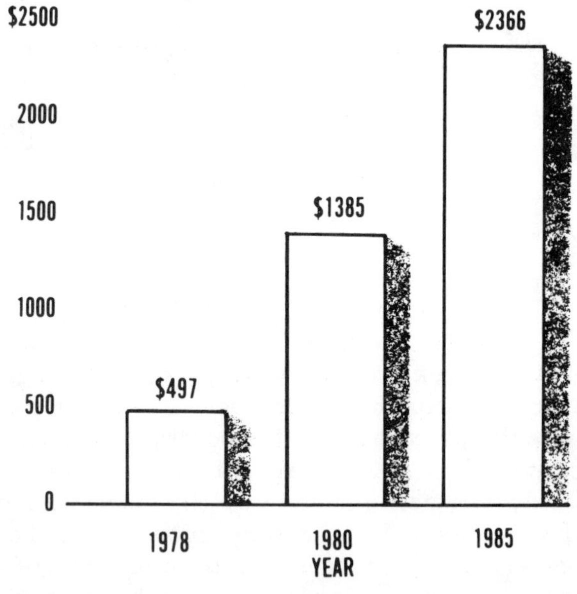


Average nonplan costs vary widely by case disposition, from $122 in claims where the injury giving rise to the need for rehabilitation was found to be nonwork-related, to upwards of $5,000 if extensive evaluation, testing and counseling is provided before services are terminated. The major cost component is the maintenance allowance (rehab TD) paid while the employee is receiving rehabilitation services.

NON-PLAN CASES—1985

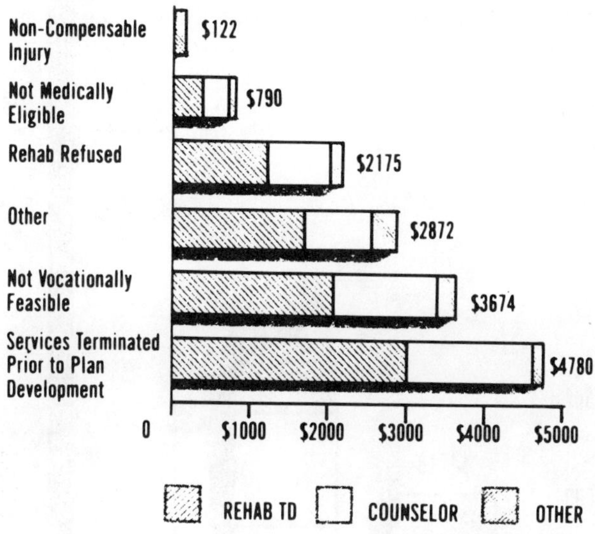


Collectively, vocational rehabilitation expenditures in nonplan cases account for 16 percent of all rehabilitation costs, a significant improvement from 33 percent in 1978. Today the major portion of the vocational rehabilitation claims dollar is being spent for rehabilitation, not ineligibility or nonparticipation determinations, but the expense of return-to-work services also shows the familiar pattern of cost increases.

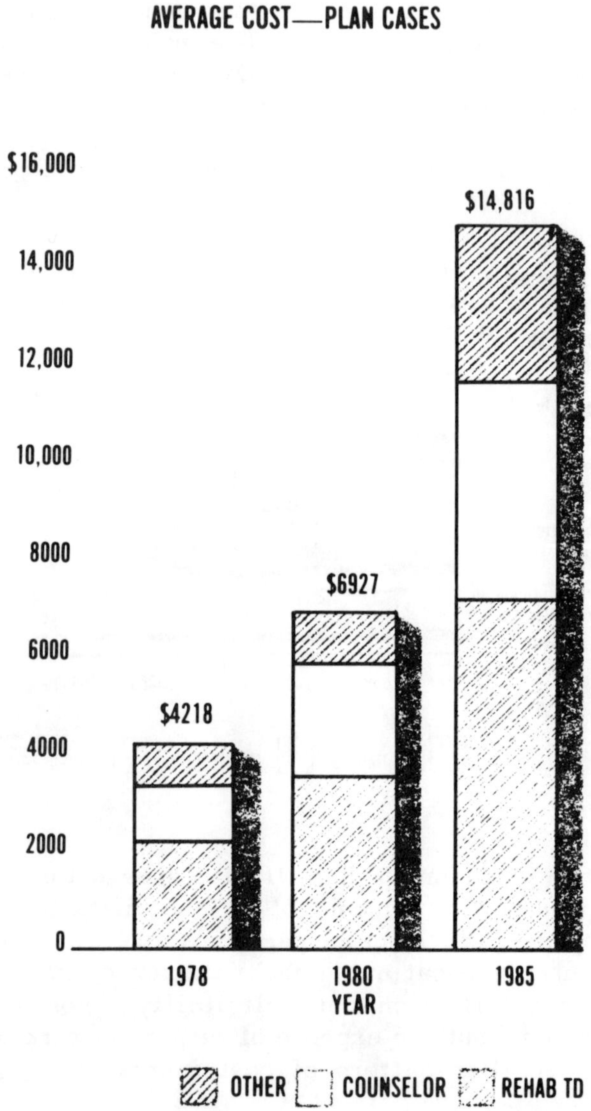


Plan cases closed in early 1985 average nearly $15,000, up 25 percent since 1978. The percentage increase, less than the corresponding figure for nonplan cases, still exceeds the growth rate of inflation, benefits and claims cost generally.

Component elements -- maintenance allowance, counselor costs and other expense -- contributed nearly proportionately to the cost increase, reflecting the effects of inflation, longer plan duration and, to a lesser extent, benefit adjustments. Over the survey periods, the weight of each cost element has shown little variation, e.g., maintenance allowance payments account for 48 percent of plan costs in 1985, down slightly from 51 percent recorded in both 1978 and 1980.

**Distributions by Plan Type:** Costs vary substantially by type of rehabilitation plan, ranging from an average of $2,081 for modified work with the same employer to $18,386 for formal schooling programs. Plan duration is the principal cost variable, and the increase in mean plan length -- 6.9 months in 1985 vs. 5.6 months five years earlier -- explains a significant portion of the cost escalation.

**AVERAGE PLAN COSTS BY PLAN TYPE**
**1985**

| Plan Type | Avg. Length of Plan (Months) | Avg. Cost Per Case |
|---|---|---|
| Modified Job, Same Employer | 5.4 | $ 2,081 |
| Alternative Work, Same Employer | 3.7 | 3,998 |
| Direct Job Placement | 4.1 | 9,698 |
| Modified Job, New Employer | 7.2 | 10,052 |
| OJT, New Employer | 5.4 | 13,382 |
| Self-Employment | 8.9 | 13,950 |
| Schooling & OJT Combination | 8.4 | 16,821 |
| Formal Schooling | 8.3 | 18,386 |

The table also illustrates an important element regarding current rehabilitation costs in California. The least expensive plans -- those involving reemployment with the same employer -- are also the least prevalent. On the other hand, the most expensive -- formal schooling -- are the most frequent.

The dominance of formal schooling plans may be influenced by several factors. First, California's economy was in deep recession in the early 1980's, when rehabilitation plans were being developed for workers in the 1985 sample, and modified and alternative work were less available (although earlier CWCI studies found similar reliance on formal schooling plans even when the economy was stronger). Second, formal training in a new field may offer the only opportunity to develop employability for injured workers with limited transferable skills, a significant segment of the rehabilitant population. Third, the employer's economic incentives to rehire an injured worker are limited and inadequate. Finally, the schooling bias may reflect the attitudes and training of some rehabilitation counselors and bureau consultants who favor certainty and structure over less formal rehabilitation activity.

Cost increases by plan type follow the familiar pattern, with the largest increment (549 percent since 1978) in the cost of direct job placement. Cost increases since 1980 range from 15 percent for alternative work with the same employer to 135 percent for on-the-job training with a new employer.

**AVERAGE PLAN COSTS**
**1978-85**

| Plan Type | 1978 | 1980 | 1985 |
|---|---|---|---|
| Modified Job, Same Employer | NA | $1744 | $2081 |
| Alternative Work, Same Employer | NA | 3477 | 3998 |
| Direct Job Placement | $1495 | 4965 | 9698 |
| Modified Job, New Employer | NA | 6675 | 10,052 |
| OJT New Employer | 3486 | 5689 | 13,382 |
| Self-Employment | 5267 | 8728 | 13,950 |
| Schooling & OJT Combination | 4603 | 8371 | 16,821 |
| Formal Schooling | 5707 | 9872 | 18,386 |

Contrary to anecdotal information, few injured workers

participate in more than one rehabilitation plan. Overall the number of plans implemented in the 1985 sample was 1.2 per worker; five individuals started three plans each and one worker started four.

**Cost Control**

Since the cost of rehabilitation plans represent the largest portion of vocational rehabilitation expenditures in California, cost control can best be approached through managing the costs of individual plans. The analysis of the 1985 study included a statistical evaluation to isolate factors that significantly contribute to total plan costs.

For example, when other variables are controlled, rehabilitation expenses will increase $9 for each $1 increase in the worker's weekly earnings over others in the sample. There's little insurers or the rehabilitation community can do to control the wage level of rehabilitation candidates, but there are other factors that can be managed. These statistically significant determinants of plan costs include:

* $75 for each additional month of delay between date of injury and the date the employee's medical condition is "permanent and stationary."
* $76 for each additional month from P&S date to date of referral for vocational rehabilitation services.
* $369 for each additional month between date of referral and start of plan.
* $726 for each additional month of plan duration.

Surprisingly, neither the age of the rehabilitant nor the severity of the injury (measured by permanent disability rating) were statistically significant contributors to total rehabilitation cost. This finding does not necessarily disprove the experience of practitioners, who have noted increased expense when either or both factors are present. Rather, the absence of statistical significance stems from the dominance of formal schooling plans in 1985 and the total lack of any pattern, by age or PD rating, as to which injured workers enter these plans.

**Prompt Reporting:** The results of the regression analysis of the 1985 data underscore the importance of prompt identification of potential rehabilitation candidates, early intervention and timely initiation of return-to-work activity -- and the cost consequences of failure. One aspect of the 1985 study documents the delays and the need for improvement.

Under California law, insurers and self-insured employers

are required to identify potential rehabilitation candidates by filing a disability status report (Form RB-1) with the Rehabilitation Bureau immediately upon knowledge that the injured employee may not be able to return to his or her usual occupation, but in no event later than 180 aggregate days of total disability. In 1985 on-time performance continues to fall well short of the requirement.

**TIME LAG—DATE OF INJURY TO RB-1 FILING**

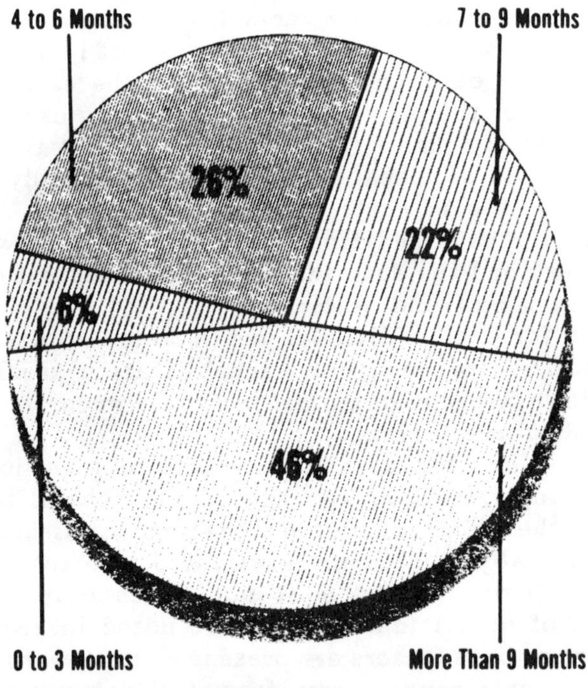


The status report, the first formal identifier of rehabilitation potential, is filed timely in only one-third of all rehabilitation cases. The remaining reports may not necessarily be reported late in every instance, since disability sometimes is intermittent -- but, clearly, the record shows that early identification and the activities that stem from it require attention.

**Results**

Any evaluation of vocational rehabilitation in Workers' Compensation would be incomplete without examining the outcome of the process. In determining effectiveness, three progressively stringent tests were devised.

The first test identifies the percentage of workers who complete a specific return-to-work program. By this measure

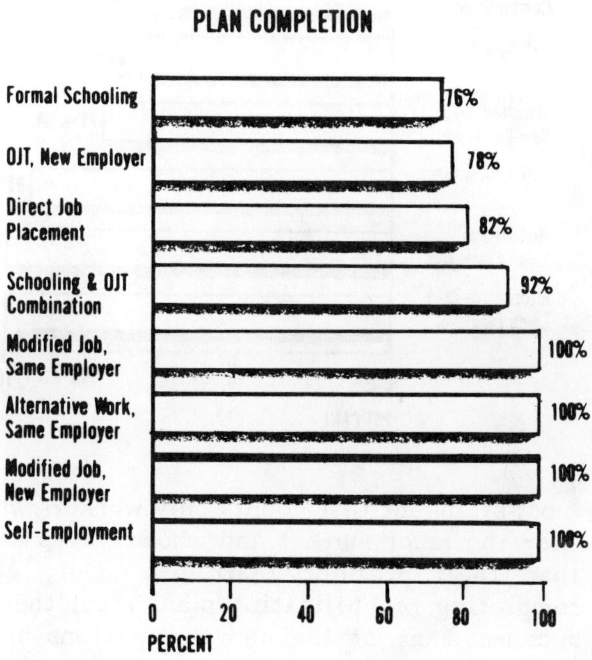


rehabilitation services were effective in restoring employability for 82 percent of enrolled workers, with completion rates varying by type of plan.

The second test of effectiveness is based on the percentage of workers who are reemployed after completion of a rehabilitation plan. By this index, the success rate is 69 percent of workers who complete a plan (and 57 percent of those originally enrolled). Again, results vary by plan type.

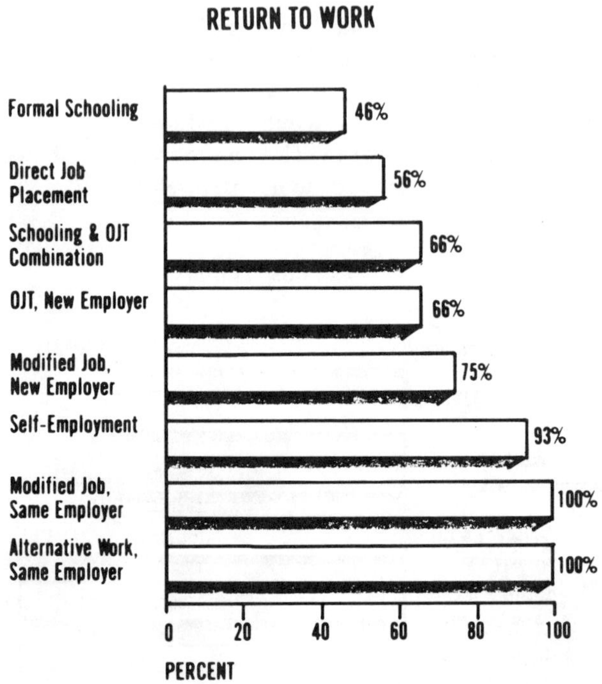


The most stringent test counts only workers who complete a plan, reenter the labor market and whose wages are equal to or greater than their preinjury earnings. Only 27 percent of workers completing rehabilitation plans meet these criteria -- in part because many of the new occupations are entry-level positions -- and no type of plan is universally successful.

The effectiveness tests suggest successful vocational rehabilitation is influenced by the length and complexity of the process. The results also provide further evidence of the inverse relationship between plan cost and plan success, a finding borne out by previous Institute research.

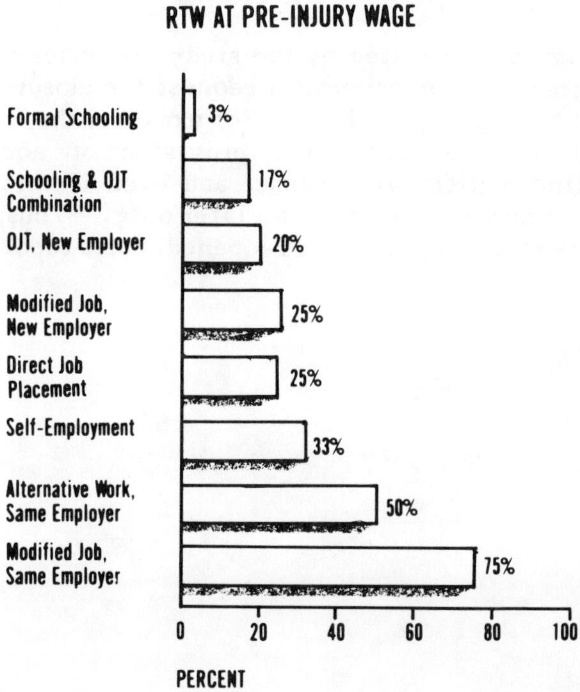


## Technical Notes

Results of the study are based on data collected from 822 cases submitted for closure to the Rehabilitation Bureau, California Division of Industrial Accidents, in the four-week period ending March 15, 1985. Twenty-nine Workers' Compensation insurers accounting for 69 percent of statewide premium participated.

In 80 percent of the cases the year of injury giving rise to the potential need for vocational rehabilitation services occurred in 1981 or later. In half the cases the year of injury is 1983 or 1984. Mean time from date of injury to rehabilitation closure is 2.3 years.

Three of every four workers in the sample are male, conforming to the distribution of the injured work force generally, and age and type of injury distributions are correspondingly similar. The mean permanent disability rating of workers in the sample is 28 percent, higher than the average for all injured workers but an expected difference given the nature of the study population.

The cost figures generated by the study are understated to an unknown degree. Submission of a request for closure (Form RB-20) may not terminate liability. For example, the Rehabilitation Bureau may not order the provision of additional services entailing additional expense, and even if the bureau closes the case, it may be reopened at a later date. Thus, to the extent that cases remain open or are reopened, costs reported are conservative.

## CHAPTER 33

# A Report Concerning the Incidence and Costs of Vocational Rehabilitation

**National Council on Compensation Insurance, Economic and Social Research Department**
**1984**

### Introduction

The purpose of this report is to review the most significant findings from a study into the use and costs of vocational rehabilitation. At the outset, it is important to note that the findings in this report are specific to vocational rehabilitation programs that are provided for by Workers' Compensation Insurance carriers.

The motivations for undertaking this study were to ascertain (1) the relative incidence of vocational rehabilitation and (2) the seriousness of the injuries for workers who participate in vocational rehabilitation programs. For efficiency and equity reasons, it can be argued that vocational rehabilitation should be used most frequently by the seriously injured workers to modify or change occupations. In particular, the most seriously injured workers should be provided the greater amounts of vocational rehabilitation to enhance reentry into the employed work force.

The data source for this study is the Call for Detail Claim Information (DCI), a data base complied and maintained by the National Council on Compensation Insurance. The study is limited to claim reports filed in 13 states during 1982: Connecticut, Florida, Georgia, Illinois, Kentucky, Maine, Massachusetts, Michigan, Minnesota, New York, Pennsylvania, Virginia, and Wisconsin. Interstate differences in the probability that a claim is included in the DCI necessitated weighing each observation by the inverse of the sampling probability.

The first section of this report reviews the incidence of vocational rehabilitation among claims for Workers' Compensation benefits. The second section evaluates the average costs of vocational rehabilitation with special attention to the evaluation, educational, and incurred indemnity expenses, as well as interstate differences. The third section discusses the level of indemnity benefits paid to by workers receiving vocational rehabilitation compared to workers not receiving vocational rehabilitation. The fourth section presents a summary of the findings.

## Incidence of Vocational Rehabilitation

The incidence of vocational rehabilitation is higher among claims that remain open for longer periods. However, the large majority of injured workers do not participate in a vocational rehabilitation program. Among claims that close within six months from the date a claim is filed with the insurer, 0.18% included vocational rehabilitation (Table 1). By contrast, among claims closed between 18 and 30 months, 4.07% of the injured workers received vocational rehabilitation. Similarly, 2.08% of the cases remaining open after six months and 11.08% remaining open after 30 months incurred vocational rehabilitation expenses.

The differences in the incidence rates by the type of benefit were not substantial. Among first report claims remaining open, vocational rehabilitation expenses were incurred in 1.55% of the temporary total injuries and 2.87% of the permanent partial injuries. Among third report claims remaining open, vocational rehabilitation expenses were incurred for 8.52% of the temporary total claims and 10.67% of the permanent partial claims (Table 1). The lack of a substantial difference between the benefit types suggests that vocational rehabilitation might serve two contrasting purposes. For workers with lingering temporary total injuries, vocational rehabilitation might be a means to modify a worker's skills without changing the worker's occupation. In contrast, for workers with permanent partial injuries, rehabilitation might require the worker for a new occupation.

The costs of vocational rehabilitation are greater the longer the duration of a claim. The total costs incurred for vocational rehabilitation averaged $764 for claims closed by the first report and $1,930 for claims closed between the second and third reports. Similarly, among claims remaining open after six months the total costs incurred for vocational rehabilitation averaged $2,151, while among claims remaining open after 30 months the same costs averaged $4,387 (Table 2). The differences between the average costs of closed and open claims were very substantial. Presumably, these differences were due to the high costs incurred for workers where the duration of the claim was expected to be long and the costs of rehabilitation very high.

**A. State Differences**

A breakdown of the vocational rehabilitation cases by state was unreliable for closed claims due to an insufficient number of observations for most state/report divisions. However, a sufficient number of observations were available to produce a breakdown of the costs of vocational rehabilitation for claims remaining open during 1982. In the present study, the total costs incurred for vocational rehabilitation expenses were the sum of the evaluation expenses (which include expenses incurred while testing or evaluating the worker's ability or aptitude for formal vocational rehabilitation), indemnity benefits specific to vocational rehabilitation participation, and educational expenses (that is, educational and direct training costs, including tuition, books, tools, transportation, and additional living expenses).

Among the 13 states, vocational rehabilitation expenses were highest in Minnesota and Wisconsin (Table 3A). For claims remaining open after the first report (6 months after the injury was reported to the insurer), vocational rehabilitation expenses averaged $4,206 in Minnesota; for claims remaining open after the third report (30 months after the injury was reported), vocational rehabilitation expenses averaged $6,819. In Wisconsin, vocational rehabilitation expenses averaged $3,676 and $6,152, respectively, for claims remaining open as of the first and third reports. By contrast, vocational rehabilitation expenses averaged $781 and $1,829 in Connecticut for claims remaining open as of the first and third reports.

A further analysis of the total costs incurred for vocational rehabilitation is provided in Appendix A. It exhibits a comparison between open and closed claims who participate in vocational rehabilitation and open and closed claims who do not participate.

Cross-state comparisons of vocational rehabilitation expenses are confounded by the amount of indemnity benefits paid to vocational rehabilitation participants. In particular, the allocation of indemnity benefits for the amount of time spent in a vocational rehabilitation program differs across states. The problem caused by the inclusion of the indemnity benefits was overcome by performing interstate comparisons limited to the evaluation and educational expenses (Table 3B). As expected, the range of vocational rehabilitation costs across states was narrowed by the exclusion of the indemnity benefits. Even though the state rankings of vocational rehabilitation costs differed slightly depending upon the report classification, some discernible patterns were observed: (1) Minnesota remained the state with the highest vocational rehabilitation costs; (2) Florida and Georgia were consistently among the states with the highest vocational rehabilitation costs; and (3) Connecticut was consistently among the states with the lowest vocational rehabilitation costs.

**B. Injury Type Differences**

A breakdown of the average total cost incurred by injury type provided some interesting comparisons. As expected, vocational rehabilitation was more costly for the more serious injury types. In Table 4, among first report claims remaining open during 1982, the average incurred costs were highest for head injuries ($3,198) and occupational diseases ($3,128), and lowest for injuries to the upper extremities ($1,596) and lower extremities ($1,700). One explanation for the high costs of vocational rehabilitation for head injuries and occupational diseases is that such disabilities very probably require a change of the worker's occupation. By contrast, the average costs for vocational rehabilitation were lower for injuries to the lower or upper extremities, which are less likely to require an occupational change.

For further detail, Appendix B provides a breakdown of the average total cost incurred for open and closed claims who participate in and who do not participate in vocational rehabilitation.

A further means to assess the seriousness of the injuries for workers participating in vocational rehabilitation programs is to compare the average durations of injured workers' claims. Average duration was indirectly assessed in the present study by computing the average total incurred indemnity benefits, which included the incurred costs for temporary total, other than temporary total, and vocational rehabilitation indemnity benefits. In Table 5, the average total incurred indemnity benefits are presented for closed and open claims. Among closed claims, indemnity benefits for workers who received vocational rehabilitation averaged at least triple the average indemnity benefits received by injured workers who did not participate in vocational rehabilitation. In particular, the average indemnity benefit was $6,499 for claims that closed between 18 and 30 months after the initial report to the insurer and $19,507 for claims remaining open after 30 months from the initial report.

The difference in average indemnity benefits was less pronounced among claims remaining open during 1982. In particular, among claims remaining open at least 42 months after the first report, the average indemnity benefit for workers participating in vocational rehabilitation was only 1.6 times the amount for nonparticipants ($62,697 vs. $39,020). However, the expectation that the most seriously injured workers eventually receive vocational rehabilitation is probably sufficient reason to suspect that the differences for open claims is understated.

The findings from the present study can be summarized as follows.

1. The incidence of vocational rehabilitation is higher among workers with permanent injuries than among workers with temporary injuries. Furthermore, among all workers who receive Workers' Compensation insurance benefits, relatively few participate in vocational rehabilitation.
2. Substantial cross-state differences were observed in the average costs of vocational rehabilitation. Evaluation and educational expenses were highest in Minnesota, Florida, and Georgia, and lowest in Connecticut.
3. The costs of vocational rehabilitation were highest for workers with head injuries and occupational diseases, and lowest for workers with injuries to the upper or lower extremities.

One of the objectives of the present study was to assess the relationship between the seriousness of a worker's injury and participation in vocational rehabilitation. The results concerning the incidence and costs of vocational rehabilitation suggest that the more seriously injured workers participate in vocational rehabilitation. Thus, at least tentatively, it is possible to conclude that vocational rehabilitation is an efficient and equitable component of the Workers' Compensation Insurance benefit system.

It is not possible, however, to conclude from the present study that the benefits of vocational rehabilitation outweigh the costs. Although the costs are relatively easy to identify, the benefits from vocational rehabilitation are very difficult to calculate accurately. Even a narrow definition of the benefits would require estimating the injured worker's earnings in the absence of the rehabilitation program. In sum, while the present study found that the more seriously injured workers are more likely to participate in a rehabilitation program, whether the benefits exceed the costs remains for further analysis.

**TABLE I**
**INCIDENCE OF VOCATIONAL REHABILITATION CLAIMS**
**A. Incidence for all Benefit types**

**PERCENT DISTRIBUTION**

| Status | Report | Total Number of Claims | No Voc Rehab | Voc Rehab | Temporary Total | Permanent Partial | Permanent Total | All Other Types |
|---|---|---|---|---|---|---|---|---|
| Closed | 1 | 748892 | 99.82 | 0.18 | 0.14 | 0.03 | 0.00 | 0.02 |
| | 2 | 189842 | 98.71 | 1.29 | 0.62 | 0.41 | 0.03 | 0.23 |
| | 3 | 29572 | 95.93 | 4.07 | 1.23 | 1.49 | 0.14 | 1.21 |
| | 4 | 3055 | 95.04 | 4.96 | 1.20 | 1.64 | 0.44 | 1.69 |
| Open | 1 | 369478 | 97.92 | 2.08 | 0.88 | 0.80 | 0.04 | 0.36 |
| | 2 | 100060 | 93.05 | 6.95 | 2.23 | 2.68 | 0.21 | 1.83 |
| | 3 | 31955 | 88.92 | 11.08 | 3.18 | 3.77 | 0.55 | 3.57 |
| | 4 | 5640 | 85.49 | 14.51 | 4.58 | 4.57 | 0.84 | 4.52 |

**B. Incidence by Benefit type**

**PERCENT DISTRIBUTION**

| Status | Report | Temporary Total | Permanent Partial | Permanent Total | All Other Types |
|---|---|---|---|---|---|
| Closed | 1 | 0.15 | 0.50 | 0.30 | 0.52 |
| | 2 | 1.12 | 1.96 | 6.18 | 0.97 |
| | 3 | 3.17 | 5.24 | 13.29 | 3.83 |
| | 4 | 4.01 | 5.25 | 20.97 | 4.65 |
| Open | 1 | 1.55 | 2.87 | 2.61 | 2.59 |
| | 2 | 5.24 | 8.03 | 8.21 | 8.45 |
| | 3 | 8.52 | 10.67 | 16.68 | 14.90 |
| | 4 | 14.27 | 13.49 | 17.67 | 15.37 |

**TABLE 2**

**AVERAGE COSTS OF VOCATIONAL REHABILITATION**

| Status | Report | Total Costs Incurred | Total Costs Paid | Evaluation Expense | Incurred Indemnity | Education Expense |
|---|---|---|---|---|---|---|
| Closed | 1 | 764.30 | 761.59 | 440.77 | 255.25 | 68.28 |
| | 2 | 1208.35 | 1166.95 | 605.18 | 449.40 | 153.77 |
| | 3 | 1930.23 | 1871.28 | 1160.98 | 512.59 | 256.67 |
| Open | 1 | 2151.22 | 535.65 | 854.11 | 987.93 | 309.18 |
| | 2 | 3414.50 | 1452.30 | 1581.12 | 1368.92 | 464.46 |
| | 3 | 4386.54 | 2209.37 | 2011.85 | 1903.32 | 471.36 |

**TABLE 3A**

**AVERAGE TOTAL COST INCURRED FOR VOCATIONAL REHABILITATION BY STATE**

**OPEN CLAIMS**

| STATE | REPORT (1,2 & 3) | | |
|---|---|---|---|
| | 1 | 2 | 3 |
| Connecticut | 780.73 | 1316.17 | 1828.88* |
| Florida | 3288.95 | 3943.43 | 4151.52 |
| Georgia | 1713.76 | 3197.31 | 3963.20 |
| Illinois | 1355.81 | 2344.94 | 1600.44* |
| Kentucky | 1466.29 | 1964.70 | 3440.43* |
| Maine | 1312.50* | 3068.89* | 3654.25* |
| Massachusetts | 1438.38 | 2557.69 | 2079.53* |
| Michigan | 1652.40 | 3273.12 | 4961.09 |
| Minnesota | 4205.98 | 4999.49 | 6818.67 |
| New York | 723.37 | 2098.15 | 4475.79* |
| Pennsylvania | 1337.23 | 2363.15 | 2605.67 |
| Virginia | 2302.36 | 3037.37 | 3098.88 |
| Wisconsin | 3676.24 | 5194.68 | 6151.67 |

**TABLE 3B**

**AVERAGE TOTAL COST INCURRED FOR VOCATIONAL REHABILITATION BY STATE EXCLUDING INDEMNITY BENEFITS**

**OPEN CLAIMS**

| STATE | REPORT (1, 2, & 3) | | |
|---|---|---|---|
| | 1 | 2 | 3 |
| Connecticut | 562.38 | 1089.34 | 1439.26* |
| Florida | 1399.41 | 2148.09 | 1991.35 |
| Georgia | 1264.57 | 2553.31 | 2521.85 |
| Illinois | 700.26 | 1879.28 | 1104.33* |
| Kentucky | 923.17 | 1330.14 | 2293.36* |
| Maine | 1228.13* | 2186.27* | 1954.25* |
| Massachusetts | 1022.86 | 1073.15 | 1232.94* |
| Michigan | 1158.99 | 1803.21 | 1895.36 |

### TABLE 4

### AVERAGE TOTAL COST INCURRED FOR VOCATIONAL REHABILITATION

#### A. CLOSED CLAIMS

| INJURY TYPE | REPORT (1, 2, & 3) 1 | 2 | 3 |
|---|---|---|---|
| Head | 1348.60* | 1965.54 | 1170.10* |
| Lower Extremities | 581.32 | 1187.12 | 1623.51 |
| Lower Back | 660.04 | 1283.52 | 2063.68 |
| Multiple Body Parts | 930.28* | 1073.30 | 2876.80* |
| Neck | 593.79* | 1194.23* | 1967.68* |
| Occupational Diseases | 1158.95* | 1599.58* | 2397.92* |
| Trunk | 2480.44 | 1057.79 | 2518.56 |
| Upper Extremities | 473.98 | 1040.55 | 1497.94 |

#### B. OPEN CLAIMS

| INJURY TYPE | REPORT (1, 2, & 3) 1 | 2 | 3 |
|---|---|---|---|
| Head | 3197.92 | 4636.81 | 7592.45 |
| Lower Extremities | 1700.09 | 2907.83 | 4533.09 |
| Lower Back | 2360.45 | 3747.04 | 4702.98 |
| Multiple Body Parts | 2713.45 | 3083.97 | 3612.26 |
| Neck | 1758.46 | 5489.69 | 2513.84 |
| Occupational Diseases | 3127.76 | 3426.54 | 5399.99 |
| Trunk | 2281.16 | 3078.30 | 4349.56 |
| Upper Extremities | 1595.99 | 2661.13 | 3257.21 |

* Based on Fewer than 20 Observations

### TABLE 5

### AVERAGE TOTAL INCURRED INDEMNITY BENEFITS

| Report | Closed Claims No Vocational Rehabilitation | Vocational Rehabilitation | Open Claims No Vocational Rehabilitation | Vocational Rehabilitation |
|---|---|---|---|---|
| 1 | 818.05 | 4340.18 | 7708.58 | 18284.35 |
| 2 | 2895.74 | 12352.35 | 16110.47 | 33462.71 |
| 3 | 6499.12 | 19507.14 | 27087.10 | 47472.25 |
| 4 | 9644.08 | 32744.23 | 39020.43 | 62696.82 |

Total Incurred Indemnity Benefits = Temporary Total Income Benefits Incurred (TEMPINC) + Total Incurred Other Than Temporary Total Benefits (TOTAL BEN) + Vocational Rehabilitation Incurred Indemnity (VOCATIND)

## APPENDIX A

### Average Total Incurred Indemnity Benefits** By State

#### A. Closed Claims

| | No Vocational Rehabilitation | | | Vocational Rehabilitation | | |
|---|---|---|---|---|---|---|
| | Report | | | | | |
| State | 1 | 2 | 3 | 1 | 2 | 3 |
| Connecticut | 556.43 | 2576.00 | 7049.70 | 2134.00* | 8560.30 | 20758.60* |
| Florida | 645.33 | 2425.08 | 5694.27 | 1107.71* | 9669.90 | 11014.70 |
| Georgia | 760.60 | 2536.88 | 6967.04 | 3049.42 | 7697.77 | 16000.80 |
| Illinois | 1059.83 | 4488.02 | 7026.76 | 7635.22* | 33478.21* | 32749.83* |
| Kentucky | 815.46 | 3171.10 | 7571.84 | 4226.37* | 16794.63* | 12802.45* |
| Maine | 874.40 | 5608.84 | 14250.57 | 34665.42* | 16521.80* | |
| Massachusetts | 794.00 | 4336.54 | 11774.06 | 2649.00* | 12403.47* | 31329.64* |
| Michigan | 1069.12 | 3740.55 | 8124.07 | 3302.94 | 14011.56 | 26744.09 |
| Minnesota | 687.97 | 2215.34 | 5364.86 | 6336.60 | 10850.96 | 18021.84 |
| New York | 789.62 | 1438.47 | 3099.77 | 2881.20* | 6589.90* | 17319.25* |
| Pennsylvania | 1035.65 | 3447.45 | 8960.93 | 4341.29 | 8460.92 | 16281.30* |
| Virginia | 782.93 | 2773.62 | 8485.85 | 3499.45 | 10749.26 | 23456.97 |
| Wisconsin | 496.72 | 1915.08 | 5009.13 | 4609.60* | 7339.13* | 12993.75* |

#### B. Open Claims

| | No Vocational Rehabilitation | | | Vocational Rehabilitation | | |
|---|---|---|---|---|---|---|
| | Report | | | | | |
| State | 1 | 2 | 3 | 1 | 2 | 3 |
| Connecticut | 7709.07 | 17116.92 | 25454.53 | 14158.50 | 24142.31 | 32284.39* |
| Florida | 5606.45 | 11559.97 | 21216.03 | 13416.09 | 21672.79 | 32693.93 |
| Georgia | 5524.91 | 12931.15 | 20645.42 | 11047.44 | 19341.02 | 26706.78 |
| Illinois | 10322.61 | 11882.14 | 15283.33 | 18162.63 | 48662.67 | 76066.44* |
| Kentucky | 11558.78 | 20840.64 | 28388.19 | 30242.53 | 42482.67 | 53087.65 |
| Maine | 11082.34 | 30307.41 | 52932.63 | 16051.37* | 49837.52* | 71585.00* |
| Massachusetts | 8935.99 | 19574.18 | 28287.99 | 18539.82 | 39678.89 | 53491.06* |
| Michigan | 7955.06 | 18207.38 | 29702.10 | 22483.98 | 41946.42 | 51797.02 |
| Minnesota | 8988.57 | 20675.97 | 36692.40 | 22275.74 | 35908.05 | 51091.63 |
| New York | 3669.61 | 9417.63 | 18974.84 | 11284.20 | 15275.42 | 37639.21* |
| Pennsylvania | 15559.34 | 35041.62 | 55942.14 | 32815.03 | 49973.70 | 71118.07 |
| Virginia | 8417.44 | 22973.06 | 39904.60 | 19732.59 | 46154.24 | 45303.99 |
| Wisconsin | 4511.73 | 10455.84 | 15390.05 | 20760.23 | 29595.50 | 38351.42 |

* Based on Fewer than 20 observations.

** Total Incurred Indemnity Benefits = TEMPINC*** + TOTAL BEN*** = VOCATIONAL***.

*** See Table 5.

## Appendix B

### Average Total Incurred Indemnity Benefits** By Injury Type

#### A. Closed Claims

| | No Vocational Rehabilitation | | | Vocational Rehabilitation | | |
|---|---|---|---|---|---|---|
| | Report | | | | | |
| Injury Type | 1 | 2 | 3 | 1 | 2 | 3 |
| Head | 591.81 | 1632.88 | 4358.83 | 3410.97* | 24088.29* | 9540.10* |
| Lower Extremities | 815.02 | 3225.76 | 6499.80 | 4092.64 | 13379.3 | 18762.56 |
| Lower Back | 807.90 | 3277.60 | 8211.20 | 4370.12 | 12497.95 | 19338.53 |
| Mult. Body Parts | 985.32 | 3702.50 | 7764.76 | 5291.18* | 15867.22 | 25950.29* |
| Neck | 956.48 | 2995.62 | 8168.62 | 4118.47* | 14536.05* | 11537.39* |
| Occup. Diseases | 1323.57 | 2595.36 | 5291.03 | 4272.37* | 9885.74* | 7219.70* |
| Trunk | 1034.46 | 3470.20 | 8245.20 | 4599.06 | 10950.75 | 34513.59 |
| Upper Extremities | 758.99 | 2459.35 | 4947.85 | 4280.95 | 8590.83 | 11405.77 |

#### B. Open Claims

| | No Vocational Rehabilitation | | | Vocational Rehabilitation | | |
|---|---|---|---|---|---|---|
| | Report | | | | | |
| Injury Type | 1 | 2 | 3 | 1 | 2 | 3 |
| Head | 7827.23 | 20678.12 | 38888.06 | 20154.23 | 29102.45 | 39760.84 |
| Lower Extremities | 6250.44 | 13413.97 | 21099.35 | 16667.63 | 35631.96 | 47251.83 |
| Lower Back | 7389.33 | 16704.73 | 27309.23 | 17794.77 | 30565.51 | 43417.86 |
| Mult. Body Parts | 12781.39 | 25275.41 | 35749.80 | 25767.41 | 50723.45 | 77442.59 |
| Neck | 7893.98 | 17253.49 | 29620.36 | 17938.23 | 39738.41 | 40446.42 |
| Occup. Diseases | 13020.36 | 22866.91 | 37519.51 | 27935.20 | 41587.09 | 79467.12 |
| Trunk | 11998.97 | 21864.95 | 33019.66 | 22334.11 | 38072.66 | 50107.89 |
| Upper Extremities | 5740.80 | 9785.66 | 17981.28 | 13832.36 | 26768.46 | 39061.21 |

* Based on Fewer than 20 Observations.

** Total Incurred Indemnity Benefits = TEMPINC*** + TOTAL BEN*** + VOCATIONAL***.

*** See Table 5.

## CHAPTER 34

### Study of Closed Rehabilitation Cases
by
Lawrence J. Deneen, Ph.D., C.R.C.
Colleen M. Deneen, M.Ed., C.R.C.

Using a Rehabilitation Research Form developed by the author, data in a total of 345 cases closed between April 1978 and March 1980 was systematically categorized. The computations and results were analyzed by an independent research technician. The study was a sequel to one done with cases closed as of September 1977 and reported at the AACD convention in Las Vegas 1979. Only the highlights are presented below.

**TABLE 1: KEY**

| | |
|---|---|
| M-D 1977 | Martin-Deneen Associates Study 1977 |
| M-D 1980 | Martin-Deneen Associates Study 1980 |
| N/A | Data Not Available |
| RTW | Return to Work |
| FT | Formal Training |
| DP | Direct Placement |
| OJT | On-the-Job Training |
| SE | Self-Employment |
| RB-2 | Formal Rehabilitation Plan |
| Med-TD | Temporary Disability Due to Medical |
| Reh-TD | Temporary Disability Due to Rehabilitation |
| D/I | Date of Injury |
| D/R | Date of Referral |
| Cost* | Cost includes counselor fees, Med-TD, and fees for FT, OJT, DP |

**TABLE 2: Status of Closed Cases**

| | Formal Plans | Medically Not Qualified | Vocationally Not Feasible | Refused |
|---|---|---|---|---|
| M-D 1977 (N=239) | 31% | 40% | 9% | 20% |
| M-D 1980 (N=345) | 38% | 27% | 17% | 18% |

**TABLE 3: Types of Plans Developed**

| | DP | OJT | FT |
|---|---|---|---|
| M-D 1977 | 36% | 23% | 41% |
| M-D 1980 | 59% | 10% | 31% |

**TABLE 4: Completion Ratio/Employability Ratio**

| | Completed | Terminated |
|---|---|---|
| M-D 1977 (N=74) | 62% | 38% |
| M-D 1980 (N=130) | 75% | 25% |

**TABLE 5: Success Ratio/Reemployment Ratio**

| | Not RTW, Job Ready | Successfully Returned to Work |
|---|---|---|
| M-D 1977 (N=46) | 11% | 89% |
| M-D 1980 (N=98) | 12% | 88% |

**TABLE 6: Completion Ratio by Type of Plan**

| | DP | OJT | FT |
|---|---|---|---|
| M-D 1977 | 75% | | 43% |
| M-D 1980 | 81% | 77% | 64% |

**TABLE 7: Success Ratio by Type of Plan**

| | DP | OJT | FT |
|---|---|---|---|
| M-D 1977 | 85% | | 92% |
| M-D 1980 | 91% | 90% | 80% |

**TABLE 8: Average Overall Cost* of Plans**

| | Reh-TD | Reh-TD and Med-TD |
|---|---|---|
| M-D 1977 | N/A | N/A |
| M-D 1980 (N=108) | $3638 | $5207 |

**TABLE 9: Average Cost* of Plans by Closure**

| | Completed RTW | Completed No RTW | Terminated |
|---|---|---|---|
| M-D 1977 | $4634 | | $5081 |
| M-D 1980 | $3685 | $5755 | $4224 |

**TABLE 10: Average Total Cost* of Plan by Type of Plan**

| | DP | OJT | FT |
|---|---|---|---|
| M-D 1977 | $3690 | $5378 | $5089 |
| M-D 1980 | $3348 | $3644 | $5745 |

**TABLE 14: Other Statistics**

| Yr. | Clients With Back Disability | Ave # Wks D/I to D/R | Ave # Wks D/R to Plan Compl-tion | Ave D/I Wages | Ave Clo-sure Wages | App Att | Def Att |
|---|---|---|---|---|---|---|---|
| M-D 1977 | 71-82% | 42 wks | N/A | $245 | $224 | 68-79% | N/A |
| M-D 1980 | 67% | 79 wks | 33 wks | $270 | $245 | 86% | 55% |

The typical (average) client is age 38, male, married, has 1.41 dependents, has worked 357 weeks with his employer, was earning $270 per week, is a union member, has completed 11.87 years of schooling, has marketable transferable skills, has an attorney, has an additional source of income of $97 per week from sources other than spouse and temporary disability, has a low back disability, has received treatment from 3.81 doctors, will enroll in a Rehabilitation Plan, and will complete the Plan and return to work earning 91% of his preinjury wages.

## Conclusion . . . The Beginning!!

Despite all the problems involved in multiple accountability and the conscious and unconscious agendas each party brings into the vocational rehabilitation process, injured workers are helped, people **do** go back to work after industrial accidents and illnesses, profitably and contentedly. Studies done by various groups including a major insurance carrier, the State of California Rehabilitation Bureau, the California Workers' Compensation Institute, representing most California carriers, and a private vocational rehabilitation firm were reviewed by one of the authors at a recent American Association for Counseling and Development convention. These studies indicate that persons were restored to employability at ratios of 62% to 94% and persons were reemployed at ratios from 85% to 92% depending on the type of plan. Some people go back to similar occupations adapted to compensate for their residual disablement. Some move on to the exciting challenge of a new career they never dreamed possible. **Section IV** of this book presented **for the first time** under the same cover national data regarding rehabilitation statistics.

It is a tribute to the work of the private rehabilitation counselor that he has created a new area of vocational rehabilitation practically from scratch. He has learned to cope with the competing pressures from many different sources. He has learned to work closely and amicably with a variety of other professionals. He has met the challenge of the industrially injured worker. Out of this comes good quality vocational rehabilitation -- the return of injured workers to satisfactory and remunerative ways of making a living.

Research of one of the authors indicates that, on the average, rehabilitated workers return to jobs paying 92% to 94% of their preinjury wage. The bottom line is success.

## Note on the Bibliography and Appendix

We have included a bibliography rather than specific references to facilitate the reading. The publications listed in the bibliography contain all source data referred to in the text. Selected footnotes are discussed at the end of each chapter.

# APPENDIX

## Certification Information

There are two certification procedures most relevant for practitioners in disability compensation systems. Having at least one of these certification designations ensures clients, carriers, attorneys, judges, and regulators that:

1. Your academic achievements have been verified through an independent process.
2. Your work experience has been investigated and verified.
3. You passed a full day of an objectively scored exam.
4. You maintain 30 hours of continued education on an average per year or a total of 150 hours for each 5-year cycle.

Certification gives credibility to professional standards, which registration does not do. Yet, certification does not carry with it the expense of licensure which must be set up through state governments.

The two designations are:

1. **Certified Rehabilitation Counselor:** Experience and education in rehabilitation counseling or closely-related fields is required. Most CRC's have a Master's degree and several years of experience in counseling disabled persons.
2. **Certified Insurance Rehabilitation Specialist:** Experience and education in working with people receiving benefits from an insurance disability system is required. Most CIRS are trained as professional nurses, counselors, evaluators, or job placement specialist and many have a graduate degree. All CIRS designated people have experience in disability compensation systems.

For more information, write:

Board of Rehabilitation Certification
1156 Shure Drive, Suite 350
Arlington Heights, Ill. 60004
(312) 394-2104

## BIBLIOGRAPHY

Azrin, N. and Besalel, V. **Job Club Counselor's Manual--A Behavioral Approach to Vocational Counseling.** University Park Press, Baltimore, 1980.

Azrin, N. and Besalel, V. **Finding a Job**, Ten Speed Press, P.O. Box 7123, Berkeley, CA 94707, 1982.

Baty, Gordon. **Entrepreneurship Playing to Win.** Reston Publishing Company, Reston, Virginia, 1974.

Beyer, R. D., Deneen, L., Hessellund, T., and Largay, D. The medical community and the workmen's compensation insurance carrier: a treatment alliance model. **Journal of Occupational Medicine,** Vol. 17, No. 5, May 1975, pp. 318-323.

Bolles, Richard. **What Color Is Your Parachute?,** Ten Speed Press, Berkeley, CA, Revised Edition, 1986.

Botterbusch, Karl F. **A Comparison of Computerized Job Matching Systems.** Materials Development Center, Stout Vocational Rehabilitation Institute, University of Wisconsin - Stout, Menomonie, Wisconsin 54751, 1983.

Brown, T., Nemiah, J., Barr, J., and Barry, H. Psychological factors in low-back pain. **New England Journal of Medicine,** 251: pp. 123 and 128, 1954.

California Association of Rehabilitation Professionals. **Guidelines for Professional Behavior,** San Francisco, CA, 1979.

Carkhuff, Robert. **Helping and Human Relations: Selection and Training,** Volume I, and **Practice and Research,** Volume II, Holt, Rinehart, and Winston, New York, 1969.

**Compendium on Workmen's Compensation.** National Commission on State Workmen's Compensation Laws, U.S. Government Printing Office, Washington, D.C., 1973.

Crystal, John C. and Bolles, Richard. **Where Do I Go from Here with My Life?** Ten Speed Press, Berkeley, CA, 1974.

Deneen, C. Job placement in a private vocational rehabilitation company with the industrially injured. Paper presented at American Personnel and Guidance Association annual convention, Las Vegas, 1979.

Deneen, L. **Job Search Skills Workshop Manual,** 1986. Martin-Deneen Associates, Inc., P.O. Box 22606, San Francisco, CA 94122.

Deneen, L. and Deneen, C. The need for facilitative human relations in the delivery of health care. In George Gazda et al. **Human Relations Development: A Manual for Health Sciences,** Allyn and Bacon, 1975.

Dible, D. **The Pure Joy of Making More Money,** Reston Publications, 1981.

Dible, D. **Up Your Own Organization,** Reston Publications, ISBN 0-8359-8086-3, revised edition, 1985.

Field, T., Choppa, T., Shafer, L. **Labor Market Access,** VSB, P.O. Box 1945, Athens, GA 30603, 1984.

Field, T. and Field, J. **The Classification of Jobs According to Worker Trait Factors** (an addendum to the 1977 edition of the **Dictionary of Occupational Titles**), VSB, P.O. Box 1945, Athens, GA 30603, 1984.

Grisso, T. and Sales, B. **Professional Psychology,** Special Issue: Law and Professional Psychology, Vol. 9, No. 3, August 1978.

Happock, Robert. **Occupational Information.** McGraw-Hill Book Company, 1976.

Hessellund, Thorvald A. The delivery of vocational rehabilitation services within workers' compensation system. Paper presented at seminar sponsored by California Workers' Compensation Institute, San Francisco, 1976.

Hessellund, Thorvald A. Establishing a private vocational rehabilitation practice. Paper presented at American Personnel and Guidance Association annual convention, Washington, D.C., 1978.

Hessellund, Thorvald A. Ethics and standards in private rehabilitation. Paper presented at the National Association of Rehabilitation Professionals Workshop at the National Rehabilitation Association convention, Chicago, 1979.

Ivey, Allen. **Microcounseling: Innovations in Interviewing Training.** Charles C. Thomas, Springfield, Illinois, 1971.

Keane, Richard. Providing Rehabilitation Services to the Insurance Industry in **Handbook of Private Sector Rehabilitation,** 1985, pp. 27-54.

Kamoroff, B. **Small Time Operator,** Bell Springs Publishing, 1985.

Lathrop, Richard. **Who's Hiring Who,** Ten Speed Press, ISBN 0-913668-55-9, 1977.

Livingston, R. The history of rehabilitation counselor certification. **Journal of Applied Rehabilitation Counseling,** Vol. 10, No. 3, Fall 1979, pp. 111-118.

**Longshore Desk Book.** U.S. Department of Labor Benefits Review Board, through the Industrial Claims Association, 582 Market Street, San Francisco, CA 94104.

Lynch, R. Vocational rehabilitation of workers' compensation clients. **Journal of Applied Rehabilitation,** Vol. 9, No. 4, Winter 1979, pp. 164-167.

Marcon, M. and Worthington, M. **Twelve Steps to Finding a Job Under $30,000 in Four Weeks.** Prentice-Hall, Englewood Cliffs, N.J., 1984.

Matkin, Ralph. **Insurance Rehabilitation,** Pro-ed, 5341 Industrial Oaks Blvd., Austin, Texas 78735.

Morin, W. and Yorks, L. **Outplacement Techniques,** Amacom, 1982.

McCroskey, Billy J., Wattenbarger, W., Field, T., Sink, Jack. **Vocational Diagnosis and Assessment of Residual Employability.** VSB, P.O. Box 1945, Athens, GA 30603, 1979.

**Medicine for Attorneys Neurology.** University of Miami Law Center/School of Medicine, Walter Beckman, L.L.D., Augusto Sarmiento, M.D. Coiner Publications, Washington, D.C., 1971.

**Medicine for Attorneys Orthopedics.** University of Miami Law Center/School of Medicine. Walter Beckman, L.L.D., Augusto Sarmiento, M.D. Coiner Publications, Washington, D.C., 1971.

Porter, T., Rubin, S., and Sink, J. Essential rehabilitation counselor diagnostic, counseling and placement competencies. **Journal of Applied Rehabilitation Counseling,** Vol. 10, No. 3, Fall 1979, pp. 158-162.

Salamone, P. and Rubin, D. Job placement: new tactics for securing job leads. **Rehabilitation Counseling Bulletin,** Vol. 22, No. 4, April 1979, pp. 338-346.

Sink, J., Porter, T., Rubin, S., and Painter, L. **Competencies Related to the Work of the Rehabilitation Counselor and Vocational Evaluator.** Vol. I, University of Georgia Printing Department, Athens, GA, 1979.

Soule, C. **Disability Income Insurance: The Unique Risk,** Dow Jones - Irwin, 1984.

**Survey of Medicine and Medical Practice for the Rehabilitation Counselor.** Jean Spencer Felton, M.D., Dorothy Cantrell Perkins, and Molly Lewin, B.A., U.S. Government Printing Office, Washington, D.C.

Taylor, L. Golter, M., Golter, G., Backer, T. **Handbook of Private Sector Rehabilitation**, Springer Publishing Co., 1985.

Truitt, J. **Telesearch: Direct Dial The Best Job Of Your Life,** Facts on File Publication, 460 Park Avenue South, NY, NY 10016, 1983.

U.S. Department of Labor, **Dictionary of Occupational Titles, Fourth Edition,** U.S. Government Printing Office, Washington, D.C., 1977.

U.S. Department of Labor, **Handbook for Analyzing Jobs.** U.S. Government Printing Office, Washington, D.C., 1972.

U.S. Department of Labor, **Occupational Outlook Handbook, 1984-85 Edition.** U.S. Government Printing Office, Washington, D.C., 1984.

Vandergoot, D., Avellani, P. and Jacobsen, R. **A Compendium of Placement Related Literature.** Human Resources Center, Albertson, New York, 1978.

Vinitsky, B. and Benjamin, J. **How To Become Happily Employed.** Career Management Press, Kansas City, MO, 1984.

Watters, G. Vocational Computer Systems And The Dictionary of Occupational Titles (A Critical Analysis), **Journal of Applied Rehabilitation Counseling,** Vol. 16, Number 4, winter 1985, pp. 10-14.

Worker's Compensation Research Institute, **Vocational Rehabilitation in Workers' Compensation: Issues and Evidence,** 245 First Street, Suite 402, Cambridge, MA 02141.

Zadny, J. and Jones, L. A survey of job-search patterns among State vocational rehabilitation clients. **Rehabilitation Counseling Bulletin,** Vol. 22, No. 1, September 1978, pp. 60-65.

Ziskin, J. **Coping with Psychiatric and Psychological Testimony.** 3rd Edition, Vol. 1 and II, Law and Psychology Press, P.O. Box 9489, Venice, CA, 90291, 1981.